MAJOR CRIMINAL JUSTICE SYSTEMS

SOME OTHER VOLUMES IN THE
SAGE FOCUS EDITIONS

MAJOR CRIMINAL JUSTICE SYSTEMS

A Comparative Survey
Second Edition

Edited by
George F. Cole
Stanislaw J. Frankowski
Marc G. Gertz

Foreword by
Gerhard O. W. Mueller

SAGE PUBLICATIONS
The Publishers of Professional Social Science
Newbury Park   Beverly Hills   London   New Delhi

The co-editors wish to express their thanks to Miss Mary Margaret Naal for her valuable editorial assistance. A separate thank you goes to Miss Shirley Moore for her patient typing.

For information address:

SAGE Publications, Inc.
2111 West Hillcrest Drive
Newbury Park, California 91320

SAGE Publications Inc.
275 South Beverly Drive
Beverly Hills
California 90212

SAGE Publications Ltd.
28 Banner Street
London EC1Y 8QE
England

SAGE PUBLICATIONS India Pvt. Ltd.
M-32 Market
Greater Kailash I
New Delhi 110 048 India

Printed in the United States of America

Library of Congress Cataloging-in-Publication Data

Major criminal justice systems.

(Sage focus editions ; 32)
Bibliography: p.
1. Criminal justice, Administration of.
I. Cole, George F., 1935-   II. Frankowski,
Stanislaw.   III. Geertz, Marc G.
K5001.Z9M34   1987   364'.9   87-23232
ISBN 0-8039-2596-4
ISBN 0-8039-2597-2 (pbk.)

Contents

Foreword

A book on major criminal justice systems would have been an impossibility a generation ago. The term *criminal justice*, by itself, would not have been properly understood. When used at all, it was used in reference to the judicial apparatus with jurisdiction in criminal matters. The use of the term *systems* in reference to criminal justice would have prompted a blank stare, because the various agencies concerned with crime prevention and control were not viewed as parts of an interdependent system. Comparison was in its infancy—at least as far as crime prevention was concerned—and was restricted to law comparison. Yet even then the systematic, dogmatic, and political differences were regarded as so overwhelming as to cause many scholars to regard comparative studies in criminal law as esoteric and virtually fruitless.

All this has changed in a single generation, largely due to the efforts of a handful of scholars, at a few research centers, in a few countries mostly in the northern tier of the world. Today, thanks to the phenomenal growth of scientific criminology, criminal justice has become a political reality that encompasses all of society's attempts to come to grips with the crime problem. The agencies of criminal justice are now being viewed as parts of a system, an entire sector of a public—and, to some extent, private—endeavor to deal with unacceptable deviance in a humane yet effective and efficient manner. Social, economic, ideological, or political differences are no longer being viewed as an obstacle to comparison. On the contrary, they are seen for what they are: variables worthy of analysis in an effort to determine why countries have such widely varying crime problems—ranging from insignificant to catastrophic.

A whole new methodology for the comparative study of criminal justice systems, all their component parts and all their strategies, had to be created. The interaction of the criminal justice sector with all other sectors of public life began to be investigated in an effort to turn criminology, as the science of criminal justice, from a theoretical discipline into a practical tool of social engineering. It is at this point that the United Nations has entered the picture. The world organization, having achieved virtual universality of representation with its 151 member states, is deeply committed to the proposition that all nations should be able to enjoy the benefit of the experience of all other nations. In the field of crime prevention and criminal justice, for which the Crime Prevention and Criminal Justice Branch is the Secretariat's administrative organ, this means that the aggregate of world experience must be presented in a meaningful and comparable manner so that each nation can profit from the success—and failures—of all other nations, so that no nation need repeat the costly mistakes made elsewhere. Experience does show that, on the natural path of socioeconomic development, crime becomes a problem whenever crime prevention and the criminal justice system are not built into the overall national development effort.

The United Nation's first world crime survey, with the participation of 66 states, has been approvingly received by the General Assembly (A/Res/32/60). For the first time nations can gauge their own position on the region-by-region charts showing both the extent of criminality and the investment in personnel devoted to crime prevention. The General Assembly has also adopted the first international plan of action, for the remainder of the twentieth century, which is calculated to guide international and national efforts for efficient crime prevention and criminal justice administration (A/32/58, adopting E/CN.5/536, annex IV).

The experiences in crime prevention and control, criminal justice, offender treatment, and criminal policy are now being widely distributed through the quinquennial world congresses of the United Nations; through the work of the interregional and regional institutes in Europe, Asia, and Latin America; through the publications of the Secretariat—including the International Review of Criminal Policy—and through regional and interregional meetings of experts. Technical assistance, providing for a transfer of technology, strategy, and experience in the field of crime prevention and control, is now available to all governments requesting it. In sum, the academic discipline of comparative criminology has become the practical intergovernmental and governmental instrument of crime prevention and control.

It is most timely, therefore, that a group of distinguished scholars from countries that played a leading role in the field—in theory and in practice—have pooled their efforts in the production of this important volume on comparative criminal justice systems. It is my fervent hope that through this volume the expertise necessary for improving national criminal justice systems by comparison may be more widely spread. I wish the authors every success in their contribution to the important world effort to reduce the human and material waste and suffering that criminality brings with it.

—Gerhard O. W. Mueller
Chief, Crime Prevention and
Criminal Justice Branch,
United Nations

Foreword to the Second Edition

The first edition of *Major Criminal Justice Systems* appeared nearly a decade ago. The world crime problem has increased significantly since then, but so has society's effort to deal with it. There are now 159 nations within the United Nations family, pooling their resources to combat crime. The First World Crime Survey has been followed by a much more detailed and informative Second World Crime Survey (1985), and the U.N. General Assembly's First International Plan of Action has been followed by such development as:

The Milan Plan of Action (for crime prevention, worldwide)
The Guiding Principles for Crime Prevention and Criminal Justice in the Context of Development and a New International Economic Order
The United Nations Standard Minimum rules for the Administration of Juvenile Justice (The Beijing rules)
The Declaration of Basic Principles of Justice (a) relating to victims of crime, and (b) relating to victims of abuse of power
And a host of other agreements, models, and guidelines

All these instruments were adopted by the Seventh United Nations Congress on the Prevention of Crime and the Treatment of Offenders (A/CONF. 121/22 Milan, 1985), at which a record number of 124 States were represented by delegations. The unanimity with which nations of diverse economic, political, and cultural orientation are tackling the world's crime problems is astounding, yet demonstrates that the danger is commonly perceived.

For a common approach to worldwide crime prevention and control to be effective, there must be a mutual understanding of, and respect for, each other's criminal justice systems and approaches. And here lies the significance of a work such as *Major Criminal Justice Systems.*

It is a pleasure to help launch the second edition of *Major Criminal Justice Systems*. While indeed a new edition, this book is also a sequence to its predecessor by adding a chapter on Nigeria, permitting the researcher to consult the first edition for information on countries that, for brevity's sake, were not included in the second edition.

All the hopes and wishes with which I greeted the first edition appear to have been fulfilled. The book found favorable acceptance by the scholarly community and a multitude of students have learned from it about the divergent experiences of the world's variegated criminal justice systems. Indeed, such a cross-cultural understanding is a prerequisite for dealing with a crime problem that has become so intricately and obviously internationalized as to require global thinking in devising crime prevention and control strategies. May *Major Criminal Justice Systems*, in its second edition, continue to play its important role in educating the young men and women who are capable of dealing with today's and tomorrow's world crime situation.

—Gerhard O. W. Mueller
Chief (Ret.) Crime Prevention
and Criminal Justice Branch,
United Nations
Professor of Criminal Justice
Rutgers University,
School of Criminal Justice

Preface

As events of recent decades have demonstrated, the world is a small space in which travel and communication make it possible for important events to transcend national and even regional concerns. The simple fact that more than 150 countries belong to the United Nations indicates that Earth is made up of an interdependent network of nations where no one country stands completely alone. This is a dramatic change from just fifty years ago, when many nations followed isolationist policies, believing that they could remove themselves from the problems of other states. Only in recent decades has it been recognized that most of the pressing social matters on the contemporary scene—pollution, resource allocation, poverty, and crime—are universal problems.

During the past decade, scholarly activity regarding crime and the administration of justice has greatly increased. Responding to the growth of crime, a concern that affects all developed countries, scholars have conducted research examining the causes of crime, the treatment of offenders, and, as indicated in the foreword by Professor Mueller, such a volume would have been an impossibility a generation ago.

As Mueller also notes, the United Nations "is deeply committed to the proposition that all nations should be able to enjoy the benefit of the experience of all other nations." This international perspective is the basis upon which this book is organized. We all need to know the experiences of other countries with regard to their criminal justice, which are now being taught in universities throughout the world. Unfortunately, there does not seem to be a comprehensive book that adequately deals with a representative cross-section of the criminal justice systems of the international community. We hope that *Major Criminal Justice Systems* will help to fill this void.

The book was designed primarily to introduce American students of crime to the criminal justice systems of some of the major countries of the world. It is intended to be introductory and descriptive, in keeping with what we believe is the level of theory and evidence currently available on criminal justice in most countries. Each chapter was written by a distinguished scholar who describes the administration of penal justice in his/her native land. The book is organized into three parts that correspond to the major legal system, and the chapters are grouped so that comparisons can be made among the countries of a particular family of law and then among these families.

Anthologies using multiple authors often run the risk that each chapter will be written along different lines and thus the opportunities for comparisons are reduced. We hope we have solved this problem by presenting eight chapters that follow a common outline. On the assumption that the book will be read principally by Americans who know about their own criminal justice system, the chapter on the United States was written in a different style so that it can serve as a benchmark for comparative purposes.

Some may question our choice of countries for inclusion. Certainly it would increase the value of the book if selections were included from countries subscribing to Islamic law, those in South America, and the world's most populous nation, the People's Republic of China. Unfortunately, we were unable to solicit chapters from scholars in these areas. We hope that future editions will benefit from the contributions of scholars from these countries.

Readers may find that some of the authors have written chapters that do not comply with the dominant scientific paradigms of the West. It is important that these chapters not be dismissed but studied so that it will be possible for the student to understand the author's perspective and the assumptions concerning law and justice in that country. It is our thesis that despite ideological, socioeconomic, and cultural differences, there exists at least one common denominator that makes our attempt as editors meaningful; the administration of justice in every country is supposed to protect the set of social relationships and values, the maintenance of which seems desirable for those holding power. As such, criminal law is used to protect these values and to prohibit, under the threat of penalty, the commission of certain forms of behavior perceived as dangerous.

As noted above, we hope that readers will become more acquainted with the criminal justice systems of a variety of countries and that the book will help to foster an international and comparative perspective among students of criminology. It is also our hope that this volume will serve as a first step toward the development of such an international approach to the problems of crime and justice.

—George F. Cole
—Stanislaw J. Frankowski
—Marc G. Gertz

Comparative Criminal Justice:

An Introduction

GEORGE F. COLE
STANISLAW J. FRANKOWSKI
MARC G. GERTZ

Given the prevalence of crime in all societies, it is perhaps somewhat strange that there has been little or no attempt to compare, at a sophisticated and systematic level, the administration of criminal justice in various countries and especially to make these analyses across the spectrum of socioeconomic systems. Certainly there has been extensive research on the causes of crime and the policies of enforcement, adjudication, and correction of offenders in specific countries, but there is lacking a body of literature that contributes to a cross-cultural theory of criminal justice. It would appear that such a comparative approach is in its infancy largely because of a number of methodological problems that have impeded development of such a perspective. It is only when these difficulties are understood that we may proceed to examine the wide implications for a comparative study of criminal justice.

Some Methodological Problems

One of the central concepts necessary for comparative analysis of criminal justice is that of system. Based on concepts drawn from the biological sciences, the systems perspective has been extensively developed by such social scientists as Parsons (1951), Blau (1964), and

Merton (1957). It gained greatest acceptance in the United States during the past two decades, while its application in Europe has been most recent. In fact, it is interesting to note that it is difficult to find a suitable equivalent of the English term *criminal justice system* in most other languages of the developed world. Traditionally, scholars have examined each component of criminal justice—police, courts, corrections— without taking into account its functional relationship to the other parts and the sociopolitical environment within which it operates. It is now recognized that there is a linkage, an interdependence, of these components, and such an analysis requires that a systems framework be used. Given the recent nature of this development, it is not surprising that there are few studies using the comparative approach and the system concept when no serious analysis exists at the national level.

All of the difficulties involved in the study of one system of criminal justice exist when ventures are made into the comparative framework. In addition, new conceptual problems appear. These difficulties are related to a variety of factors, including the assumption that seemingly identical organizational structures are in fact the same, that language differences may play tricks on us, and that the cultural settings within which the systems operate produce very different outputs. As a result, one may be easily misled into assuming that two institutions perform the same function in different countries because they bear the same name and the "official" statement of their operations would seem to indicate that they are identical. The exact work of a given institution can be grasped only when the researcher has a full knowledge of the legal system of which criminal justice is a part, the political and cultural environment in which it functions, and the actual operations of the system as compared to formal statements describing the operation. Given these problems, it is necessary to analyze the institutions of a given country at both the normative, or formal, level and then at the substantive level, where it is possible to take into account the operations in practice.

Herrmann (1977), for example, notes that each criminal justice system has to face the fact that there cannot be a full trial for every case. In common law countries this problem is solved through extensive use of the guilty plea, while the Federal Republic of Germany has developed a "penal order procedure," in which the prosecutor asks the judge for issuance of such an order. From a formal perspective, the guilty plea and the penal order have nothing in common. In fact, German scholars have emphasized that the guilty plea could never be reconcilable with the criminal procedures of that country, yet when one studies the actual functioning of the two practices one finds striking similarities.

A second reason for the slowness with which scholars of criminal justice have used the comparative approach may be related to philosophical assumptions concerning the nature of law. It is suggested that those using the common law approach have been influenced to take a more pragmatic or realistic view of criminal justice. Certainly the works of American scholars such as Pound, Llewellyn, and Cardozo influenced a legion of researchers who wanted to understand the law in action rather than the law on the books. Scholars have argued that, by comparison, European thought—for some time influenced by the German idealism of Kant and Hegel—emphasized a highly speculative mode of thinking that concentrated on building abstract concepts without reference to the social context. This approach reached is peak at the beginning of this century; it was argued that the law as passed by legislature was elevated and thus considered as an absolute value with the concomitant demand that there be obedience. The continental approach seems to have greatly influenced the development of a socialist way of viewing law, especially in the Soviet Union during the Stalinist period. Here one has the sense that the law was viewed as omnipotent and that absolute obedience was the utmost duty of each citizen. It was stated that socialist law was always just, always proper, since it was passed in accordance with the will of the people. One result of these philosophical assumptions has been that empirical research on the administration of justice has been a fairly recent phenomenon in many countries.

In addition to these reasons for the slowness with which a cross-national approach to the administration of justice has developed, it is necessary to consider several concepts that have heuristic value for comparative studies. As will be developed in a later portion of this essay, it seems useful to divide the criminal justice systems of the developed world according to three families of law—common, civil, and socialist. By clustering systems in this manner it is then possible to make comparisons that we will call *internal* and *external*. A comparison of at least two systems of criminal justice belonging to the same legal family—for example, the American and the English—may be called an internal cross-national comparison. Alternately, comparisons between or among systems of different legal families may be defined as external cross-national comparisons.

At a different level of analysis, it may also be important to compare only portions of two systems—courts of the USSR and Japan—while on other occasions cross-national statements about two or more criminal justice systems in their entirety may be appropriate. The first we will designate as *micro*; the latter would be *macro* comparison. Even though it may be desirable to study a particular institution in different countries, it must still be recognized that they are lined to other parts of their criminal justice systems and to the sociopolitical environment.

The Value of Comparative Criminal Justice Research

Why should we undertake the enterprise of comparative research? Some might argue that crime in one's own country is such a serious problem that only the dilettante would try to understand the administration of criminal justice in similar nations, let alone those with completely different legal and political structures. On the contrary, it can be argued that comparative research in the field of criminal justice is not only a desirable undertaking but one that is necessary. At the pragmatic level, it is possible to show that certain operations in other states will have direct application if adopted in one's own country. At a theoretical level, it can be hoped that progress in the development of a science of criminology will be advanced through comparative undertakings. To understand the ramifications of these proposals, let us look at a few of the expected values of comparative research in more detail.

International Cooperation

As already mentioned, through comparative research a knowledge of foreign systems of criminal justice is attained. This knowledge is, in fact, a prerequisite for obtaining the other value to be discussed, but it is also profitable in itself. Comparative research expands our knowledge of the contemporary world with its complexity, speed of communication, and the internationalization of many social problems. It is hoped that such knowledge contributes to a better understanding of other countries and their cultures. It contributes to a more international, less parochial perspective. But although these are valued goals, it must also be recognized that crime has become an international concern. Since the end of World War II we have become much more aware of the extent to which criminal operations are carried out on a transnational basis.

International terrorism, air hijacking, and drug smuggling have all become recognized as problems that require international cooperation if they are to be prevented. With the ease of modern transportation comes increased problems that have emerged with regard to foreign nationals committing offenses abroad. Often cultural differences are the basis for commission of the crime, but questions of extradition and the execution of foreign judicial orders require an understanding by criminal justice officials of the procedures of the other nation.

Understanding One's Own System

Just as it is important to learn about the criminal justice system of others, it can also be stated that through the comparative approach we can achieve a better understanding of our own system. There is a common tendency to be uncritical of the system in one's own country if one is ignorant of the ways of others. There is an inclination to think that the solutions to problems in one's own legal order are the only possible answers. This can lead to idealization of one's native legal institutions and the tendency to treat them as inherent in the general nature of law. In the words of Lepaulle (1922: 858), "Where one is immersed in his own law, in his own country he is unable to see things from without, he has a psychologically unavoidable tendency to consider as natural, as necessary, as given by God, things which are simply due to historical accident or temporary social situations." Here is a leading scholar who admitted that he never completely understood French law until he came to the United States to study another system. As discussed by David and Brierley (1968: 8), legal parochialism is "irreconcilable with a truly scientific spirit since it impoverishes, and indeed is dangerous to the development and application of national law." The discovery of other legal possibilities thus not only stimulates students' curiosity and imagination but also puts into question the solutions defined by their own national law. They are compelled to question the soundness of the solutions, norms, and many other aspects of their own law, to inquire into the whys and wherefores of the institutions.

It is especially important that we gather knowledge of a foreign system when our own is derived, through transplantation, from that other system. Americans recognize that their legal institutions have their roots in those of England, yet through time certain aspects have changed. Visiting English, for example, often see in the American state judicial system a model of the prereform courts of their native country. Likewise, Americans can get a much better insight into their institutions—for example, public prosecution—when they become aware of the historical background of the colonial period. Similarly, after World War II Japan inherited criminal procedures that borrowed heavily from the United States. It is highly probable that the inability of these procedures to function under Japanese conditions was caused by a lack of knowledge of the American criminal justice system and culture as a whole. Such an example of legal transplantation is of particular importance for many Third World countries that have attempted to adopt elements of either the common law or continental systems, institutions from the colonial periods, and new procedures based on customary law, to create a system that meets their needs and conforms to their values.

Finally, the comparative approach to criminal justice forces us to identify and explain the differences and similarities of our own and other systems. As a result, there may be a greater appreciation of the fact that the reason for particular legal institutions and practices must be understood as evolving from the socioeconomic and cultural environment. As Kamba (1974: 493) noted, "Comparative law serves to emphasize the interdependence between law and other social phenomena." Given this reality, it becomes clear that the machinery of criminal justice is actually an instrument of social control and is thus influenced by and influences social life in numerous ways.

Reform of One's Own System

Every nation has portions of its criminal justice system that can be improved. One of the values of comparative research is the opportunity to benefit by learning of the experiences of others who may have faced similar problems. As Maine (1871: 4), one of the early exponents of comparative law, said, "The chief function of comparative jurisprudence is to facilitate legislation and the practical improvement of law."

Currently, those countries with a high degree of industrialization and urbanization face a number of similar crime problems, such as increases in white-collar criminality, crimes of violence, and those related to the use of drugs. The criminal justice systems of these countries face similar difficulties, such as court congestion, law enforcement inefficiency, and correctional ineffectiveness. Socialist countries also have many shared problems—alcohol-related, economic criminality, and motor vehicle offenses are growing concerns. Although the criminal justice systems of these countries function quite smoothly in terms of the efficiency of courtroom procedures, in some of them the number of incarcerated offenders compared with the general population is very high. Finally, in the Third World there are problems of corruption and abuse of power as these countries move toward full economic and political independence.

It is obvious that knowledge of the experiences of other nations is invaluable when attempts are made to reform existing systems. Although procedures and institutions used in one culture may not flower in the same manner in another environment, often elements can be shifted, resulting in improvements in attempts to prevent crime and administer justice in the new setting. Likewise, knowledge of the experience of others can point to actions that should be avoided. However, it must be emphasized that when the procedures of one country have been adopted by another without adjustments for local circumstances, the effects are often disastrous. As observed by Tallon (1969: 265-266):

> Assuredly, to resort to a foreign legislation is not an innovation. . . . Its aim is not to find a foreign institution which could be easily copied, but to acquire ideas from a careful survey of similar foreign institutions and to make a reasonable transportation of those which may be retained according to local conditions.

Unification and Harmonization of Laws

One of the early reasons espoused for the comparative study of criminal justice was that it would lead to unification and harmonization of laws on a cross-national basis. As early as the 1900 Paris International Congress of Comparative Law, it was urged by Lambert that the purpose of comparative law was to prove

> material which would form the basis of a general unification of those national systems of law which have attained the same degree of development or "civilization" and their replacement by an international common law [Kamba, 1974: 501].

This hope, which reflects much of the international sentiment following World War I, has not been realized, but there are indications that in some specialized areas unification of laws is possible. The harmonization of the laws of several countries with others has a greater potential for fulfillment.

A distinction must be made between unification, the adoption of identical laws by different countries, and harmonization, the elimination of major differences by minimizing existing legal obstacles. Efforts to bring about these goals can be seen at the international, regional, and national levels. For example, the United Nations has been active in promoting the adoption of minimum standards for the treatment of prisoners. Likewise, regionally or culturally linked nations—for example, the Scandinavian countries and members of the European Economic Community—have attempted to coordinate many activities in the criminal justice field. At the national level, especially in federations such as the United States, model codes have been developed to guide state legislatures so that their actions will be consistent with those of their sister states. Even in a unitary country such as the United Kingdom, where there are separate criminal justice systems for England and Wales, Scotland, and Northern Ireland, attempts are made to ensure the coordination among these entities.

Although the dreams of many who have advocated the unity of law at an international level have not been realized, there are many examples of nations seeking to unify or harmonize their criminal justice systems with those of others. What must be emphasized is that knowledge of comparative law is a prerequisite for such activities.

Scientific Progress

Thus far we have outlined a number of purposes that might justify the study of criminal justice systems on a comparative basis. Each function may be viewed as oriented toward the achievement of some instrumental purpose that would improve the rule of law. However, knowledge of the major criminal justice systems of the world and the use of the comparative perspective are important for the development of theories that will contribute to the broader purposes of science. For, as Rheinstein (1952: 92) argued, comparative law belongs to the realm of the exact sciences "when its cultivator tries to observe, describe, classify and investigate in their relations among themselves and to other phenomena, the phenomena of law." Thus the comparative approach to law uses the scientific method.

The mere knowledge of the functions and processes of criminal justice systems in a number of countries will not contribute to science unless the comparative approach is undertaken in a systematic manner. This means that research on criminal justice must conform to the accepted standards of the scientific enterprise in which findings accumulated following specific experimental procedures are used to develop concepts that can link hypotheses in order to develop theories. This movement from the plane of observation to that of the theoretical is essential if we are to understand our world. Use of the comparative approach as a means of studying criminal justice is one of the most important tools that can be used to achieve that goal.

In seeking to contribute to a scientifically based theory of criminal justice it is important that regularities observed in one system be examined to determine if they are found in other countries. For a theory or model to be viewed as reliable it will be necessary for its validation to be accomplished on a cross-national basis. As explained by Clinard and Abbott (1973: 2), the aim of comparative research "is to develop concepts and generalizations at a level that distinguishes between universals applicable to all societies and unique characteristics representative of one or a small set of societies."

Classification of
Criminal Justice Systems

The division of this book into three sections denoting the common law, civil law, and socialist criminal justice systems follows the typology normally accepted by Western specialists in the field of comparative law. According to this scheme, elaborated by French scholar Rene David (1968), there exist in the contemporary world three main systems, which may be called groups or "families" of law. David uses two criteria in formulating this scheme. First, he asks if someone educated in one law would be able to handle another. If this is not possible, the two laws must belong to different families. Second, laws cannot be considered as belonging to the same family if they are based on opposing philosophical, political, or economic principles and they seek to achieve two entirely different types of societies. When used cumulatively, these criteria, David argues, result in the threefold division of the criminal justice systems of the developed world. In addition, he notes that there are supplementary systems based strictly on religious tenets found, for example, in the Muslim countries, as well as those emerging systems in the developing countries of Africa and Asia that are evolving out of their colonial past.

Many scholars contend that a distinctive category of socialist law does not exist, since the foundation of the legal systems of the Soviet Union and the countries of Eastern Europe can be traced to the continental (Romano-Germanic) family. Similarly, the threefold classification is usually criticized by socialist scholars (Szabo and Peteri, 1977) who, drawing inferences from their Marxist view of the world, point out that the typology is based only on formal elements, such as the sources and structures of law, organization of the judiciary, and ways of legal reasoning. They claim that we must understand the essence of law, and thus the continental and Anglo-Saxon legal systems are merely various appearances of the same type of law based on a particular social order. Thus from a socialist perspective the basis for the demarcation should result in two legal families, one based on the private ownership of the means of production and the corresponding social system (common law and continental). As Szabo said, "Any approach differing from this will blur the differences arising from the social categories and is likely to lead, owing to its false start, to false conclusions" (Szabo and Peteri, 1977: 13).

Some "bourgeois" scholars seem to be of the same opinion. For example, E. L. Johnson (1969: 51), an English specialist on the Soviet legal system, says that

> although we correctly place Soviet law within the continental group of legal systems, there is another factor of the greatest importance to be considered, for Soviet law claims to be an entirely new type of legal system based on the Marxist political philosophy and the socialist type of economy.

He believes that, from this perspective, Soviet law bears no resemblance to continental systems, since it has aims and purposes different from those of capitalist states.

With regard to this controversy the name of Karl Renner, the Austrian jurist, is often mentioned. Renner elaborated the doctrine of the "neutrality of legal concepts." In his view, legal concepts, like bricks, can be used for the construction of a building that can serve different purposes. In the same way, legal concepts may be used to construct various legal systems. Johnson (1969: 5), for example, claims that "the fact that the traditional civil law concepts have now been used for the purpose of constructing a system based on Marxist philosophy and socialist economics seem to many a striking justification of Renner's thesis." Hungarian scholar Szabo (Szabo and Peteri, 1977) also emphasizes the correctness of Renner's observation that the legal institutions will, in time, undergo functional changes, while their normative definition remains the same.

Another viewpoint, such as the one advanced by French comparative law specialist Marc Ancel, suggests that there are two main types of legal systems in the developed world: one found in Western countries, including the common law and continental systems, based on the ideas of liberalism and individualism and on Christian traditions; and the socialist system, being the reflection of current socioeconomic conditions, viewed in an instrumental way as a tool in building a new society and not as an expression of any abstract concept of justice. Ancel (1971) points out that the unity of the Western system has deep historical roots. For example, immediately following the American Revolution some leaders, such as Jefferson, urged that the common law be rejected and that the French pattern be adopted. At the time, it must be remembered, the French legal structure had been greatly influenced by the French Revolution. The arguments advanced by the two American jurists Story and Kent won, however, and there was popular support for retaining the common law. It was pointed out that the common law system as well as the French legal reforms aimed at the protection of civil liberties and rights. It is clear, says Ancel, that the ideological unity of the Western world stems from an older period. In conclusion, he claims that in the contemporary world there are two basic types of legal systems—the liberal and the socialist. As Ancel notes, in the future a third type probably will emerge to serve the needs of the peoples of Africa and Asia. This form, while retaining some elements of customary law, probably will be a model with characteristics placing it between Western liberalism and the socialist structures of the East.

In summary, we are brought back to this question: Is the socialist system a distinctive system or is it just a continental one adapted to other circumstances? It is our belief that the thesis supported by the majority of scholars reflects reality: The socialist law, because of its distinctive philosophical background and ideology and the radically different functions it is supposed to perform, should be considered as a separate type of law as opposed to the common law and the continental law that exist in other developed countries. It is with the knowledge of this controversy that we have adopted the traditional three-system division in this book. In our view this formulation is a reflection of the reality of the existing world order—at least as far as the countries under discussion are concerned.

REFERENCES

ANCEL, M. (1971) Utilite et Methodes du Droit Compare. Neuchatel: Editions Ides et Calendes, Universite de Neuchatel.

BLAU, P. (1964) Exchange and Power in Social Life. New York: John Wiley.

CLINARD, M. B. and D. J. ABBOTT (1973) Crime in Developing Countries. New York: John Wiley.

DAVID, R. and J. E. BRIERLEY (1968) Major Legal Systems in the World Today. London: Free Press.

HAZARD, J. (1951) "Comparative law in legal education." University of Chicago Law Review 18: 264.

HERRMANN, J. (1977) "Teaching and research in comparative and international criminal law." Reveue International de Droit Penal 48: 304.

JOHNSON, E. L. (1969) An Introduction to the Soviet Legal System. London: Methuen.

KAMBA, W. J. (1974) "Comparative law: a theoretical framework." International and Comparative Law Quarterly 23: 485.

LEPAULLE, P. (1922) "The function of comparative law." Harvard Law Review 35: 838.

MAINE, H. J. (1871) Village Communities in the East and West. New York: Holt, Rinehart, & Winston.

MERTON, R. (1957) Social Theory and Social Structure. New York: Free Press.

PARSONS, T. (1951) The Social System. Glencoe: Free Press.

RHEINSTEIN, M. (1952) "Teaching tools in comparative law." American Journal of Comparative Law 1: 95.

SZABO, I. and Z. PETERI (1977) A Socialist Approach to Law. Budapest: Akademiai Kiado.

TALLON, D. (1969) "Comparative law: expanding horizons." Journal of the Society of Public Teachers of Law 10: 265.

PART I

Common Law Systems

The common law system originated in England following the Norman Conquest and today is found in all English-speaking countries with the exception of Scotland and South Africa. Through colonial expansion it was transferred to those Third World countries formerly linked to England. However, in many of these countries, particularly those with a Muslim population and in India, the transplantation was not complete, with the result that portions of the common law system existed along with the traditional rules of law.

Common law is referred to as "judge-made law," in that it developed out of decisions made in individual cases that then became precedent for the resolution of future disputes. It is thus characterized by an emphasis on solving the present case rather than on articulating a rule of conduct for the future. Thus it is less abstract than the legal rule found in the civil law systems. For common law jurists, matters concerning the administration of justice, evidence, procedure, and the execution of penal decisions are more important than the articulation of substantive rules.

Part I begins with a description of criminal justice in the United States. Because it is assumed that most readers will be American students, this chapter should serve as the basis for comparisons with the other countries discussed in the book. The English and Nigerian chapters describe the systems that are the most similar to that of the United States in that they are both based on common law. There are, however, obvious differences in governmental structure and such measures of development as urbanization and industrialization. In particular, it must be noted that England is a unitary political system, while the United States and Nigeria are federations. England and the United States are both industrialized and urban countries compared with Nigeria, which gained independence in 1960 and is less developed. What are of interest are the ways that the common law system has been adapted to fit the circumstances of each of the countries.

1

United States of America

GEORGE F. COLE

It is generally agreed that the amount of crime in the United States rose dramatically from the mid-1960s through the mid-1970s; then the rate of growth started to level off and the incidence of some offenses began to decline. The surge in crime during that decade drew the attention of the public and governmental leaders to this enduring social problem. Presidents Johnson and Nixon, two prestigious national commissions, and Congress encouraged the states and municipalities to launch a variety of efforts to control crime. Public expenditures for the police, courts, and corrections escalated and new technologies and procedures were adopted. Neighborhood crime watches, prosecutions of career criminals, diversion, and community corrections were some of the more innovative approaches that emerged.

Today it may appear that because crime is not rising at the rate it did a decade ago it is no longer such a serious matter. This assumption would be incorrect, for the public continues to place crime near the top of the list of problems about which it is most concerned, and the activities of criminal justice agencies are still using extensive public resources in this seemingly never ending fight.

Over the past twenty years there have been shifts in the criminal justice picture; situations and problems that were only dimly perceived have moved closer to center stage. Public attitudes have changed remarkably with regard to the nature of the criminal sanction and the ways in which punishment should be imposed. In the 1960s and 1970s the rehabilitation of offenders was the dominant concern; now the public leans toward retribution. As a result, arrest rates are higher, sentences are more severe, and the size of the imprisoned population has skyrocketed.

General Information

The United States of America comprises 250 million people who live in 50 states and 5 territories, contains almost every topographical feature, and extends from the frozen wastes of the Arctic to the semitropical zones of Puerto Rico. During the past half-century there has been a continuing shift of the population from rural to urban areas. In addition, black citizens, who prior to World War II lived mainly in the South, have moved in great numbers to the northern cities. There have been other population shifts from the older sections of the Northeast to the Sunbelt of the Southwest. More Spanish-speaking citizens are now living in many parts of the country, particularly as a result of migrations from Puerto Rico, Cuba, and Mexico. Given this heterogeneity in a multiracial "nation of immigrants," it is of interest that public opinion surveys have shown there is near-unanimity as to the major sociopolitical values. These studies note a high level of agreement among the citizenry on the types of behavior that should be labeled as criminal.

Criminal Justice in
a Federal System

A federal governmental structure was created in 1789 with the ratification of the U.S. Constitution. This instrument created a delicate political bargain in which it was agreed that the national government would have certain powers—to raise an army, to coin money, to make treaties with foreign countries, and so on—but that all other powers would be retained by the states. Nowhere in the Constitution does one find specific reference to criminal justice agencies of the national government, yet the Federal Bureau of Investigation is widely known, criminal cases are often tried in U.S. district courts, and the Federal Bureau of Prisons operates institutions from coast to coast that hold offenders who have violated national laws.

For conceptual purposes it is useful to think of two distinct criminal justice systems: national and state. Each performs enforcement, adjudication, and correctional functions, but they do so on different authority and their activities are vastly dissimilar in scope. Criminal laws are primarily written and enforced by agencies of the states, yet the rights of defendants are protected by the constitutions of both state and national governments. Although approximately 85% of criminal cases are heard in state courts, there are certain offenses—narcotics violations and transportation of a kidnap victim across state lines, for example—that are infringements of both state and federal laws.

As a consequence of the bargain worked out at the Constitutional Convention, the general police power was not delegated to the federal government. No centralized national police force with broad enforcement powers may be established in the United States. It is true that the national government has police agencies such as the FBI and the Secret Service, but they are authorized to enforce only those laws prescribed under the powers granted to Congress. Because Congress has the power to coin money, it also has the authority to detect and apprehend counterfeiters, a function performed by the Secret Service of the Treasury Department. The FBI, part of the Department of Justice, is responsible for the investigation of all violations of federal laws, with the exception of those assigned by Congress to other departments. The FBI has jurisdiction over fewer than 200 criminal matters, including offenses such as kidnapping, extortion, interstate transportation of stolen motor vehicles, and treason.

The role of criminal justice agencies following the assassination of President John F. Kennedy in November 1963 illustrates the federal-state jurisdictional division. Because Congress had not made it a federal offense to kill the president of the United States, Lee Harvey Oswald would have been brought to trial under the laws of the state of Texas. The Secret Service had the job of protecting the president, but apprehension of the killer was the formal responsibility of the Dallas police and other Texas law enforcement agencies.

As the components of U.S. society have become interdependent, with constant movement of people and goods across state lines, federal involvement in the criminal justice system has increased. No longer is it useful to assume that acts committed in one state will not have an impact on the citizens of another state. This is seen especially in the area of organized crime, in which gambling or drug syndicates are established on a national basis. Congress recently passed laws designed to allow the FBI to investigate situations where local police forces are likely to be less effective. For example, under the National Stolen Property Act, the FBI is authorized to investigate thefts of over $5,000 when the stolen property is likely to have been taken across state lines. In such circumstances jurisdictional disputes are possible because the offense is a violation of both state and national laws. The court to which a case is brought may be determined by the law enforcement agency making the arrest. It is possible for a defendant to be tried under state law and then retried in the federal courts for a violation of the laws of the national government. In most instances, however, the two systems respect each other's jurisdictional lines.

It is important to emphasize that the U.S. system of criminal justice is decentralized. Two-thirds of all criminal justice employees work for county and municipal units of government. This is not a result of the fact that any one subunit of the system, such as the police, is primarily employed at the local level. It is a result of the fact that, with the exception of corrections, at least a majority of the workers in each of the subunits—police, judicial, prosecution, public defense—have ties to local government. It is in the states and communities that laws are enforced and violators are brought to justice. Consequently, the formal structure and actual processes are greatly affected by local norms and pressures—that is, the needs and demands of local people who are influential and the community's interpretation of how much and how far the laws should be enforced.

Extent of Criminality

One of the frustrations of studying criminal justice is that there is no accurate means of knowing the amount of crime. Surveys that have asked members of the public if they have ever committed a breach of the law indicate that there is much more crime than is reported. Until recently, measurement of crime was limited to those incidents that were known to the police. Beginning in 1972, however, the LEAA sponsored ongoing surveys of the public to determine the amount of criminal victimization experienced. Comparing these studies with what appears in the *Uniform Crime Reports* (UCR), maintained by the FBI and published annually, one sees a significant discrepancy between the occurrence of crime and offenses known to the police.

The UCR are one of the main sources of crime statistics. Authorized by Congress in 1930, this national and uniform system of compiling crime data is the product of a voluntary network through which local, state, and federal law enforcement agencies transmit to Washington information concerning eight major crimes, "Index Offenses," and 21 other offense categories. Scholars have pointed out that UCR data concern only those crimes reported to the police, that submission of the data is voluntary, that the reports are not truly uniform because events are defined according to differing criteria in various jurisdictions, and that upper-class and "white-collar" crimes are not included.

The public most fears crimes of violence, such as murder, rape, and assault, yet these make up only about 9% of the incidents annually cited by the UCR. These are also the crimes that have been committed at fairly constant rates over the years, although some rates, such as that for murder, are lower now than in times past. It is the crimes that involve theft and burglary that have increased most dramatically. But here the reports may fool us. Property crimes may have mounted statistically not because there are more criminals but because more things are insured, because there are more opportunities for criminal activity in an affluent society, and because the FBI's definition of "serious" crime (theft of more than $50 in valuation) is inconsistent with the realities of inflation.

Although questions have been asked about the accuracy of data concerning crime, it is broadly accepted that crime rose precipitously in the United States during the late 1960s but that it has now leveled off and begun to decline for some categories. We may take heart from the fact that crime rates have not continued skyward during the 1980s, but we must also be aware that the fear of crime remains vexatious. Opinion surveys still show that more than 40% of the public believe that they cannot walk safely in their neighborhoods at night, and that they worry a great deal about being robbed or beaten. The level of the fear of crime is perhaps of as much concern to criminal justice scholars and planners as is the actual level of crime.

Agencies of Criminal Justice

Society has commissioned the police to patrol the streets, prevent crime, arrest suspected criminals, and enforce the law. It has established courts to determine the guilt or innocence of accused offenders, to sentence those who are guilty, and to "do justice." It has created a correctional system of prisons and programs to punish convicted persons and to try to rehabilitate them so that they may eventually become useful citizens. These three components—law enforcement, law adjudication, and corrections—combine to form the U.S. system of criminal justice. It would be incorrect, however, to assume that system to be monolithic or even consistent. It was not fashioned one piece at a time. Rather, various institutions and procedures that are the parts of the system were built around the core assumption that a person may be punished by government only if it can be proved by an impartial process that he or she violated a specific law. Some of the parts, such as trial by jury and bail, are ancient in origin; others, such as juvenile courts and community-based corrections, are relatively new. The system represents an adaptation of the institutions of the English common law to the social and political environment of the United States.

Public organizations numbering 20,000 with 670,000 employees and total annual budgets of over $3 billion in four levels of government are charged with enforcing the law and maintaining order in the United States. The local nature of police efforts can be seen in the fact that the federal government contains only 50 law enforcement agencies and the states have 200. The other 19,750 are dispersed throughout the counties, cities, and towns.

The responsibilities of law enforcement organizations fall into four categories. First, they are called upon to "keep the peace." This is a broad and most important mandate, and involves the protection of rights and persons in a wide variety of situations ranging from street-corner brawls to domestic quarrels. Second, the police must apprehend law violators and combat crime. This is the responsibility the public most often associates with police work, yet it accounts for only a minuscule portion of police time and resources. Third, the agencies of law enforcement are expected to engage in crime prevention. Through public education about the threat of crime and by reducing the number of situations in which crimes are most likely to be committed, the police can lower the incidence of crime. Finally, the police are charged with providing a variety of social services. In fulfilling these obligations, a police officer recovers stolen property, directs traffic, provides emergency medical aid, gets cats out of trees, and helps people who have locked themselves out of their apartments.

Entrusted with the enforcement of a list of specific federal penal statutes, police organizations of the national government are part of the executive branch. Other than the FBI, which has the broadest purview—investigation of all federal crimes not the responsibility of another agency—there are also (1) units of the Treasury Department concerned with violations of laws relating to the collection of income taxes (Internal Revenue Service), alcohol and tobacco taxes, and gun control (Bureau of Alcohol, Tobacco, and Firearms), and customs

(Customs Service); (2) the Drug Enforcement Administration of the Justice Department; (3) the Secret Service, a division of the Treasury concerned with counterfeiting, forgery, and protection of the president; (4) the Bureau of Postal Inspection of the Postal Service, which deals with mail offenses; and (5) the Border Patrol of the Department of Justice.

Each state has its own police force, yet here also the local nature of law enforcement may be seen by the fact that state police forces were not established until the turn of the century, and then primarily as a wing of the executive branch that would enforce the law when local officials did not. In all states this force is charged with the regulation of traffic on the main highways, and in two-thirds of the states it has been given general police powers; yet in about only a dozen populous states is it adequate to the task of general law enforcement outside the cities. Where the state police are well developed—such as in Pennsylvania, New York, New Jersey, Massachusetts, and Michigan—they tend to fill a void in rural law enforcement. The reluctance of Americans to centralize police power means that the state forces generally have not been allowed to supplant local officials. For the most part they operate only in areas where there is no other form of police protection or where the local officers request their expertise or the use of their facilities.

Sheriffs are found in almost every one of the more than 3,000 counties in the United States. They have the responsibility for law enforcement in rural areas, yet over time many of their functions have been assumed by the state or local police. This is particularly true in portions of the Northeast. In parts of the South and West, however, the sheriff's office remains a well-organized force. In 33 of the states, sheriffs have broad authority, are elected, and occupy the position of chief law enforcement officer in the county. Even when the sheriff's office is well organized it may lack jurisdiction over municipalities and incorporated areas. In addition to having law enforcement responsibilities, the sheriff is often an officer of the court and is charged with holding prisoners, serving court orders, and providing bailiffs.

Police departments exist in over 1,000 cities and 20,000 towns, yet only in the cities where they have sufficient resources can it be said that they perform all four of the law-enforcement functions. Although established by local government, the police of the cities and towns are vested by state law with general authority. Usually, the larger the community, the more police workers it employs. Nearly one-third of the police personnel in the United States are employed by the 55 cities with populations over 250,000, resulting in a ratio of officers to residents of 2.9:1,000, which is almost twice the average for cities of less than 100,000. In the metropolitan areas, where law enforcement may be fragmented among agencies of all governmental levels, jurisdictional conflict may inhibit the efficient use of police resources. The United States is essentially a nation with small police forces, each operating independently within the limits of its jurisdiction.

The United States has a "dual court system": a separate judicial structure for each of the states in addition to a national structure. In each of the systems is a series of trial and appellate courts, with the United States Supreme Court being the only body in which the systems are "brought together." It is important to emphasize that the U.S. Supreme Court, although commonly referred to as "the highest court in the land," does not have the right to review all decisions of state courts in criminal cases. It hears only those cases in which a federal statute is involved or in which a right of the defendant under the U.S. Constitution is alleged to have been infringed. This usually means the accused claims that one or more of his or her due process rights were denied during the state criminal proceeding.

With a dual court system, interpretation of legal doctrine can differ from state to state. Although states may have statutes with similar wording, none of them interprets the laws in exactly the same way. To some extent these variations reflect varying social and political conditions. They may also represent attempts by certain state courts to solve similar problems through different means. But primarily the diversity of legal doctrine results simply from fragmentation of the court system; within the framework of each jurisdiction the judges have discretion to apply the law as they believe it should be applied, until overruled by a higher court.

The national court system is arranged in a hierarchical manner, with the district courts at the base, the courts of appeals at the intermediate level, and the Supreme Court at the top. The 94 district courts are the tribunals of original jurisdiction, or the first instance. Distributed throughout the country, with at least one in each state, they constitute the judicial body that hears the great majority of civil and criminal cases arising under federal law.

Above the federal district courts are 12 United States courts of appeals, each with jurisdiction for a geographic portion of the country, and one for the District of Columbia. Created in 1891 as a means of reducing the case burden of the Supreme Court, this intermediate level of the judiciary hears appeals from the district courts and from administrative bodies such as the United States Tax Court and the National Labor Relations Board. From three to nine judges are assigned to each court of appeals, and normally three jurists sit as a panel.

The Constitution gives original jurisdiction to the U.S. Supreme Court for only a few types of cases; hence the primary task of the high court is to hear appeals from the state courts of last resort and the lower federal courts. But as the highest appellate court, it still retains discretion over the cases it will hear. Each year it rejects as unworthy of review three-fourths of the 2,000 cases reaching it. With nine justices appointed for life, the Supreme Court is probably the most influential judicial tribunal in the world, exercising review and attempting to maintain consistency in the law within the federal structure.

One of the difficulties in describing the structure of state courts is that although they all are somewhat alike, they are all somewhat different. The laws of each state determine the organization of these courts; thus their names, their relationships to one another, and the rules governing their operation vary considerably. Still, one usually finds three levels of courts and a close resemblance between the pattern in the states and the organizational framework of the national judiciary. It should be emphasized that the state courts operate under the authority of state constitutions and should not be considered "inferior" to comparable courts in the national structure.

The courts of first instance, often referred to as the "inferior" trial courts, have powers limited to arraignment of all cases, preliminary hearings involving crimes that must be adjudicated at a higher level, disposition of summary offenses (where a jury is not allowed), and, in some states, trial of persons accused of some misdemeanors. Generally, the law defines the jurisdiction according to the maximum jail sentence that may be imposed. Six months in jail is commonly the greatest penalty that these courts may confer.

Especially in urban areas, the observer at these courts finds very little that resembles the dignity and formal procedures of higher bodies. These are not jurisdictions of record (no detailed account of the proceedings is kept), and the activities are carried out in an informal atmosphere. In most urban areas endless numbers of people are serviced by these courts, and each defendant gets only a small portion of what should be a defendant's "day in court."

The courts of general jurisdiction are above the courts of first instance and have the authority to try all cases, both civil and criminal.

They are courts of record and follow the formal procedures of the law. In large metropolitan areas it is common to have divisions specializing in different kinds of cases. In addition to the original jurisdiction that such courts exercise, and which is their principal function, they also act on appeals, hearing defendants who contest decisions made at the inferior level.

The appellate courts have no trial jurisdiction but hear only appeals from the lower courts. In some states only the state's supreme court is found at this level; in others there may be an intermediate appellate court in addition to the highest judicial body.

On any given day, approximately 2.5 million offenders are under the care of the U.S. system of corrections. Through a variety of institutions and treatment programs at all levels of government, attempts are made to restore people to society. Of interest is the great number of approaches employed by correctional personnel to bring about the rehabilitation of offenders. The average citizen probably equates corrections with prisons, but only about one-third of convicted offenders are actually incarcerated; the remainder are under supervision in the community. The use of probation and parole has increased dramatically, as has the creation of community-based centers, where those who have been incarcerated may maintain ties with families and friends so reintegration into society can be more successful.

The federal government, all of the states, most counties, and all but the smallest cities are engaged in the correctional function. In small communities facilities are usually limited to jails that are used to hold persons awaiting disposition. As in the police and court functions, each level of government acts independently. Although the states operate prisons and parole activities, probation is frequently tied to the judicial departments of counties or municipalities.

Substantive Criminal Law

In the U.S. system of justice, violators of the laws are prosecuted and tried according to rules. The ancient Latin maxim, *nullum crimen, nulla poena sine lege* (there can be no crime, and no punishment, except as the law prescribes), is basic to the system. The criminal code therefore not only embodies a view of the forbidden behavior and the punishment to be administered but describes the ways officials may deal with defendants.

The mere description of criminal offenses does not give a full understanding of the law's content. The criteria used to decide whether a specific act is a crime must be more precise than the statements of the general characteristics of a body of rules. More important, it is necessary to understand the principles buttressing these definitions because the principles assist in differentiating those who should be labeled offenders. For every crime there are theoretically seven interrelated and overlapping principles. Ideally, behavior cannot be called a crime unless all seven principles are present:

(1) Legality—a law defining the crime
(2) *Actus reus*—behavior of either commission or omission by the accused that constituted the violation
(3) *Mens rea*—a guilty state of mind
(4) Fusion of *actus reus* and *mens rea*—the intention and the act must both occur
(5) Harm—a crime has a harmful impact on certain legally protected values
(6) Causation—a causal relationship between the act and the harm
(7) Punishment—the sanctions to be applied for the proscribed behavior must be stipulated in the law

Over time the seven principles of a crime have been interpreted to meet changing conditions. In particular, the concept of a guilty state of mind (*mens rea*) has been adapted to the lessening of religious influences (sin) on the law and the emergence of psychology as a prominent field of knowledge. The concept of *mens rea* as an actual consciousness of guilt has been abandoned in favor of intentional, or even reckless or negligent, conduct. The new doctrine, called "objective" *mens rea*, asks "not whether an individual defendant has consciousness of guilt, but whether a reasonable person in the defendant's circumstances and with the defendant's physical characteristics would have had consciousness of guilt." The traditional notion of *mens rea* has thus been replaced by the requirement that the act be voluntary and that the so-called general defenses be inapplicable. The general defenses include such conditions as insanity, immaturity, intoxication, coercion, and mistake of fact. In contemporary terms, *mens rea* has evolved into a concept of objectivity, without the ethical or moral connotations originally attached to it.

Sources of Criminal Law

In recent years there has been increased academic debate concerning the sources of criminal law. This question has come to the forefront as minority groups have become more vocal and as the sanctions imposed on white-collar offenders has been contrasted with those imposed on street criminals. Why are some types of human behavior and not others declared criminal by law? What are the social forces that are brought to bear on legislators as they write the criminal code? Why are activities that are labeled criminal during one era found to be acceptable in another? Such issues require the development of a theory explaining the sources of the criminal law because they have an impact on the assumptions concerning the nature of crime and the sources of criminal behavior.

For much of U.S. history there was a tendency to think of crime as pertaining only to criminals rather than to some other units of society. Most Americans seem not to separate the concept of crime from that of "criminal" and believe that criminals are a group set off from the mainstream of society. In Puritan Massachusetts crime was viewed in theological terms, and the criminal was a creature of the devil. Most provisions of the Puritans' legal code were annotated to show the Biblical source of the injunctions. In a later era, medically oriented persons saw crime as arising from some biologically inherited abnormality. Psychologists in the nineteenth and twentieth centuries described crime as resulting from mental or personality defects. More recently, social scientists have looked to social situations—neighborhood, school, gang, and family—as predisposing persons to be either law-abiding or criminal. Throughout all of these approaches runs the idea that criminality is a characteristic of individuals and not a consequence of a label imposed by the community.

It is most important to recognize that the definition of behavior as criminal stems from a social process in which rules are developed and applied to particular people. This means that before a person can commit a crime, there must first be a community and process that has called the commission of that act criminal. In addition, someone must have observed the act or its consequences and applied the community's definition to it. Third, a crime implies a victim. Finally, punishment implies that someone is responsible for carrying out the community's will. All of this signifies that crime is a social phenomenon arising from the complex interactions of a number of individuals and social situations.

Theories have been developed to explain the focus and functions of criminal laws and the social processes by which they evolve. These ideas may be divided into a consensus model and a conflict model. The consensus model argues that the criminal law is a reflection of the will or values of society. This assumes that the society has achieved a well-integrated and relatively stable agreement on basic values. Studies have shown very high public agreement on the seriousness of crimes, and the norms concerning crime seriousness are widely diffused throughout the subgroups of society. The conflict model emphasizes the role of political interests in the formulation of the law and points to the dominance of powerful groups in structuring the law to meet their own needs. As an example, it has been shown that a variety of elements influenced the development and enforcement of prohibitions against narcotics, including the relations among nations, controversies between druggist and physician interest groups, the bureaucratic politics of enforcement agencies, and the fear of racial and ethnic minorities.

At this point in the development of a sociology of law it is impossible to reach a conclusion as to the theoretical value of the consensus and conflict models. Certainly with some laws, especially those prohibiting crimes that are *mala in se*, there is consensus in most Western societies as to the values espoused. It is also very easy to demonstrate how the laws prohibiting cattle rustling, the consumption of alcohol, vagrancy, and the sale of pornography—crimes *mala prohibita*—have their sources in the political power of special interests. Because the great bulk of criminal violations are now those of the latter type, attention logically focuses on the conflict model.

Criminal Procedure

Although a formal diagram of the criminal justice process may appear streamlined, with cases of the accused entering at the left and swiftly moving toward their disposition at the right, the fact remains that the system is detailed and fraught with detours. At every point along the way decision makers have the option of moving a case on to the next point or dropping it from the system. The formal blueprint of the administration of justice does not include the influences of the social relations or political environment within which the system operates.

The popular and even the law book conception of the criminal justice machinery supported by a due process ideology and reinforced by the "Perry Mason" image of an adversary system oversimplifies in some respects and overcomplicates in others. Theory holds to an ideal of law enforcement in which the police arrest persons suspected of committing infractions of the law and promptly bring them to a magistrate. If the offense is minor, the magistrate disposes of the case immediately; if it is serious, the accused is held for further action and is admitted to bail. The prosecutor is next given the case and charges the offender with the specific crime after a preliminary hearing of the evidence. If the defendant pleads not guilty to the charge, he or she is bound over for trial. In the courtroom a "fight," supervised by the judge, is staged between adversaries—defense counsel and prosecutor—so that the truth becomes known. If the jury finds the defendant guilty, the judge or the jury determine the sentence and correctional officials impose the prescribed sanctions.

Although many cases do proceed as described above, for most cases this conception of the criminal justice flow makes fundamental assumptions that do not correspond to reality. It fails to take note of the many informal arrangements that occur through negotiations among the principal actors. Only a small number of cases ever reach the trial stage. Rather, decisions are made early in the process on the basis of discretion, so that cases that may not result in conviction are filtered out by the police and prosecutor. In addition, is some jurisdictions up to 90% of the defendants plead guilty, thus obviating the need for a trial. Through bargaining between the prosecutor and defendant, a guilty plea is exchanged for reduction of the charges or a sentencing recommendation. The size of the prison population can be used as a justification to influence sentencing or parole decisions.

Social scientists have recognized that discussion of an organization solely in terms of its structure is inadequate for a full appreciation of its dynamic process. Although the term *organization* suggests a certain bareness—a lean, no-nonsense construct of consciously coordinated activities—all organizations are molded by forces tangential to their rationally ordered structures and stated ends. The formal rules do not completely account for the behavior of the actors because an informal structure also exists that results from the social environment and the interaction of the actors. Organizations have formal decision-making processes, but these may serve mostly to legitimize organizational goals and act to enhance the symbolic needs of authority. Emphasis on the prescribed structure may neglect the fact that the achievement of goals is dependent upon the behavior of actors who have their own requirements, which may run counter to the manifest aims of the organization. Further, it must be recognized that the organization itself has survival needs that must be fulfilled. Thus the realization of system aims is but one of the several important purposes of the organization. The system makes adaptive responses to meet its needs because informal arrangements arise to meet the goals of both the organization and its actors.

The administration of criminal justice may be characterized by certain essential features. First, it should be noted that it is an open system; new cases, changes in personnel, and different conditions in the political system mean that it is forced to deal with constant variations in its milieu. Second, there is a condition of scarcity within the system; shortages of resources, such as time, information, and personnel, are characteristic. Every case cannot be processed according to the formally prescribed criteria. This affects the subunits of law enforcement—police, prosecutor, courts—so that each competes with the others for the available resources. Central to this analysis is the politics of administration; the varied range of interactions between an agency and its environment that augment, retain, or diminish the basic resources needed to attain organizational goals.

The President's Crime Commission has referred to the legal process as a continuum—an orderly progression of events. Like all legally constituted structures, there are formally designed points in the process where decisions are made concerning the disposition of cases. To speak of the system as a continuum, however, may underplay the complexity and the flux of relationships within it. Although the administration of criminal justice is composed of a set of subsystems, there are no formal provisions for the subordination of one unit to another. Each has its own clientele, goals, and norms, yet the outputs of one unit constitute the inputs to another.

We should not be surprised by the fact that conflicts exist among the various actors in the criminal justice process. Each sees the problem of crime and the administration of justice from a different perspective. The daily experiences, social background, and professional norms of the police officer, prosecutor, defense attorney, and judge exert an influence on the way each makes decisions. The police officer who has seen the agony of crime victims and risked his or her life to protect society may be unable to understand why defendants are released on bail or why prosecutors may be concerned by the police officer's lack of attention to detail in collecting evidence, and the judge may be upset by a failure to maintain the civil liberties of defendants. A characteristic of the criminal justice process is that each participant is dependent upon others for assistance in doing his or her work. At every stage, from arrest to sentencing, a variety of actors with different viewpoints and goals are involved in making decisions about the disposition of each case.

Given the fragmentation of the system, we may ask how decisions are made. As interdependent subunits of a system, each organization and its clientele is engaged in a set of exchange relationships across boundaries. The necessary interactions among participants means that bargains are made that stipulate the conditions under which a defendant's case will be handled. The police, charged with making decisions concerning the apprehension of suspects, interact with the prosecutor's office when presenting evidence and recommending charges. The defendant, through counsel, may exchange a guilty plea for a reduction of the charges by the prosecutor. Likewise, the courts and prosecutor are linked by the decision to bring charges, the activities of the courtroom, and disposition of the case.

Although the formal structures of the judicial process stress antagonistic and competitive subunits, the interaction of exchange may strengthen cooperation within the system, thus deflecting it from its manifest goals. For example, although the prosecutor and defense counsel occupy roles that are prescribed as antagonistic, continued interaction on the job, in professional associations, and in political or social groups may produce a friendship that greatly influences role playing. Combat in the courtroom, as ordained by the formal structure, not only may endanger the personal relationship but may also expose weaknesses in the actors to their own clientele. An outcome, rather than the unpredictability and professional distance stressed by the system, is that decisions on cases may be made to benefit mutually the actors in the exchange.

The most distinctive feature of the administration of criminal justice is that it is marked by a high degree of discretion. As in few other social organizations, discretion in law enforcement and judicial agencies increases as one moves down the administrative hierarchy. In most organizations, the observer usually finds the lowest-ranking members performing the most routinized tasks under supervision, with various mechanisms of quality control employed to check their work. With the police, prosecutor, and lower-court judges, discretion is exercised more frequently by those who are newest to the organization, who maintain the primary organizational contact with the public, and whose work is usually shielded from the view of supervisors and outside observers. Thus the patrol officer has wide discretion in determining whom to arrest and on what charges; the deputy prosecutor makes vital decisions concerning indictment; and lower-court judges operate without the dominating influence of higher courts.

A final characteristic of the administration of justice is that the process resembles a filter through which cases are screened: Some are advanced to the next level of decision making; others are either rejected or the conditions under which they are processed are changed. As the President's Crime Commission noted, "Approximately one-half of those arrested are dismissed by the police, prosecutor, or magistrate at an early stage of the case." Other evidence is equally impressive, showing that a preponderance of adult felony arrests do not go to the grand jury for indictment. Typically, jury trials account for a minuscule percentage of the guilty convictions in criminal courts. Sentences are mostly imposed following a plea of guilty.

Criminal justice is greatly affected by the values of each decision maker, whose career, influence, and position may be more important than are considerations for the formal requirements of the law. Accommodations are sought with those in the exchange system so that decisions can be made that are consistent with the values of the participants and the organization. A wide variety of departures from the formal rules of the ideology of due process are accepted by judicial actors but are never publicly acknowledged. Because of the strain of an overwhelming caseload and the adversary nature of the formal structure, members of the bureaucracy can reduce stress while maximizing rewards by filtering out those cases viewed as disruptive or as potential threats to the established norms. Because defendants pass through the system and the judicial actors remain, the accused may become secondary figures in the bureaucratic setting. The administrative norms are so well established that judges may agree that defendants surviving the scrutiny of the police and prosecutor must be guilty.

Execution of Penal Measures (Corrections)

Throughout most of this century the espoused purpose of the criminal sanction in the United States has been the rehabilitation of offenders. As recently as 1973 a national commission demonstrated the almost complete acceptance by the correctional community of this medical model by recommending additional measures to implement the rehabilitation goal more fully. During the past decade, however, there has been a rethinking of the medical model as critics have pointed to the ineffectiveness of treatment programs on recidivism, to the pervasiveness of the discretion required by this goal and its impact on civil rights, and to evidence that rehabilitation has had little bearing on the control of crime.

Legislatures in over thirty states have now revised their penal laws so as to substitute for the goal of rehabilitation, sentencing, and correctional forms that emphasize deserved punishment. To implement this new focus, reformers have persuaded legislators to restrict the discretion exercised by judges and correctional officials by instituting definite sentences, sentencing guidelines, and mandatory parole release. The remaining states have kept the major structures of the rehabilitative goal: indefinite sentences, treatment programs, and discretionary parole release.

Fines, probation, and incarceration are the basic forms of criminal sanction imposed in the United States. These apparently simple categories of legally authorized punishments do not reveal the complex problems associated with their application. Although the penal codes stipulate the sentences that should be imposed for specific crimes, judges are given great leeway to determine the appropriate punishment. The discretionary nature of the administration of penal sanctions extends to probation and correctional agencies, which are able to grant reductions so that offenders are released from supervision prior to completion of their sentences.

Fines are widely used for less serious offenses and are often tied to probation. The focus of corrections in the public mind is the prison, but probation is the sentence received by over 60% of adult offenders. Probation allows offenders to live in the community under supervision, with an officer of the court available to assist with problems of employment, housing, and family matters. Rates of incarceration have ballooned during the past decade, so that now over 200 of every 100,000 Americans are in state or federal prisons; in 1986 this equaled 503,000 individuals. More than 208,000 Americans were being held in local jails. Following the 1976 decision by the Supreme Court in *Gregg v. Georgia*, thirty-five states reinstituted the death penalty. Although about 1,900 persons are now awaiting this penalty, capital punishment orders have been carried out sparingly—by 1986, fewer than seventy.

Methods of dealing with criminal offenders have come a long way since the reform activities of Philadelphia's Quakers, but uncertainty remains about the methods that should be used. With the rate of recidivism about constant, more and more doubts are being expressed about the value of the rehabilitative models. As crime rates fail to drop, questions are voiced as to the deterrent effect of correctional methods.

Of all the subsystems of criminal justice, corrections appear to be going through the most sustained soul searching. Changes made in corrections policy will have important consequences in the ways that law enforcement and adjudication goals are pursued in the future.

2

England

JOHN C. FREEMAN

General Information

England, for the purposes of this chapter, is taken to include the Principality of Wales. Northern Ireland and Scotland, while part of the United Kingdom, have a largely separate system of criminal law and are therefore excluded. England and Wales together make up about 50-thousand square miles and have a population of about 49 million. Thus the country has a relatively high density of population (1,000 per square mile). Immigration, coming largely from the countries of the British Commonwealth, has resulted in a nonwhite population widely estimated at about 2 million. London is England's capital with a population of slightly less than 7 million.

Despite an invasion by the Romans (in 55 B.C.), there has been no significant reception of Roman Law. The influence of Roman Law doctrines in Scotland was much more pronounced. England may now be described as a country with a Christian tradition and as a constitutional monarchy with an unwritten and hence flexible constitution. Legislation, to become effective, must be passed by the House of Commons (composed of 650 elected members) and the House of Lords and then receive the Royal assent. In practice, the latter cannot be withheld, and the blocking powers of the House of Lords are extremely limited.

The members of the House of Commons are democratically elected, all citizens over the age of 18 years being eligible to vote. Elections must be held at least once every five years; most of those elected belong to either the Conservative or the Labor Party, although other elements are now gaining political strength. An independent and permanent Civil Service is a strong factor in maintaining a fairly consistent and progressive policy toward criminal justice whichever party is in power.

There is no Ministry of Justice in England. The functions normally exercised by such a ministry in other countries are carried out chiefly by the Home Office (whose minister, the Secretary of State for the Home Department, is one of the principal members of the Cabinet) and by the Lord Chancellor's Office (The Lord Chancellor also being a senior cabinet minister, as well as being head of the judiciary and presiding over the House of Lords).

The Criminal Law Revision Committee and various ad hoc committees review the criminal law and make recommendations for change. In 1965 a Law Commission for England and Wales was created with the express task of keeping the law up-to-date. Some major reforms in the criminal law have been instigated by this body in recent years.

Scope of Criminal Sanctions

In common with all developed countries, England has seen a great growth of criminal law in recent years. The handful of major crimes against the King, persons and property that emerged many centuries ago when criminal law parted from civil law, has grown into the usual profusion of restraints and punishments thought to be required by a sophisticated modern state. Many offenses were created in the nineteenth century in response to social pressures and many more have been created recently to impose some limits on the potential harm of motor vehicles and kindred contemporary vexations.

In company with other nations with a similar inheritance, England is now scrutinizing its straggling criminal law quite closely. The work of the Law Commission has already achieved much consolidation and the abolition of many obsolete crimes. A Criminal Policy Department exists within the Home Office. Persistent consideration is being given to decriminalization and to the future shape of the criminal law. In the future, more attention may be paid to offenses against the environment and to certain far-reaching white-collar crime. At the same time there may be corresponding withdrawal from the enforcement of criminal sanctions for petty crimes against individuals. It is, of course, unrealistic to imagine that all social problems are solved by a withdrawal of criminal law. They merely become the responsibility of an alternative agency (the frequent offense of drunkenness being a case in point), although the decriminalization thesis may win some acceptance in England for other good reasons.

As in other jurisdictions, the borderlines of criminal law and morality do not coincide. The 1960s and 1970s saw some relaxation of criminal law regarding homosexual behavior, abortion, and suicide, for example, following a jurisprudential debate on the nature and purpose of criminal sanctions. The discussion that had begun in the last century with the clash of views of J. S. Mill and Sir James Fitzjames Stephen was revived more recently between Professor H.L.A. Hart and Lord Devlin, with Lady Wootton and others joining in. Put broadly, the liberal position is that, unless conduct can be shown to be harmful, it should not be punished by criminal law. The opposing camp sees social morality as a "seamless web" that is capable of suffering detriment, however minor, by even small personal infractions. The present decade finds conservative, not to say reactionary, opinions to be on the ascendant.

General Description of the Legal System

England is a common law country, and courts are bound by earlier decisions of superior courts on similar facts. Many crimes, including some of the most serious (such as murder) are still not defined by statute, but modern Acts of Parliament are gradually replacing the common law, as well as creating many new offenses. Two contemporary trends may be noted. First, Parliament, with increasing frequency, lays down the outline of legislation to be filled in by delegated or subordinate legislation, often in the form of multitudinous rules and regulations promulgated by ministerial departments. Road traffic legislation and the Bail Act of 1976 are two examples. Second, legislation is sometimes passed by Parliament to become effective when later announced by ministerial decision. As in the case of the Children and Young Persons Act of 1969, it is not unusual for many sections of Acts to remain inoperative for years because of changes in policy, lack of resources for implementation, or other reasons.

Amount, Structure, and Dynamics of Criminality

Social attitudes change. Sir William Blackstone, in his widely published *Commentaries* at the turn of the eighteenth century, listed as most grave those crimes immediately injurious to God and His holy religion and second those violating and transgressing the law of nations, yet a recently successful prosecution for blasphemous libel was the first in many years and there was widespread public dismay that such a crime should still exist at all. English criminal law has often been criticized for apparently placing more emphasis on offenses against property than offenses against the person, and there is wide concern that persons convicted of a serious robbery, for example, may serve longer terms of imprisonment than some who have murdered.

Perhaps the biggest change in crime and criminal law has resulted from the Industrial Revolution, organization, and the need to control and administer an increasingly complex society. With motoring offenses running at about half the court convictions in England and Wales, underdeveloped countries wishing to curtail conviction statistics might well eschew the introduction of the motor vehicle.

The *British Crime Survey*, a victimological survey of some 10,000 households conducted in the 1970s and 1980s, has shown that the offenses causing most anxiety are burglary (mentioned by 44% of respondents), "mugging" (robbery in the street; 34%), and sexual attacks (23%). This research also gave some insight into the "dark figure" of unreported crime, revealing it to be far greater than even well-kept official statistics disclosed. The *Criminal Statistics, England and Wales, 1984*, which show a generally increasing rate of law breaking, are subject to all the usual caveats raised by criminologists regarding such data. Thus although they show an increase in notifiable offenses of violence reported to the police from 64,000 in 1974 to 114,000 in 1984, sociological scrutiny makes it impossible to conclude that contemporary society is in fact any more violent than was the case 50 or indeed 500 years ago. The number of rapes throughout the whole of England and Wales reported to the police in 1984 was the relatively tiny number of 1,433 (an increase of 381 over ten years). Although many incidents are undoubtedly still unreported, changes in law and practice in recent years have facilitated reporting and the mass media of communication have done everything possible to focus attention on this crime, to increase reporting, and, coincidentally, to generate panic. The fact remains that a high proportion of rapes are committed in the victim's own dwellings and by persons known to the victims, so that the chances of public attack of the kind by a stranger in any part of England are very remote indeed. Although the reporting and "clear-up" rates of homicide are very high, the number of persons convicted of murder in 1983 was a mere 149 and there has hardly been any increase in this number over very many years. The general pattern of crime is similar to that observed in other countries of comparable socioeconomic development, with a high rate of offending against property and apparently some increase in offending by females. Juvenile crime has not been seen as growing, possibly because police diversionary methods such as "cautioning" have prevented incidents from entering the official statistics.

Structure and Functioning of Law Enforcement Agencies

There are over 120,000 police (including some 11,000 women) organized in 43 regular forces throughout England and Wales. The largest force is the Metropolitan Police Force of London, which has almost 27,000 police covering an area with a radius of about 15 miles. There is no *national* police force. Responsibility for, and control of, the police is shared between local and central government. The year 1984 saw the creation of the Police Complaints Authority to deal independently with citizens' grievances. An issue remains as to how far the working of the police should be subject to democratic control.

In 1986 a new organization came into operation under the Director of Public Prosecutions. Called the Crown Prosecution Service, it is intended to introduce more consistency and professionalism into the prosecution process, which had previously been very much in the hands of the police.

The legal profession in England and Wales is divided into two. Barristers (counsels) are chiefly advocates before the higher courts and provide opinions on difficult questions of law. Solicitors, usually practicing in partnerships, sometimes appear in certain courts but more often simply give advice on everyday legal affairs. The services of barristers may be obtained only through the intermediary offices of a solicitor. The most senior barristers are designated Queen's Counsel and most judicial appointments are made from the ranks of the barristers. In 1985 there were 5,367 barristers in practice, including 696 women, and in the same year 46,490 solicitors were practicing, of whom 6,262 were women. Free, or substantially subsidized, legal aid is widely available to defendants.

About 98% of those convicted of crimes are dealt with by magistrates' courts, of which there are about 640 throughout the country. They are staffed by over 27,500 lay magistrates (justices of the peace), who voluntarily take time off from their normal occupations to do this work.

In addition, about 55 stipendiary magistrates (full-time salaried lawyers) man some of the courts in large urban areas. Appeal from the magistrates' courts lies to the Divisional Court of the Queen's Bench Division of the High Court. Above the magistrates courts are the Crown Courts, which have original jurisdiction in serious criminal cases. Further affects may be taken to the Court of Appeal (Criminal Division) and thence to the House of Lords in certain cases. In the Crown Courts the judge sits with a 12-man jury that is the arbiter of facts at the trial. Judges of the higher courts are appointed by the Crown, and the removal of a judge from office would be constitutionally extremely difficult and exceptionally rare. Persons under the age of 17 years are brought before juvenile courts where 3 specially appointed lay justices sit. Both sexes must be represented on such a bench.

Substantive Criminal Law

General Principles of Liability

It goes almost without saying that in England there can be no conviction for crime save for proven infractions of preexisting laws. An apparent attempt in the House of Lords to recognize the power of the courts to create new heads of liability retrospectively was widely criticized and eventually denied. So far as statutory offenses are concerned, a number of presumptions have been acknowledged by the courts—for example, (1) against alteration of the common law, (2) that penal statutes are to be strictly construed, (3) against e.c. retrospective effect, (4) that *mens rea* is required for liability, and so on.

Classification of Offenses

Offenses in England may be classified in different ways for different purposes. Many distinctions are largely procedural. Crimes may be regarded philosophically as dealing with things either *mala en se* or *mala prohibita*; they may be thought of as either statutory or common law. The ancient divisions of treasons, felonies, and misdemeanors were abolished by the Criminal Law Act of 1967 and replaced by the new categories of arrestable offenses and nonarrestable offenses that made more sense according to contemporary standards.

Perhaps the most useful (though confusing) distinction exists between indictable and nonindictable offenses, the former being eligible for trial by jury. Although this provides an apparent guide to the seriousness of an offense, indictable offenses could include relatively minor thefts, robberies, and assaults; in certain circumstances many such crimes may be tried summarily before the magistrates. The Criminal Law Act of 1977 explains which offenses are triable only summarily, which are triable only on indictment, and which are triable either way.

Age of Criminal Responsibility

Although persons under the age of 17 years are dealt with in juvenile courts, they are considered in law to be fully responsible for their crimes if they are over the age of 14. Children under the age of 14 are not held to be liable unless, in addition to having the normally required mental element, they also have "a mischievous discretion." This latter is generally taken to be present if a child admits to knowing that what he or she was doing was wrong. Children less than ten years of age are entirely exempt from criminal liability.

Liability of Corporations

A corporation is recognized as having a legal existence with rights and duties separate from that of its members. Corporations may now be regarded as generally liable to the same extent as an individual. This result has been achieved by extending the doctrine of vicarious liability and by visiting responsibility upon the high officers of a company who direct its activities. Although it has been remarked that a corporation has no body to be kicked nor soul to be damned, this has not prevented the imposition of appropriate sanctions.

The Mental Element

While *mens rea* remains, in general, an essential element in criminal liability, nevertheless there have been many offenses in the last 50 years that have been held to be offenses of strict (sometimes wrongly called "absolute") liability. This doctrine has been held to be necessary in the public interest: It is said to promote higher standards of safety, hygiene, and welfare by dispensing with the need to prove intent and thus facilitating prosecution. This is seen as working injustice on, for example, an honest trader who is already doing his or her best, or indeed upon anybody who has taken all reasonable care to do nothing wrong. In more recent statutes, defenses equivalent to due diligence are beginning to appear, as the injustice of the full rigor of the strict liability doctrine becomes apparent even to the common layman. There has been, in general, no liability for negligence in English criminal law.

Attempt and Conspiracy

The law of attempt and conspiracy has become very complicated and confused. Since mere intention to commit a crime is in itself insufficient for liability, there must be evidence of the commission of some act directly connected with the offense for attempt to be charged. But some acts of the accused that may show the necessary connection might be considered too remote to constitute a true attempt. In truth, no one theory seems yet to have been consistently accepted and the matter is surrounded by a considerable incrustation of academic literature. The law of conspiracy has also been widely criticized. According to the common law, one was guilty of conspiracy who agreed with another to commit an unlawful act or a lawful act by unlawful means. The Criminal Law Act of 1977 now provides, in effect, that a charge of conspiracy can be lodged only in respect to an agreement to commit a criminal offense.

Defenses

If the accused, being brought to trial, is found incapable of pleading, understanding the charge, and following the proceedings, he or she may be found unfit to plead on arraignment under the Criminal Procedure (Insanity) Act of 1964, but even if he or she is well enough to stand trial he or she may still wish to raise insanity as his or her defense. This happens very rarely. The rules are ancient and amount to this:

> That every defendant is presumed sane until the contrary be proved to the satisfaction of the jury. It should be ascertained whether the accused was laboring under such a defect of reason from disease of the mind as not to know the nature and quality of his act. If he is found to have understood the nature and quality of his act, the court has further to be satisfied that he knew that it was wrong.
>
> If the accused is found to be suffering under an insane delusion, he is under the same degree of responsibility as he would have been on the facts as he imagined them to be [*R. v. M'Naghten*, 1843, 10Cl. & F.200].

In 1957 the Homicide Act was passed, which borrowed from Scots law the doctrine of diminished responsibility. This is a limited defense, which provides that murder may be reduced to manslaughter where the accused is "suffering from such abnormality of mind (whether arising from a condition of arrested or retarded development of mind or any inherent causes or induced by disease or injury) as substantially impaired his mental responsibility."

For practical purposes, this defense seems virtually to have replaced insanity that is still based on the outmoded psychiatric understanding implicit in the old *M'Naghten* rules. There is also some suspicion that pleas of guilty to manslaughter based on diminished responsibility are being accepted in lieu of pleas of not guilty to murder. The flexible sentencing powers of the courts, which may impose up to life imprisonment for manslaughter (which sentence is mandatory for murder), ensure that elements of justice and security are satisfied and a court enabled to deal mercifully with, for example, a "mercy killing."

Automatism, in the sense of involuntary movement of the body or limbs, or acts done while unconscious or in a convulsion or spasm, may be a defense.

Irresistible impulse as such is no defense, but it might amount to diminished responsibility.

An honestly held mistake of fact might serve as a defense. A mistake of law never will (even though the state of the law at any given time must surely be regarded as a fact!).

Self-induced (as opposed to involuntary) intoxication due to drink or drugs, which falls short of bringing about actual insanity, seems to be a defense only where it negates specific intent in crimes held to require this.

Fear of dire threats and some other forms of duress may be a defense to some crimes, but not to murder. Coercion is a somewhat obsolete defense available only to wives who commit offenses under the moral persuasion of their husbands.

The supposed defense of necessity is illustrated by one of the most poignant cases in English legal history. A sailing vessel, the *Mignonette*, was shipwrecked in 1884. Some survivors were 20 days at sea in an open boat, with virtually no food or water. Then, on the point of starvation, they killed and ate the youngest of their number, a cabin boy. They were later rescued, to be tried and convicted of murder. Inevitably, they were sentenced to death, although their sentences were later commuted to imprisonment for six months. But still from that day until the present, however, no place has been found for any defense of necessity.

Punishment and Penal Measures

For the purposes of the present discussion, penal measures are taken to embrace all the sentencing options open to the courts from absolute discharge to capital punishment.

A recent Home Office Working Paper describes policy objectives as follows: (1) to protect society from the dangerous offender, (2) to reduce the incidence of offending (particularly amongst juveniles), (3) to reduce the prison population and the use of imprisonment, and (4) to improve the efficiency and enhance the humanity of the system. This policy rests on a number of assumptions about the efficacy of general and particular deterrence; it reveals a certain official ambivalence toward the positive and negative consequences of imprisonment; it illustrates also the now evident conflict between the two philosophies of treatment and punishment or "just deserts."

Currently, efforts are being made to introduce more consistency into sentencing by courts at all levels. The Court of Appeal is providing guidelines and more training is being given to magistrates. There is also a discernible tendency to fetter the power of the executive to interfere with sentences and for courts to pass sentences that reflect the gravity of the crime more than the "needs" of the offender.

It is important to note that there are no general minimum penalties laid down by law, although there may be statutory limits on maximum sentences.

Principal Penal Measures
and Sentencing Trends

Capital punishment for murder has not existed since the Murder (Abolition of Death Penalty) Act of 1965. It still survives in theory for the obsolescent offenses of high treason and piracy with violence. Public opinion, in this matter as in many others, is divided, volatile, and unreliable. A poll on maintaining capital punishment in 1938 showed 50% to be in favor. By 1947 this had become 68%, yet by 1955 the tide had turned and another poll showed 65% to be opposed. It seems just possible that a survey conducted nowadays might show a majority in favor of capital punishment, at least for certain crimes, but although attempts have been made to pass laws through Parliament to reintroduce this sentence, these have been defeated again and again in recent years. Whipping was abolished in 1948. The gravest punishment at the present time is life imprisonment, which is mandatory upon conviction for murder and may also be passed on conviction for certain other very serious crimes, such as manslaughter, rape, and violent robbery. It serves as an indefinite preventative measure. Life imprisonment does not necessarily imply incarceration for the term of one's natural life.

Life imprisonment is, in effect, a sentence of custody of indeterminate length from which the offender will be released when the executive so decides. Those convicted of murder and released during the years 1980 and 1982 had served on average 10.5 years, but many life sentence prisoners remain in prison for much longer periods, in some cases for more than 20 years.

Of the range of sentences available, the fine remains by far the most frequently used. In 1984, 83% of all offenders were fined. In the case of summary offenses, nearly 96% of cases received fines, but even in indictable matters 41% of both men and women convicted were given fines. The efficacy of the fine as a penalty is well-known in many legal systems and it has a long history in English Law. It gives a court a relatively easy form of tariff to apply, although adherence to tariff principles has to be tempered by the defendant's means to pay. The Swedish day-fine system has been considered but not adopted in England, largely because of difficulties of administration.

The inability of offenders to pay fines in present economic circumstances when the level unemployment is very high has led to a very discernible decline in the use of fines and to a corresponding intensification in the quest for appropriate alternatives. Imprisonment remains a possible sanction in extreme cases for those who are fined but do not pay. Thus although imprisonment for soliciting by prostitutes was abolished in 1982, some prostitutes still find themselves in prison simply because they are unable to pay the fines awarded them. Again, some offenders continue offending, simply to make the money to pay the penalties.

In days long gone the courts themselves used to benefit from the revenue generated by fines. Now that money goes into the general coffers of the state. As such, it makes no reparation in the form of direct benefit or recompense to the victim. In current parlance, reparation is seen as being either general or individual. Individual reparation predicates some redress for the immediate victim of the offender's crime. Courts have power to order restitution or to make orders for compensation. The latter can either be attached to other penalties, or made as the only order following a conviction. Once again, the efficacy of a compensation order is governed by the offender's ability to pay. In certain cases, for example, large-scale fraud, it is possible for the crime to be regarded as an act of bankruptcy. Such an adjudication would enable the assets of the criminal to be traced and realized for the benefit of those who were the victims.

The reparative principle is now receiving attention that is long overdue. It is being said that although it might not be appropriate for an offender to make redress to his or her victim, yet he or she can provide reparation in a more general way through a community service order. Although only 8% of men and 3% of women received CSOs for indictable crimes in 1984, this in fact amounted to some 34,000 orders. Offenders cannot be placed on a CSO against their will, but if they consent and are found by the Probation Service to be suitable, they may spend up to 240 hours of their spare time in unpaid activity for the community of a kind to which no paid labor would be attracted. Although the reconviction rates following this type of sentence are very little different from any other, there have been most significant successes and advantages on other dimensions.

The Probation Service that is responsible for organizing or administering a number of sentences that are intended as alternatives to custody is principally concerned with supervising those individuals who are made the subject of probation orders. A probation order is an alternative to any other penalty and means that for a period of not more than three years an offender is subject to the guidance and supervision of one of these officers. The role of the probation officer in England involves a somewhat uneasy balance between that of a controlling authority and a counseling friend. As well as being able to give advice, social skills training, emotional support, and so on, the Probation Service has some access to tangible benefits such as accommodation and money. It also has a duty to bring back to court those who are breaching the terms of their probation orders. In 1984, 7% of males and 16% of females were placed on probation for indictable crimes. These percentages represent nearly 36,000 orders.

Occasionally, the mere experience of having been arrested and brought to court is considered a sufficient sanction in itself and no further penalty is awarded. In such circumstances, a discharge may be given. An absolute discharge is occasionally hassled when an offense is a purely technical breach of law, or where circumstances in mitigation are massive. More commonly, the discharge is conditional, that is, if offenders are able to keep out of trouble for a period laid down by the court, but not exceeding three years, they will hear no more about it, but if they do commit any further offenses the matter for which they were discharged can be brought up again and they can be punished for it. In total, 12% of males and 24% of females were discharged for indictable crimes in 1984.

The ultimate sanction for serious criminality committed by those aged more than 21 years remains imprisonment. The government has stressed again and again the desperate need to reduce the prison population and some of the laws passed by Parliament have had the same intention. The higher courts too, while recognizing that some cases are so grave that there is no alternative, have also repeatedly stressed that where possible prison should not be used and if it is seen as inevitable, then the period of custody should be as short as possible consistent with justice. Yet despite seeming unanimity on the part of the legislature, the executive, and the judiciary, the prisons are more overcrowded than ever before. The prison population in mid-1986 was 46,687 with some 13,000 sleeping two to a cell and 4,000 sleeping three to a cell originally built for just one person. Many of the institutions are one-hundred or two-hundred years old, unsavory in every respect. There have been riots on the part of prisoners and strikes on the part of staff. The imprisonment rate for 1982 in the U.K. as a whole was 104 per 100,000 of the population and reckoned to be the highest in Western Europe.

This sad and worrying state of affairs occurs despite systems of remission and parole. The former means that offenders who are of good behavior while serving their sentence will have their custody reduced by up to one-third and the latter is a scheme for still earlier release subject to the approval of the Home Secretary as advised by the Parole Board. It is also possible for some prison sentences to be suspended, either wholly or in part. The statistics for 1984 show that 10% of males and 3% of females convicted of indictable offenses were sent to prison. These data have been used to suggest that women are more favorably treated by the criminal justice system than men.

In addition to these penalties, there is other action that the courts can take, in appropriate cases, such as ordering deportation, disqualification from driving, deprivation of property used for criminal purposes, residence in a hospital, and so forth. Special measures are available against juvenile offenders that are mentioned below.

Perhaps it is worth noting that the courts have available to them a power to "bind over" people to be of good behavior, which is a centuries-old remedy of rather a preventative kind and also a power to defer sentence where an individual has been found guilty but the court wishes to allow time before deciding upon a sentence. Offenders may use this period (not more than six months) as an opportunity to reform themselves in certain ways suggested by the court, after which they may expect a lighter (sometimes nominal) punishment.

Inevitably, when sanctions are listed, questions are raised as to their efficacy. In this connection it might be of interest to note the findings of a Home Office study published in 1976:

> It has seemed, therefore, that longer sentences are no more effective than short ones, that different types of institutions work about equally as well, that probationers on the whole do no better than if they were sent to prison, and that rehabilitative programmes—whether involving psychiatric treatment, counseling, casework or intensive contact and special attention, in custodial or non-custodial settings—have no predictably beneficial effect.

Special Categories of Offenders

Offenders who are aged less than 17 years are brought before the Juvenile Courts. Like adults, they may be subject to absolute or conditional discharges, bound over, fined, or ordered to pay compensation. If they are subjected to a financial penalty the payment will normally be the responsibility of a parent.

Additionally, they may be ordered to spend some of their Saturday afternoons at attendance centers, or may be placed under supervision, which is generally undertaken by a social worker employed by the local authority instead of the Probation Service. The juvenile courts also have power to sentence boys over the age of 14 to detention centers, where they may be held in custody for not more than four months; if custody for more than four months seems to be deserved, those aged between 15 and 21 who have committed grave crimes or who have long records of serious delinquency may be sentenced to youth custody. As the powers of the Juvenile Court are limited in this respect, it is possible for juveniles charged with very grave crimes to be ordered to be tried in the Crown Court under the Children and Young Persons Act 1933, s.53. The use of this power has been increasing markedly in recent years.

The effective limit of a juvenile court's powers is reached when it makes a care order, which places the ordinary powers of the parents in the hands of the local authority whose social workers decide in case conferences the best disposition of their charges under the age of 18. They will consider placement of the children in community homes and schools, foster placements, return to their natural parents, and other options.

Much emphasis has been placed on intermediate treatment that, as part of a supervision order, is meant to provide a juvenile with a range of challenging activities. It is intended to impose some structure on a young person's life and to make some demands of him or her, short of a truly custodial sentence.

The maximum duration of sentences of imprisonment laid down for certain offenses may be exceeded by the courts in the case of some recidivists by means of extended sentences.

The Mental Health Act of 1983 enables courts to make hospital orders or guardianship orders with respect to mentally disordered offenders. Where a mentally ill person is convicted of an offense punishable by imprisonment the court may hospitalize him or her or assign guardianship to a social services agency. In certain cases where the protection of the public is required, a restriction order may be added to a hospital order so that a patient is not discharged without the consent of the Home Secretary, or the Mental Health Review Tribunal.

The Misuse of Drugs Act of 1971 draws a distinction between those who possess controlled drugs and those who supply them. Drugs are thus listed in classes. For example, class A includes the opiates, class B contains cannabis, and class C such substances as benzphetamine. If someone comes before the courts for possession of a small amount of cannabis for his or her own use, he or she would normally be fined. At the other end of the range, someone convicted of trafficking in heroin could expect a custodial sentence of several years. When appropriate, offenders are given probation and/or referred to special treatment centers. Special treatment has been provided in some penal institutions but, particularly for those addicted to hard drugs, the success rate cannot be claimed as high.

No law—certainly not the penal law—has yet proved capable of significantly affecting alcoholics. At present, they pass through the Magistrates' Courts getting small fines or drying out in prisons for short terms. Successive legislative endeavors have attempted to better the situation. A few experimental treatment centers have been set up to provide an alternative to prosecution, but they are expensive to operate effectively and the prognosis remains poor.

Special hospitals exist for those who are mentally ill and dangerous, although some of them may have been found by the courts to be not guilty on the grounds of insanity. The head of one of these was said recently to have observed that he could release half of his inmates with complete safety to the public forthwith: His difficulty was that he could not tell which half. Many regarded as psychopathic are detained in prison and, indeed, their response to treatment elsewhere is so minimal that this has been deemed the best place for them. Other persons clearly regarded as dangerous at the present time include terrorists, bombers, and similarly violent political fanatics who have been given very long terms of imprisonment following conviction for the gravest kinds of violence. In other respects, the whole concept of dangerousness is undergoing continued and urgently needed reappraisal.

Discharged Offenders

Those discharged from institutions may have after-care provided by the Probation Service. The Rehabilitation of Offenders Act of 1974 provides that many people convicted of certain classes of crimes may regard their convictions as "spent" after given periods of crime-free life. They may not have to reveal or admit their convictions, and can be protected from any unjustified revelation of their spent convictions being made by other people.

Parole

Parole was introduced by the Criminal Justice Act of 1967. The legislation provides that prisoners may become eligible for consideration for release on license (and supervision undertaken by the Probation Service) after they have served one-third of their sentence, or 6 months.

Diversion from Criminal Justice

In England there are many ways of limiting the entry of offenders to the criminal justice system and where some have found their way in, of removing them before they have gone the whole distance. Instead of bringing an offender to court the police may, at their discretion, administer a caution. Even for indictable offenses, 23% of those dealt with were formally cautioned by the police in 1984. The cautioning rate for juveniles is much higher than for adults and a far greater proportion of females is cautioned as contrasted with men. The Crown Prosecution Service initiated in 1986 is expected to serve as an additional filter. Schemes of mediation are developing. These are mainly directed toward reparation and reconciliation with victims prior to sentence, but also to serve as an alternative to prosecution in certain cases.

Criminal Procedure

General Principles

The system of criminal trial is adversary in nature, with the burden of proof resting on the prosecution. The presumption of innocence is paramount, and the rule against double jeopardy is fully recognized, so that no man can be charged twice for substantially the same offense.

Phases of Criminal Proceedings

It has been explained that Magistrates' Courts hear and dispose of about 98% of all criminal cases. The magistrates do, however, also sit as examining justices in serious indictable cases. They determine whether there is a *prima facie* case against the accused such as to justify his or her subsequent trial in a Crown Court. The sentencing power of magistrates is very limited. As the present time they may not impose more than six months' imprisonment or, in general, a fine of more than 2,000 pounds.

The process of the trial proceeds in stages. First, the prosecutor outlines his or her case with a short speech and calls witnesses and other evidence to support it. Then, the defense may submit that the case is insufficient for conviction as it stands. If this application is rejected, the defense witnesses and evidence are called and the defense then makes a final speech. At that stage the magistrates give their decision or, if the case has been a trial before the Crown Court, the judge sums up the evidence for the jury and explains to them the law, leaving the jury to decide upon the facts. Each witness is examined by the side producing him or her, cross-examined by the other side, and then reexamined by the first side again. The court has little power to call evidence of its own volition.

Rights of the Accused

Appeals lie from the Crown Court to the Court of Appeal (Criminal Division) and from there to the House of Lords, if a point of general public importance is involved. While it is possible for an accused person to appear in the courts without any representation, it is most common, especially in the more serious cases, for barristers or solicitors to be engaged. If the accused is unable to afford the fees, they are met by legal aid. It is a fundamental right that every defendant should be entitled to a lawyer of his or her choice.

The laws regarding arrest, search and seizure are too complicated to be expressed in a short compass. Basically, the law protects the citizen's right to free movement and a citizen can be restrained only on clearly defined grounds. Save in the case of serious crime or where provided by statute, the police have no general power of arrest without warrants judicially granted, nor to detain suspects or witnesses. Private citizens have certain powers of arrest. In no case must more force be used than is reasonably required and on being arrested the person must be told the grounds.

So far as search and seizure are concerned, subject to exceptions, the police have no power to search anyone not under arrest, nor in general have they any power to enter and search premises, save by authority of a search warrant. The power to seize property is similarly curtailed. It is right to observe, however, that statutory exceptions to these important freedoms are becoming increasingly common—some would say too common. Unlike the position in some other jurisdictions, in cases where police in England have obtained evidence unlawfully, the courts have a discretion to receive that evidence notwithstanding the improper mode by which it was obtained. Some of the protections intended to be afforded to individuals are contained in what are known as the *Judges' Rules*.

Pretrial Detention

Where the police arrest a suspect, they must either release the suspect on bail or bring him or her before a Magistrates' Court. Detention of persons in custody should be the exception not the rule and bail may be granted by the courts with or without conditions. If a sum of money is stipulated by a court as a surety that a person will attend for his or her trial, the money does not have to be produced unless the accused absconds, in which case some or all of the money may be ordered to be forfeited.

Of the 2,197,000 persons proceeded against for all types of offenses in 1984, 70% came in answer to a summons, 25% were arrested and bailed, and 5% were arrested and held in custody. Even this relatively small proportion of persons being held in confinement pending trial adds considerably to the problem of overcrowding in the prisons, although those on remand are housed separately from those convicted. Efforts are being made to reduce trial delays and to increase the numbers granted bail. Not many cases are kept waiting for trial for more than a few weeks at the most.

Lay Participation
in Criminal Proceedings

The contribution of the laity in criminal proceedings is extensive, through jury service and through the lay magistracy. As already mentioned, more than 27,500 lay justices (justices of the peace) sit in 640 courts in different parts of the country and they may also sit with the Judge in the Crown Court. This office of Justice of the Peace is an ancient one, with a more or less direct lineage going back to 1362 and still further in a less direct way. They are appointed by the Lord Chancellor and serve until the age of 70. They have, as a rule, no formal legal training, though they do nowadays undergo short courses prior to appointment, and they are kept up-to-date through publications and by ad hoc lectures and conferences. They are guided on law by lawyers appearing before them and by trained clerks of the court.

There are many criticisms of the lay magistracy. It is not as representative of all social classes as it might be, but the demands are onerous for certain categories of workers. In many ways, it is perhaps remarkable that the quality of these benches of unpaid, part-time justices is as good as it is.

Certainly, by years of experience, many become very capable and give good service. There is, after all, a right of appeal to the Divisional Court of the Queen's Bench Division of the High Court by way of complete rehearing of a case, and the infrequency of such appeals may reflect general satisfaction with the outcome of the trials. At the present time, it is difficult to see how the necessary judicial manpower could be provided if the vast amount of work now undertaken by lay magistrates were to be placed in professional hands.

This principle of trial by one's peers, or lay participation in criminal justice, is also preserved in the ancient jury system. Juries of 12 people are used in the Crown Courts and most citizens aged between 18 and 65 are eligible to serve. People in certain occupations are barred from taking part, as are people with some kinds of criminal records. Juries are now able to reach majority verdicts.

Juvenile Courts

Those under 17 years of age may be brought before a Juvenile Court. The courts are less formal than adult Magistrates' Courts, although, understandably, some children and their parents may still be bemused by what is going on around them. The Children and Young Persons Act of 1969 represents a difficult compromise between those who see the Juvenile Courts as another arm of social services with a protective role toward children in trouble and others (largely lawyers) who see it as an affront to justice that children may be dealt with in ways that they (the children) perceive as punitive under the guise of welfare and treatment in the child's best interests. The position at the present time remains that the procedure of the juvenile courts is very little different from that in the adult courts, except that the atmosphere is more relaxed, some strict rules are a little less rigidly enforced, and the courts—uniquely in the English criminal justice system—are not open to the general public.

Execution of Penal Measures (Corrections)

The aims of penal measures no doubt embrace the usual hodge-podge of objectives: deterrence (general and individual), prevention, reformation, retribution, denunciation, compensation, expiation, and so on. The sentences may not always be overt in taking these goals into account, but they are behind every sentence in greater or lesser proportion according to circumstance. The concept of reparation is gaining in importance and the "just deserts" model is on the ascendant.

Execution of Deprivation of Liberty

It is for the judiciary to pass sentence in England and it is not the practice from prosecutors to call for any particular sentence or form of punishment. Once the court has pronounced sentence, however, the role of the judge is virtually at an end in that case.

The executive still plays a large part in the delineation of the sentence. Thus, for example, after a judge says a prisoner is to be imprisoned for five years, an executive decision determines where the sentence will be served, whether under open conditions or closed; what "treatment" might be accorded the convicted person in prison, whether he or she will receive the usual one-third remission for good conduct or be deemed to forfeit any part of it; whether he or she will be paroled; and so on. Similarly, once a juvenile court has used its gravest powers (the making of a care order passing parental rights to the local authority), it is a matter for the authority as to how those rights are exercised, whether the child is allowed home, placed in an institution or elsewhere, and, if so, for how long. A number of other situations make it true to say that the control of sentences is balanced between the judiciary and the executive. The judge is to some extent left to create a sentence framework to be filled in by others.

Administration and Supervision
of Penal Institutions

The Home Secretary is the minister ultimately responsible for penal institutions and the treatment of offenders in England and Wales. Prison policy and the administration of custodial institutions are carried out by the Home Office Prison Department, and probation is administrated by the Home Office Probation and After-Care Department.

In 1981 an independent Inspectorate of Prisons was established to Report to the Home Secretary on the treatment of prisoners, conditions in prisons, and on any other matters relating to prisons.

Classification of Offenders

Offenders may be classified by age. Those under the age of 17 years are regarded as juveniles and treated accordingly. Between the ages of 17 and 21 they are regarded as young adult offenders and only over the age of 21 years are adult processes and institutions fully applicable. All offenders are segregated according to sex. In general, there are separate institutions for each sex. In the case of adult offenders this is certainly so. Some dispositions, such as detention centers, are not available for females.

So far as adult prisoners are concerned, they are segregated into those convicted and those unconvicted, and those convicted are separated into security categories that considerably influence the type of prison to which they may be sent and the regime to be employed there:

Category A: Prisoners whose escape would be highly dangerous to the public or to the police or to the security of the state (approx. 1%).

Category B: Prisoners for whom the very highest conditions of security are not necessary but for whom escape must be made very difficult (approx. 30%).

Category C: Prisoners who cannot be trusted in open conditions but who do not have the ability or resources to make a determined escape attempt (approx. 50%).

Category D: Those who can reasonably be trusted to serve their sentences in open conditions (approx. 20%).

Types of Penal Institutions

The main distinction is made between open and closed prisons. Most are of the latter category. Some are very modern (and the building program continues), but many were built during the last century or earlier. Most are seriously overcrowded—more than one-third of those in custody sleep two or three to a cell that was originally designed for one. There are prisons especially designed for those on remand, for those with psychiatric problems, for those deemed suitable for certain industrial conditions, and others. There are also prisons with special units to contain certain prisoners in Category A. All prisoners receive one-third remission of their sentences, so long as they do not forfeit all or part of this by infringing rules while in custody.

While former philosophies of treatment and training have been undergoing a reappraisal, the government has not adopted either "humane containment" or "human warehousing" as alternatives. It has been said that the goal of imprisonment should be "positive custody" to indicate that it is the rhetoric alone that should be changed and not all the admirable and constructive things done in its name.

Rights and Duties
of Incarcerated Offenders

These are governed largely by the ordinary law of the land and by the Prison Rules. Infringement of the rules amounting to offenses against the criminal law may be prosecuted by the governor of an institution and if his or her own powers of action are insufficient, penalties that are more severe may be imposed by visiting magistrates. Inmates also have the right to bring complaints to the visiting magistrates.

Rule 43, which provides for the segregation of certain prisoners under certain circumstances, may be invoked by prisoners themselves to obtain enhanced protection from victimization by fellow inmates.

Some prisons operate a "hostel scheme." Here a segregated part of the prison is set aside for a small number of offenders in the concluding months of their sentences, and those selected are able to sleep in the "hostel" at night, while working freely in the community outside the prison by day. There are other schemes for the employment of inmates outside institutions. Work to occupy prisoners in prison is in increasingly short supply.

Execution of Noncustodial Measures

These depend in almost all cases on the administrative support of the Probation Service and have been outlined already. Great efforts continue to be made to find valid alternatives to custody and to reduce the numbers of those going "inside" by inserting more rungs in the ladder leading to incarceration. Unfortunately, there is always a tendency for new types of sentences to be used as alternatives to alternatives and not as alternatives to prison.

3

Nigeria

ROSELINE A. EKPENYONG

General Information

Situated on the western coast of the African continent, Nigeria occupies a total surface area of 356,700 square kilometers, which is about one and a half times that of Texas.

Like most African countries, Nigeria is a country of heterogeneous cultures and traditions, of complex historical background, and ethnolinguistic and religious pluralism that have significant bearings on the country's judicial and criminal justice systems. Similarly, the Islamic and Christian religions, though predominant, share the rich religious panorama with the traditionally potent indigenous African religions.

Despite the discrepancies in estimated population (figures range from 91 million to 100 million in 1984) demographers generally concur that Nigeria is the most populous African nation. Its potential for further population expansion is strong as well, with high gross reproduction and birth rates. The declining death rate, the improvement in health services and facilities, and in the general living standards also will contribute to future growth.

The estimated 1983 population density for the whole country was 25 persons per square mile. Large cities across the country attract prospective migrants in search of job opportunities. The southern portion of the country is by far the most densely populated. The migratory flux follows the traditional rural urban shifts. There is also a sizable interstate flow of seasonal, temporary, and permanent migrant farmers and rural labor force from one rural area to another.

Despite the urban congestion, the structure of the population is typically rural. The economic structure is, in fact, agricultural.

Nigeria, historically, is an artifact of British imperialistic expansion in Africa. In 1960, the country attained political independence from Britain and within the commonwealth of nations. Nigeria, a Republic, now has one central and nineteen state administrative structures.

The 1963 Republican Constitution was designed after the British Westminster Parliamentary model. It recognized three arms of government, four regional legislatures, and a central one at the federal capital of Lagos. It adopted a bicameral system both at the regional and at the central legislatures. Nigerian civil war occurred from 1967 to 1970 and thirteen uninterrupted years of military rule from 1966 to 1979 followed.

The postbelligerent period was marked by efforts by the military to further a political Renaissance founded on the ideals of national consciousness, unity, and harmony. The new Constitution of 1979 was an effort to achieve these goals through the abandonment of the Westminster model and the adoption of a facsimile of the United States executive model. It was engineered by the military in preparation for the 1979 return to civilian rule. While the 1979 Constitution and 1983 military takeover had significantly modified the executive and legislative structures, the criminal justice philosophy and praxis were left almost intact. This means that the Nigerian criminal law and, to some extent, the criminal justice system still bear the imprints of their late nineteenth-century and early twentieth-century colonial heritage, the eighteenth-century deterrence doctrine and penology in which they were rooted.

At each seizure of power, the military has introduced decrees to abrogate the existing Constitution. Similarly, the laws, the political and administrative bases have been suppressed, the legislative and executive bodies abolished, and the decentralized formula of governance abandoned. In fact, a peculiar feature of the military rule has been the concentration of legislative and executive powers at the center. The nineteen-state system has been maintained, with 85 military governors representing the federal government in each state. Yet power delegation under the military is not conterminous with decentralization or state autonomy. Under the military, as the area of exclusive federal legislative powers broadens, the sphere of concurrent and residual jurisdictions drastically shrink.

The general administration is typically centralized around the head of the federal military government and three councils, that is, the Supreme Military Council (Armed Forces Ruling Council under the Babangida administration, August 1985), the Federal Executive Council and the National Council of States. Members of these councils may be drawn exclusively from the cadres of high-ranking military and police personnel or could be of both military and civilian membership. The Supreme Military Council plays an all-encompassing role in matters of national policies, security, legislation, supervision, and appointments. The day-to-day implementation of policies developed within the Supreme Military Council is the assigned responsibility of the Federal Executive Council.

Another peculiarity of the military regimes is the effort to leave the judiciary unaltered. Though known for their predilection for revocations and enactment of decrees, they have usually respected the integrity of the judiciary. Clearly, this has not exempted them from certain arbitrary decisions that have blatantly violated certain basic rights of the citizens and especially of suspects and critics of their mode of administration and decision making. The practice of establishing special tribunals vested with judicial powers is credited to the military and there have been many such tribunals, not without the resentment of the judicial authorities and legal practitioners. Recently, decrees have been passed introducing new special tribunals. The special military tribunals of 1984 were to try the former civilian politicians. A public officer's protection against false accusation decree made it a media offense to levy certain criticisms against the military rulers. These tribunals were the most recent in a series of others passed to regulate exchange control or punish armed robbery. The penalties, needless to say, are usually very severe and many include the death penalty.

Extent and Dynamics of Criminality

Nigerian crime statistics suffer from serious flaws in reliability and validity and pose a challenge to the researcher. The crime statistics are infrequently and inconsistently published. The procedures for reporting and recording crime information are deficient and unsystematic.

In Nigeria, there is no official agency of accounting for crime rates, distribution, volume, and pattern in a regular and comprehensive manner. The only source of official crime reporting is the *Nigerian Annual Abstract of Statistics*. The mode of data compilation and presentation, the titling procedure, and the crime classification criteria vary from one volume to another of this series. The interest is oftentimes on the number of sentences, of court dispositions, and the like. There is no cross-referencing of crimes with other significant variables. In some instances, crime information is contained under the prison statistics, that is, with regards to admissions, cases awaiting trial, investigations closed. The focus is clearly on police or prison performance rather than on crime facts. Causing additional problems for researchers is the fact that many crimes go unreported due to poor police public relations. In other cases, crimes are not reported as a sign of respect for an informal code of friendship or good neighborliness that prohibits the exposure of others to the embarrassment of official actions. In many cases, the fear of the police releasing information on the accused and the possible reaction of the offender may restrain the accuser from reporting. In still other cases, the vulnerability of the police to bribery and corrupt practices and police abuse of officers affect the number of violations known and eventually recorded. A good bribe to the police can terminate an investigation, and make evidence or a report disappear. It is even alleged that the impunity with which the criminals perpetuate the misdeeds is partly due to police connivance or participation in some of these crimes. Police reportedly ignore certain crimes and even rent their uniforms to criminals who stop, harass, and rob unsuspecting citizens or drivers on the highways.

Given such inadequacies, it may be safely assumed that official measures of crime are grossly inaccurate. They underestimate the extent, seriousness, demographic, and ecological distribution of crime. On the other hand, inertia, misconceived and dubious penal policy, the lack of economic and technical resources retard or even nullify scholarly efforts at developing dependable unofficial crime reports.

There are, however, many empirical indicators that there is a continuous crescendo in crime, especially in the last two decades. Media accounts, the fear expressed and lived out by the public, a perusal of the few scholarly writings, and the intimidatory anticrime statements by government authorities leave no doubts that there is more crime today than in the past. Much more than mere volume, the fear of crime is justified by the fact that crime is more sophisticated, more vicious, more brutal and violent today than had hitherto been. Crime statistics by the Minister of Police Affairs in May 1980 reported that armed robbery alone had claimed 4,513 lives nationwide in the eight months before that date. More than any other social cancer, crime is the premier problem of big cities.

It has been estimated that the general crime rate per 100,000 people increased by 21% between 1961 and 1975. Person victimization and property victimization rose by 54% and 33%, respectively, during this time period. A note of caution needs to be made in respect to these astronomic figures. The two time periods, in fact, coincide with the adverse political events spawned by the controversial 1963 census that culminated in the mass killings, the military coup d'etat, the attempted secession, and civil war. The availability of arms in the aftermath of the war, especially among the unskilled and poorly educated demobilized soldiers is a plausible reason for the violent and heinous nature of many crimes and the volume too.

No matter what the amount of adjustments in these figures, one can hardly elude the fact that the country is overwhelmed by a tangle of crime pathology that cuts across class, age, gender, and geographic areas. More women are in crime today than before. More are getting involved in the drug and prostitution network and in foreign exchange crime and currency contrabands. Similarly, more and younger children are committing a higher number of more and serious crimes. The school drop-out rate seems on the increase.

The magnitude and pace of change in the county have precipitated sociostructural dislocations and institutional asymmetries that also generate crime.

Despite elaborate national development plans, no government has succeeded in reducing the gap between rural and urban areas. Young but unskilled rural dwellers continuously increase the exodus to the already saturated urban areas.

Today's crime is no longer limited to elite malpractice, bribery, corruption, misuse of office, and embezzlement that made headline news in the pre-civil war years. In the large urban areas, to talk of constant danger of fatal assault is by no means an overstatement. There is danger of losing one's car, and maybe life also, to armed car thieves in the urban traffic congestion. Vehicles have been stopped on urban streets by groups of armed robbers on vehicle looting missions that often culminate in the death of car owners or occupants. Incredible as this may sound, there have been instances where robbers have raided, looted, and stolen from communities or villages after having given the latter advance verbal or written "notices of intent to rob." Postal thefts are still to be estimated as are the looting of cargoes from ships at the ports. There are daily media reports of crimes such as child abductions, highway robberies, pirating, illegal sales, and bunkering of the Nigerian crude oil by employees (top level, of course!), smuggling and peddling of consumer and luxury items, drug and prostitution rackets, currency black market, mugging, assault, pick-pocketing, purse snatching, the taking of jewelry from the owner's person, rape, and bank hold ups.

Though to be taken with due caution, the 1981 Annual Abstract of Statistics shows that between 1972 and 1979 prison admission for the 16-20 age bracket was higher than for any other age group. Clearly, the crime situation is not to be ignored, yet a rational and guided government policy is not even in the making.

Structure and Functioning of Criminal Justice Agencies

Jurisdiction over law enforcement and the administration of justice is shared by different agencies including the courts, civilian and military police, other specialized enforcement units and special tribunals.

The Police

A distinctive feature of the Nigerian law enforcement and criminal justice machinery is the centralization of organization and administration. Section 194 of the Constitution provides that the responsibility of law enforcement, the maintenance of public order and safety, crime control and prevention, and general security should fall on the Nigerian Police Force (NPF).

The NPF grew out of the unification of the early colonial constabularies. Until the early 1970s, Nigeria operated a dual police system as inherited from the colonial power. In 1972, the local forces were disbanded or absorbed into the regional force due to allegations of corruption, abuse of power, vulnerability to the whims of traditional political elite, inefficiency, poor educational qualification, and participation in political unrest. Though the 1979 Constitution recognized the NPF as the single law enforcement body, policing power has been shared with different units not directly under the NPF. In 1967, the Armed Forces and Police (Special Power) Decree, extended that power to the military personnel by conferring the power of arrest without warrant to any member of the armed forces above the rank of sergeant. It was justified on the grounds of state of emergency. The state of emergency has existed much longer than envisaged. The military police usually operate alongside the regular police.

The NPF is a centralized force whose organization and administration is the exclusive responsibility of the central government. The National Assembly is responsible for providing the legal definitions of the organization and its administrative set up.

Generally, the force operates at two levels through a national headquarters and state commands. Nationally, the NPF is under the command of an Inspector General of police and has its headquarters in Lagos. The Inspector General may be appointed or dismissed only by the chief executive, in consultation with the Federal Police Service Commission. In each of the 19 states, contingents of the force are situated in the state capitals under the command of a State Commissioner of Police. Generally, the powers and responsibilities of members of the NPF must be defined by law. Thus while the president and state governors hand down orders to the inspector or commissioner, the latter may decline or suspend the execution of such orders.

The police responsibilities over the enforcement of law and the administration of justice include crime detection and prevention, the apprehension of offenders with or without warrants, the temporary custody of offenders, and the conduct of criminal prosecution. Through the use of foot and car patrols, road blocks, and the search of suspected vehicles and persons, the crime prevention task is presumably implemented. The members of the police force do not usually carry guns. In situations where unusual force is needed to quell some riot or other mass disturbances, the Mobile Unit of the NPF usually act as the commando unit. In many instances, the armed military police intervenes alongside the regular civilian unit.

The crime-torn and congested capital city of Lagos, which is also the national headquarters of the NPF, has the largest police contingent. It is also the most specialized unit. Prior to 1976, intelligence, counterintelligence, and internal securities duties were assigned to the special branch of the NPF. The assassination in 1976 of the then military head, Murtala, prompted the creation of a separate and autonomous security unit, called the National Security Organization (NSO).

By Constitution, criminal prosecution responsibilities lie within the Office of the Attorney General. For minor violations that are brought before the lower magistrate's courts, the customary and area courts, the police may conduct criminal prosecutions under the directions of the attorney general if the cases involve issues of fact, not legal technicalities.

Police responsibility in the administration of justice also involves the warrant apprehension and detention of suspects, and the search and seizure of criminal evidence. The police may arrest without a warrant if there is reasonable suspicion that a suspect is harboring or transporting stolen or unlawfully obtained articles.

In the exercise of these powers, the police have been accused of various misdeeds that obstruct the course of justice. They reportedly abuse their powers of prosecution, arrest, search, seizure, and investigation by using those powers in an abusively discretionary way. The police allegedly solicit and request bribes or other emoluments, extorting sums of money or other favors from crime suspects. No systematic study of police corruption is available, but it is reported that some crimes are even committed with the connivance or participation of the police. It is also alleged that crime evidence and reports are destroyed by the police, arrested persons released, criminal charges and prosecutions dropped in exchange for bribes or other benefits. Similarly, false charges are reportedly made against innocent and ignorant citizens, criminal investigations suspended, and driver's licenses issued or renewed without the legally mandated driver license tests.

Poor educational standards, the lack of the appropriate professional qualification, the recruitment of low-skill demobilized soldiers, and low-salary scale, which has lagged behind the national minimum, are allegedly at the root of the misdeeds of the police and the high attrition rates.

The multitiered judicial system spreads out in a pyramidal hierarchy. At the peak of the pyramid is the highest court of the land, the Supreme Court. At the base are some thousand district-level customary and area courts. Between the two ends are three additional tiers of intermediate-level courts. Nigerian courts can be grouped in terms of their location in the hierarchy, which usually coincides with the government that controls them, that is, federal or state. They are also grouped in terms of their assigned jurisdictions.

The Constitution recognizes six superior courts of record: the Supreme Court, the Federal Court of Appeal, and the Federal High Court are the federal courts. Under the state government are the State High Courts, the Customary Court of Appeal, and the Sharia Court of Appeal. The establishment of the latter two is the discretion of each state, but their presence need be underscored. They exemplify the recognition that customary laws (including the Islamic Maliki Laws) regulate many important domains of life.

TABLE 3.1
The Courts

		Supreme Court			
		Federal Court of Appeal			
Federal High Court	State High Court	Customary Court of Appeal		Sharia Court of Appeal	
Magistrate/ District Court	Customary A and B (West)	Customary 1 and 2	Upper Area	Juvenile Court	Coroner's Court
Customary		Customary B and C		Area Court 1, 2, 3,	

Generally then, the Supreme Court is at the top, followed by the Federal Court of Appeal, while the third tier is occupied by the Federal High Court, the State High Courts, the Customary Court of Appeal, and the Sharia Court of Appeal.

All federal courts are superior courts. Apart from the three state superior courts, there are also some seven inferior courts at the state level. The High Courts and their equivalents are followed by the magistrate/district courts, the customary/area courts, the juvenile court, and coroner's court. Below these are the lowest courts, that is, the customary/area courts of different grades.

Added to this traditional judicial structure, the military popularized the use of administrative tribunals and commissions of inquiry distinguishable in terms of their decision-making or fact-finding responsibilities. In most of these tribunals, a high-ranking member of the armed forces and a police officer must be present. Their sentences, which include death, must usually be confirmed before execution by the head of the federal military government or military governor.

The Supreme Court has both appellate and original jurisdiction. The Constitution, however, limits its original jurisdiction to disputes between the federation and a state, or between states, or any other matters, except criminal, that may be assigned to it by the National Assembly. It has exclusive appellate jurisdiction over appeals from the Federal Court of Appeal in criminal and civil proceedings involving issues of law, and for cases that require interpretation or application of the Constitution. It deliberates on death sentences in criminal proceedings imposed or affirmed by the Federal Court of Appeal, hears cases involving violations of conditions of membership to elected offices, and other cases as may be prescribed by state enactments.

By constitutional definition, the Federal Court of Appeals has exclusive appellate jurisdiction over appeals from high court and courts of equivalent status. The composition of the court demonstrates the importance of local customary laws. To resolve the climate of tension in the constituent assembly created by the proposal to establish a Muslim Sharia Court of Appeal of equivalent status to the Supreme Court, it was constitutionally mandated that at least three of the fifteen justices of the Federal Court of Appeal must be learned in Islamic personal law and at least three in customary law.

The Federal High Court is the lowest level of federal courts. Established under the 1979 Constitution to replace the Federal Revenue Court, the Federal High Court occupies the same intermediate hierarchical status as the State High courts, the Customary and Sharia Courts of Appeal. Unlike the latter, the jurisdiction of the Federal High Court is limited to matters of federal government revenue or other matters as may be assigned by the National Assembly.

The State High Courts rank highest in the hierarchy of state courts. There are 19 such courts. Depending on local population size and volume of cases, a state may be divided into any appropriate number of judicial divisions of the High Court under one or two judges. Within these divisions, judges may also hold circuit sessions and assizes in places other than that of the judicial division of the High Court. The 1979 Constitution confers unlimited original and general jurisdiction to State High Courts over civil and criminal proceedings and original jurisdiction over the fulfillment of conditions to elected offices. In addition, it hears appeals from magistrates' courts, district courts, and also from customary and area courts.

The Sharia and Customary Courts of Appeal are at the highest echelon of the customary courts. Insofar as they are not repugnant to natural justice, equity and good conscience, or not in conflict with any other written law, the Constitution recognizes the need for the application of local customary laws in any part of the federation. Generally, in the exercise of their original or appellate jurisdiction, customary courts enforce and supervise the observance and application of these laws as may be prescribed by law. Neither the Sharia nor the Customary Courts of Appeal have original jurisdiction.

Manned by a Grand Kadi and Deputy Kadis, the Sharia Court exists only in the northern states, though constitutionally it may be established by any state that requires it. The court exercises appellate and supervisory jurisdiction only in civil proceedings. It hears appeals from upper-area courts on matrimonial, divorce, and probate matters and testaments in accordance with Islamic personal law, whether or not all parties to the proceedings are Moslems. In cases involving non-Moslems, the latter must have requested that the case be heard by the court of first instance in accordance with Islamic personal law.

Established by the 1979 Constitution, Customary Courts of Appeal may be established by any state though they are mainly found in the southern states. They exercise appellate and supervisory jurisdiction in civil proceedings involving issues of customary law. Their appeal cases usually come from the lower customary courts.

Magistrate and district courts operate at the state level within state magisterial court districts. Magistrates' courts are characteristic of the south while the north has district courts. They are typically of two or three grades. They exercise original jurisdiction over criminal and civil proceedings depending on the specific court. Grades are arranged according to the seriousness of the criminal case and the applicable sentence. Generally, trials are summary. Upper-area courts and customary courts occupy the same status as the magistrates courts and have almost identical jurisdictions. Appeals from these courts are directed at the State High Court.

At the lowest level of the judicial system are the lowest customary and area courts found in the southern and northern states, respectively. They exercise original jurisdiction over civil matters involving local customary laws and local government rules. They may also handle minor criminal violations with sentences of six months to five years and as prescribed by the state governor. Between 80% and 90% of all cases are reportedly handled by these courts and they are preferred over other courts because of their timely disposal of cases.

The Nigerian judicial system is rather complex. The attempt has been to maintain an open judicial system in which the principle of procedural due process is at least recognized. At each abrogation of the Constitution by a new military junta, it is not difficult to envisage the violation of fundamental bill of rights and due process safeguards guaranteed by the Constitution. The complex nature of the system is also justified on grounds of the need to recognize the force of unwritten native laws and local customs and the inalienable rights of people to be tried under them.

General Description of the
Legal and Criminal Justice Systems

The precolonial legal order was based on the unwritten yet popularly acknowledged and respected canons of indigenous native law and custom. Colonialism brought with it a corps of written laws and a machinery of justice that were grounded in the colonial metropolitan common law, equity doctrine, and nineteenth-century Victorian values and ideals. The latter laws together with the English Parliamentary and Imperial statutes on the one hand, and the indigenous customary laws on the other, formed the basis from which the Nigerian law evolved. The subsequent formulation of a Nigerian legislation and Nigerian case law added to the other sources of the Nigerian legal system.

Notwithstanding later indigenous legislative enactments, Nigerian law is largely received law. Section 45(1) of the Colonial Interpretation Act extended to Nigeria the English common law, equity doctrine, and other statutes of general application in force in England on January 1, 1900. Received laws were generally very broadly defined. This means that the entire legal superstructure was anchored in the English common law rules and equity doctrine. There was, however, the provision that through local statutory enactments, the equity doctrine could be replaced, amended, or superseded.

The Nigerian criminal code is perhaps the one area of codified laws that shows some appreciable local effort to depart from and replace the English law. It is the one area where there has been some concerted effort to incorporate local values, ideals, needs, and circumstances into the law-making process.

Prior to the colonial period, criminal violations and disputes were handled by the village, the family, or native tribunals in accordance with the time-honored, yet unwritten, customary criminal laws. Retribution, but also compensation, reconciliation, and the peaceful resolution of conflicts formed the core of the traditional philosophy of justice, even if rather severe penalties were frequently handed down on perpetrators or serious offenses. In the north, where Islamic religious beliefs and teachings prevailed, a different body of more formalized laws prevailed, that is, the Maliki law or the Moslem law of crimes. The customary law of crimes was left almost unaltered despite the introduction of colonial common law of crime. The latter was applicable only to the colony of Lagos while the rest of the country remained under the jurisdiction of the native tribunals and laws.

In 1916, a Nigerian criminal code was adopted for the whole country. It was modeled after the Queensland criminal code. Its adoption meant that a dual system of criminal adjudication had been erected in the country. The inevitable conflicts and inconsistencies that emerged between the colonial and customary laws were exacerbated in the north by the existence of the Islamic laws. Islam is more than a religious practice. Its influence permeates all aspects of daily life including the administration of justice, which was founded on the body of Islamic law, called the Maliki law. Then, as today, many acts are considered primarily because they are offensive to the Islamic religious and moral beliefs and laws. Islam condemns alcohol consumption and adultery. In the Islamic customary courts, they are punishable as criminal offenses. In the non-Islamic areas of the country, these same acts have no legal consequences.

In recognition of such cultural diversities, a Northern Penal Code was adopted in 1959. Distinct in certain details from the Southern Criminal Code, it was a way of accommodating the different needs of a Moslem society and of minimizing the potential sources of incongruities and conflict between the two sources of criminal law. A new dimension to criminal justice system duality had been created, with an in-built tendency for conflicts.

At independence, the country inherited the British Parliamentary system of government, a legislative structure, and a judicial and criminal justice system. The criminal justice and judicial systems replicated the British systems, but were also entrenched in traditional native laws and customs.

A law enforcement body, the Nigerian Police Force, developed from the unification of the early colonial constabularies. The colonial type of centralized law enforcement system has remained to the present day.

Under the 1979 Constitution, matters relating to the administration of justice, the maintenance of law, public safety, public order, internal security, and prison services fall within the legislative powers of the central government. The National Assembly also enjoys exclusive legislative powers over such critical areas as fingerprinting, identification, and maintenance of criminal records, patents, currency, coinage, and legal tender.

The settling of disputes between state governments or between the latter and the federal government falls within the federal legislature's sphere, and is handled through the Supreme Court. Federal courts are all superior courts with appellate responsibilities over civil and criminal cases, with only few exceptions. Inferior courts belong to the state and local governments, though three of the six superior courts also operate at the state level. State courts may have appellate as well as general and original jurisdiction over both criminal and civil cases.

The criminal justice system and its administration are under the control and organizational provisions of the federal government. Both the regular and special security sectors of policing are directly under the central government though there are usually smaller units within each state. The prison service is under the central administration of the Nigerian Prison Services. The Nigerian Prison Services emerged as a unified system throughout the federation through the Prisons (Control) Decree of 1966 enacted by the federal military government. Hitherto, Nigeria operated a two-tiered prison system. The federal prisons were controlled by what later became the Federal Prisons Department. The native authority prisons in the North and West were run by local authorities, while inspection and advisory functions were handled by the Federal Prisons Department. Section 31 of the 1980 Prisons Act provided for the free movement or transfer of inmates between the two systems. Generally, under the Native Authority Prisons Order-In-Council, convicts with short prison terms from the High Courts or magistrates' courts could be housed in the native authority facilities. Ordinarily, convicted offenders from the area or customary courts were accommodated in these prisons unless the sentences exceeded two years. In that event, they would be sent to the federal prisons.

Despite the adoption of the Executive Presidential System, the administration of law, and of the criminal justice system, the civilian administration was based on the centralization formula. Aspects of the system that were already under a central administration before that date were retained. The military administrations have emphasized and have strengthened the centralization of authority in all spheres, including the administration of justice.

Substantive Criminal Law

Sources of Criminal Law

Prior to the advent of colonialism, local communities depended on unwritten customary rules and laws to regulate criminal violations. While the South applied relatively simple rules of conduct, the Moslem

North had a body of well-defined, advanced, and written law of crimes associated with the jurists of the Maliki school.

The imposition of colonial rule was subsequently accompanied by the adoption of a Nigerian Criminal Code that was modeled after the Queensland code. In recognition of the peculiar nature of the Maliki and other customary laws, and their significance to the local communities, customary laws were permitted to apply in the native tribunals. By 1960, however, a separate penal code was adopted in the North that was modeled after the Moslem Sudanese Code.

Nigerian criminal law derives its origins from the two criminal codes, remotely from the English common law, and other local enactments that define specific offenses and the appropriate penalties.

Classification of Offenses

There is no common scheme for classifying offenses between the northern and southern states. The southern codes have incorporated some elaborate and formal systems of developing legal and judicial categories of offenses. The grouping system adopted in the northern codes is quite broad. One way of classifying offenses that cuts across regional codes and, therefore, is universally applicable is by use of the national administrative framework. One can then distinguish between federal and state offenses. Acts that are in violation of federal government laws are classified as federal offenses, whether the laws are civilian parliamentary acts or the decrees of a military government. State offenses involve subject areas that are, by constitution, the legislative competence of the state.

Another way of classifying offenses is to adopt the criteria incorporated in the regional codes. The Criminal Procedure Act of the southern states distinguishes between indictable and nonindictable or summary offenses. By law, indictable offenses are triable on information by a High Court only. The fact that an accused may consent to a summary trial in a magistrate's court does not make these offenses triable and punishable by summary conviction. In addition, an individual may be arrested without warrant by a police officer where there is reasonable suspicion of an indictable offense having been committed or by a private citizen where the offense was committed in his or her presence. Indictable offenses carry a minimum of two years' imprisonment.

Section 3 of the Southern Code also established three general categories of offenses distinguishable in terms of their seriousness on procedural and substantive grounds. Though the Northern Penal Code makes no provision or mention of this classification, it is nonetheless of common application. Under Section 3, simple offenses are those that are punishable with a prison term not exceeding six months. Misdemeanor offenses are punishable with not less than six months and not more than three years' imprisonment. Felonies are punishable with a prison term of at least three years.

Offense classification under the Northern Criminal Code is very loose and is limited to an appendixed enumeration of offenses according to the designated court of trial. Another judicial typology involves the distinction between bailable and nonbailable offenses. Bailable offenses are those punishable either with a fine only, or with a maximum of three years' imprisonment, which may also be in conjunction with a fine or by itself. A nonbailable offense is a more serious offense that is punishable with death or a term of at least three years' imprisonment. By virtue of the federally applicable police act and powers of arrest, the classification based on simple misdemeanor and felony offenses is used also in the North despite its absence from the Penal Code.

General Principles

There are no common law crimes in Nigeria. Yet, by colonial accident, the Nigerian criminal law has derived many of its legal principles from the English common law. Controversial as it may be, the common law doctrine of *mens rea* remains the principle in the administration of criminal law in Nigeria. Though not expressly incorporated into the Nigerian Code, the Nigerian courts invoke this doctrine to establish the mental component of a criminal act. Substantively, an act is criminal to the extent that criminal intention, knowledge, or other state of mind can be proven against the culprit. With the exception of mitigating factors or legitimate defenses such as accident, mistake, claim of right, self-defense, compulsion, provocation, age, insanity, and the like, there can be no conviction for an offense without proof of fault or the presence of a mental element. The application of the *mens rea* doctrine to Nigerian law has been questioned by legal analysts. Inherent in the Nigerian notion of criminal responsibility is the principle of no liability without fault. Section 24 provides that, subject to the express provisions of this code relating to negligent acts and omissions, a person is not criminally responsible for an act or omission that occurs independently of the exercise of his or her will, or for an event that occurs by accident. Except for all cases of legitimate defenses, criminal responsibility is predicated upon the principle of no liability without fault. Liability can be imposed only for acts or omissions that are willed or are perpetrated intentionally by the culprit. Liability may not be upheld where, despite intentionality of the act or omission, the result or consequence of which was accidental. Similarly, except otherwise provided by the law (S. 7, 8, 9: Criminal Code), the law does not impose vicarious liability. Clearly, the Nigerian law contains all the core ingredients for establishing universal principles of criminal responsibility. Unfortunately, the recourse to the *mens rea* doctrine has been a major obstacle.

Actus Reus

As a corollary of *mens rea*, there is also a statutory provision for the presence of an *actus reus* or the physical element. While the *mens rea* is the cognitive and intentional element, the *actus reus* is the act or the omission or the result of these or even the objective circumstances surrounding them. When placed in the context of Section 24 of the Nigerian Criminal Code, the two elements lead to the conclusion that for there to be crime, both the *mens rea* and the *actus reus* must be present. A person is thus criminally responsible and liable to punishment for a criminal act or omission known and willed by him or her regardless of the motive.

Defenses and
Mitigating Circumstances

The Criminal Code provides that certain states or circumstances may be introduced by the accused as defenses or as mitigating factors. General defenses completely exonerate the individual from criminal responsibility. In other cases, referred to as special defenses, certain acts may be invoked as special defenses or more appropriately as mitigating factors to punishment. Under the Nigerian law, insanity, intoxication, immaturity, mistake of fact, extraordinary emergencies, and automatism, when introduced by the accused, are general defenses. Provocation and defense of truth for public benefit against a charge of defamation are instances of specific defenses.

The Nigerian law provides for and acknowledges two types of insanity defenses. One based on the accused's present incapacity, concerns the ability of the accused to stand trial—to follow the proceedings, comprehend the charge, instruct his or her defense, and make a plea. The other concerns the sanity of mind of the accused at the moment of committing the criminal act or omission. A person may be absolved from criminal responsibility by reason of insanity if certain evidentiary conditions are proven by the defense:

(1) Presence of a mental disease or natural mental infirmity when the crime was committed.
(2) The disease or infirmity had, in fact, resulted in or produced in the accused:
   (a) lack of capacity to comprehend his or her action or omission;
   (b) lack of capacity to know the act or the omission should not be done;
   (c) lack of capacity to control his or her actions.

The decision to proceed or suspend a trial because of an insanity defense is entirely at the discretion of the judge in spite of the expert medical opinion.

Age of Criminal Responsibility

Age constitutes an exception to the general principle of criminal responsibility. It is generally provided that children under 7 years cannot be convicted of any offense because of noncriminal responsibility. Criminal responsibility may be upheld for children between 7 and 11 years if it can be shown that they had the capacity to know criminal nature and the consequences of their acts or omissions. Children of age 12 and above are given full criminal responsibility for their acts or omissions.

For the purpose of defining court jurisdiction, the Children and Young Persons' Act classifies a person under 14 as a "child." Those between 13 and 17 are described as "young persons." Both groups fall under the jurisdiction of the juvenile court.

Attempt and Conspiracy

To emphasize the deterrent or preventative philosophy underlying the criminal law, it is provided that certain preliminary acts or accessories to any offense be given identical weight as the crime itself. Thus to attempt or to conspire to commit a crime constitutes an offense.

For a crime of attempt, it must be proven that the accused had the intent to commit the offense or criminal omission. The accused must intend the act, must know that the act is an offense, and must at least have initiated the criminal act or the means appropriate for its fulfillment. Criminal liability rests not in intention only but requires knowledge that the act is inappropriate.

The attempt to procure another to commit a crime and the conspiracy between two or more to do the same are also sufficient grounds for criminal liability. If there is proof of a procurer's intent to commit a crime and if the procurer was capable of the offense, then the attempt to procure another to commit an offense is a criminal offense. Conspirators are doubly indictable for the offense of conspiracy and also for the specific act if the latter is a crime in law and is successfully executed. The law, however, protects the right of workers to strike albeit this may be in violation of employment contracts.

Corporate Liability

Under the 1968 Companies Decree, the incorporation of a company makes it a legal entity. Just like an ordinary person, a corporation enjoys the status of a legal personality distinct from that of its shareholders. Except when a corporation acts *ultra vires*, it may be held criminally liable.

The Nigerian Criminal Code does not specify and nature and extent of corporate criminal liability, yet court decisions and statutes have clarified the terms of liability. The presence of a guilty mind or *mens rea* can be established only through a fictional process and in a more restrictive manner. A corporation is criminally liable for a criminal act or omission when the latter is willed by those managing and directing the corporation. First, it is presumed that since the state of mind of the corporate managerial cadre represents that of the corporation, the latter is also criminally liable. Second, the provision does not allow the corporations' will to be expressed by the agents and servants. Third, it provides that corporate liability is not conterminous with vicarious liability.

Penal Measures

The analysis of a society's penal system and sentencing policies cannot be divorced from an understanding of their origins, the philosophy and values that sustain them. Nigeria operates a dual criminal code and a penal system that bear the imprints of the country's colonial past, the inevitable influence of the indigenous customary rules and values and the efforts to develop a body of Nigerian jurisprudence.

Punishment rather than treatment is unequivocally recognized as the purpose of the criminal law. The introduction of the punishment ideal into the Nigerian criminal law dates back to colonial times. Over and above the largely unwritten customary criminal law, the colonial administration introduced a new penal system and philosophy rooted in the eighteenth-century deterrence doctrine. A criminal code was imposed that was more a reflection of the values of the colonial metropolis than of the Nigerian society. The postindependence civilian and military efforts at Nigerianization have left unaltered the substance and form of the inherited penal system. At best, the limits and scope of the customary criminal law have been drastically reduced or certain traditional violations, customary rules, and practices have been incorporated in the modern code. At worst, the punishment and deterrence ideals have been retained as the only guidelines and rationale for criminal sanctions.

Since punishment is the purpose of the criminal law and sanctions, proof of culpability or criminal responsibility makes every proven offender liable to punishment. Legal exceptions to this rule are permissible by reason of age or other legally acceptable handicaps. Based on the principle of "*nulla poena sina lege*," Section 33(12) of the 1979 Constitution included in the Bill of Rights the provision that no punishment can be administered on an offender unless "the penalty therefore is prescribed in a written law." While this is clearly protective of the constitutional guarantees extended to an offender, it upholds the provision of Section 3(2) of the Northern Penal Code law that "no person is to be liable to punishment under any native law or custom." Regrettably, this also precludes and suppresses from the modern penal system the more benevolent features of customary penal philosophy, such as appeasement, peacement resolution of disputes, reconciliation, and certain alternatives to punishment.

The major penalties include capital punishment, imprisonment, fines, and caning. Though there are indications as to the type of penalties appropriate for specific offenses, or the permissible exceptions from certain penalties, sentencing guidelines are generally quite vague. The earlier statutory provisions indicated maximum punishment but a mandatory sentence was rarely used. The military rulers enforced a dormant sentencing policy based on a mandatory sentence, a minimum sentence, and judicial discretion.

The court has no discretionary power over mandatory sentences. Where minima are indicated the court has discretionary powers over only the maximum sentences that must strictly respect the specified minimum. Yet the minimum sentences, in many cases, are very severe.

Before, during, and after the colonial administration, the death penalty has figured in the repertoire of punishment options specified in both the criminal and penal codes. It was usually limited to the crimes of treason and murder. In 1970, because of the increase of violence and brutality of crimes, the Gowon administration enacted the Robbery and Firearms (Special Provision) Decree. The decree provided that any offender who was "armed with firearms, or any offensive weapon, or is in company with any person so armed, or at or immediately after the time of the robbery the said offender wounds or uses any personal violence to any person" would be put to death by hanging or by the firing squad. Subsequent military administrations have increased the number of offenses for which the death penalty is mandatory, including armed robbery and drug offenses. The death sentence is carried out publicly.

The civilian government of Shagari seemed to have been less convinced of the deterrent impact of the death penalty, yet its position on the issue remained unclear. Public executions were discouraged, yet it is hard to account for the trend and volume that continued under the civilians. Generally, the law has always exempted youths below 17 years and pregnant female convicts from the death sentence.

Incarceration constitutes the most frequently used form of severe punishment for most offenses. It may be given as the sole form of punishment in the first instance, or in default of the payment of a fine or in conjunction with a fine. A prison sentence is carried out in a prison facility and runs from the day of its pronouncement. A conditional discharge or bind over may be imposed in place of a prison term. In case of conviction for multiple offenses and, therefore, different prison terms, the terms may be carried over consecutively or concurrently as per court order.

Once a prison term is imposed, early release can be granted under the remission, commutation, parole, or license policies, or through presidential pardon. Commutation and pardon are very infrequently used. The parole option has remained a dead letter in the Nigerian penal system. Despite the powers granted to the chief executive under the Prisons Act to make provisions for parole release, this has never been done. The only early discharge option is the remission policy. However, its aim is primarily to ease prison overcrowding rather than to provide a community alternative to imprisonment. The remission policy permits that a maximum of one-third of a sentence be deducted from the total sentence, or a life sentence be fixed at twenty years, in recognition of good conduct and industry. In effect, the loss of remission has become a frequent form of prison discipline dreaded by inmates.

Fines, corporal punishment, and conditional or probationary discharges are the only recognizable alternatives to imprisonment within the discretionary powers of the judges. These may be imposed as penalties in the first instance, or as supplements to, rather than as alternatives to, incarceration. In case of default in the payment of fines, a prison sentence may be ordered. The imposition of a fine is strictly a retributive and deterrent measure rather than an alternative in the strict sense. The rationale is to order payments in offenses such as postal, tax, and similar violations.

Corporal punishment may be imposed as a supplementary or substitute penalty for all offenses except capital crimes. Caning and haddi lashing constitute the two forms of corporal punishments. The number of strokes to be administered, the choice between the two, and the exceptions depend on the court order, the type of crime, the circumstances, and the place where the crime occurred. Both the Southern Criminal Procedure Act and the Northern Criminal Procedure Code recognize and permit corporal punishment. The offender may be whipped on the buttock with a birch, rod, or cane. The eastern states restrict corporal punishment to juvenile offenders only. In other parts of the country, whipping may be ordered only for male adults below forty-five years of age. In the North, there is no age limit, though females may not be caned and the strokes may not exceed twelve. Corporal punishment may be ordered in conjunction with a prison sentence for a wide variety of property crimes.

The haddi lashing is a form of corporal punishment whose aim is more symbolic than physically painful. It is to be lightly inflicted on the shoulders and in public in accordance with the rules for crimes against the Moslem law. Eighty lashes may be ordered for alcohol-related offenses, a hundred for unlawful sexual relations, such as adultery, or the use of obscene language against the person of a female. Since haddi lashing must not inflict lacerations or serious physical pain and injury, the deterrence goal is to be fulfilled through the public disgrace and embarrassment of the ritual.

The deterrent impact of corporal punishment is controversial despite the alleged public predilection for its use. First, the punishment enthusiasts justify the lack of deterrent impact on the fact is has been usually limited to very minor infractions. Second, judges reportedly are reluctant to order up to the statutory maximum number of strokes.

Given the punitive orientation underlying the penal system, it is not difficult to see how probation would have limited use, despite its statutory provision. In principle, adult offenders may be granted probation based on consideration of their past criminal record, the gravity of the offense, the risk involved, and the ease of probation supervision. In affect, probation has been more readily applied with juveniles for whom rehabilitation and social welfare are preferred over punishment.

Except for prison records, there are no reliable statistics on sentencing trends and the distribution of the different penal measures. Clearly, the penal system is sustained by a strictly punitive philosophy. The various official pronouncements of decision makers further reinforce this punishment-deterrence ethos and cast serious doubts as to the chances of a rehabilitative ideal in the Nigerian penal system. The inherent regimentary life and authoritarianism of the military leave no room for this eventuality. On the other hand, the civilian administrators showed no intention of discarding deterrence despite their recognition of its ineffectiveness. The general public seems convinced that severe penalties are the only answer to police ineffectiveness and the ever increasing threat of crime. At every available opportunity, the public has administered what is commonly known as "jungle justice" or the *lex talionis*.

Criminal Procedure

Sources of the Rules of Criminal Procedure

In Nigeria, the established rules of criminal procedure have diverse statutory origins. Though revoked under Decree No. 1, 1984, by the military junta that took over power in 1983, the 1979 Constitution provided for the procedural due process safeguards of the accused. Sections 32 and 33 of the 1979 Constitution provide that the fundamental due process rights to fairness and justice, personal liberty, and to a fair hearing are guaranteed to individuals in their confrontation with the state. In addition to the constitutional procedural guarantees, two often quoted sources of criminal procedure rules are the Criminal Procedures Act and the Criminal Procedure Code. The Act applied throughout the federation until 1960 when the Criminal Procedure Code was adopted and made applicable to the northern states. Though certain provisions of the Criminal Procedure Act are still applicable in the entire country, it remains the rule of criminal procedure in force only in the southern states.

In addition to the above sources, procedural rules, especially for criminal appeals, are also contained in the rules of individual courts or in the enabling enactments of these courts. Such is the case with special courts (juvenile court, for example) or the special tribunals largely established by the military through special decrees. Such decrees often contain criminal procedure rules that violate the constitutional due process rights guaranteed under the 1979 Constitution.

General Principles

Section 33(5) of the 1979 Constitution provides that "every person who is charged with a criminal offense shall be presumed innocent until he is proved guilty." The presumption of innocence of an accused is a fundamental principle in a criminal trial. Given a nonguilty plea, the onus of proof is on the prosecution to provide all the elements of the offense to prove beyond reasonable doubt that the accused committed the offense. The Evidence Act places the onus of proof on the defense when only the insanity and intoxication defenses are raised. Then the onus still lies with the prosecution to disprove the defense raised by the accused.

Parties to Criminal Proceedings

In criminal as in civil proceedings, there are always two parties, that is, the accused and the complainant or prosecutor. By law, a court cannot initiate a criminal trial on its own motion; a complaint must be made by someone. This may be by the police, by native authorities, or the Office of the Director of Public Prosecution, depending on the seriousness of the case and the level of the court. Generally, criminal proceedings are nominally brought by the state.

Most criminal prosecutions are brought by the police in the name of the State Commissioner of Police. Police prosecutions are limited to cases involving issues of fact. Police prosecutions are usually brought in the name of the State Commissioner of Police. For more serious cases brought usually before the Superior Courts, or complex trials in the magistrates' court, prosecutions are brought only by registered legal practitioners (state counsel) in the office of the Director of Public Prosecutions. By Constitution, the Attorney General is vested with the power of control over criminal prosecutions. The attorney general may exercise this power through the director, a state counsel, or a private legal practitioner duly briefed by him or her.

Where the onus falls on the Attorney General, the prosecution is brought in the name of "The State" or of "The Republic" for state or federal cases, respectively. Section 342 of the Criminal Procedure Act also provides for private prosecutions by private citizens where the state declines prosecution, yet the possibility of having to bear the costs should the accused be acquitted or discharged makes this provision seldom used.

As the other party to the criminal trial, the accused is constitutionally (S. 33 [5]) guaranteed the right "to defend himself in person or by legal practitioners of his own choice" except where the court is presided over by lay people in the customary courts.

Phases of Criminal Proceedings

The phases in criminal proceedings vary with the type of trial, that is, summary trial or trial on information. Summary trials involve summary convictions or less serious offenses and are in the magistrate's courts' jurisdiction. Trials on information involve indictable or more serious offenses, and, by law, are in the High Court's jurisdiction. However, trials on information are preceded by preliminary investigations in a magistrate's court. These investigations are to assess the quantum of evidence in favor of the charge and determine whether the state should take the accused to trial before a high court for an indictable offense. An indictable offense may be tried in a magistrate's court only by express consent of the accused.

Most criminal cases are brought before the magistrate's court and the process of disposition occurs in stages. For misdemeanor and simple offenses, a complaint is filed by the police in the magistrate's court with an application for a summons or for an arrest warrant. For serious offenses, the suspect may be arrested without warrant and served with a charge by the police. The second phase involves the arraignment of the accused. The charge is read and explained to the accused who is requested to plead to the charge. In cases of indictable offenses, subsequent to the charge being presented but before the plea is taken, the accused may be informed of the right to choose to be tried either by a high court or a magistrate's court. For summary proceedings, the accused may enter into any of these pleas:

(a) a guilty plea, whereby he may be convicted and sentenced, or
(b) not guilty plea that places the burden of proof on the prosecution and opens a criminal trial, or
(c) not guilty to the offense charged but guilty to another not charged that may lead to conviction and sentencing, or
(d) special pleas for the very or similar offense and that may involve
   (1) an *autrefois acquit*, that is, accused previously tried, and acquitted,
   (2) an *autrefois convict*, that is, accused previously tried, and convicted,
   (3) an *autrefois pardon*, that is, accused previously tried, convicted, and sentenced but subsequently pardoned.

The pleas proceed in conformity with the Constitutional safeguards against double jeopardy.

A nonguilty plea opens the trial stage with the prosecution's presentation of his or her case through examination, cross-examination, and reexamination of the sworn witnesses called in by the prosecutor to prove the charge. A submission of no case may be presented for insufficient evidence under Section 286 of the Criminal Procedure Act. The court may uphold the submission and discharge the accused or overrule it and call upon the defense. If overruled or where it was never made and the accused fails to rest his or her case on the prosecution's, the defense portion of the trial commences with the examination, cross-examination, reexamination of witnesses, and evidence of the accused. The prosecution may introduce evidence in rebuttal of additional evidence by the defense. The court may also recall and reexamine witnesses or may, on its own, introduce evidence not called upon by either party. Following the final addresses by the parties the court enters a verdict.

Under the military, certain aspects of the procedural principles, rights, and stages were modified or even suppressed for certain offenses, such as armed robbery, exchange control, telephone, or postal offenses, or more recently, offenses associated with oil pipeline or the media. In the case of media offenses, a 1984 Public Officers Decree shifted the burden of proof to the accused in charges involving the publishing or reporting of false information or information that brings ridicule or disrepute on the government or its officials.

Rights of the Accused

The fundamental rights of every individual to life, to dignity, to personal liberty, fair hearing, privacy, freedom of thought, conscience, religion, and expression are guaranteed under Sections 30 through 39 of the 1979 Constitution. In recognition of the need to guarantee fairness and justice to individuals in their dealings with the state, the Constitution provides for specific procedural due process rights from the pretrial arrest and detention stage to sentencing.

Under Section 32 (2, 3, 4) of the Constitution any person who is under arrest or under detention has the right to remain silent, to a timely notice of charges within 24 hours in a language that he or she understands, and to a timely court appearance.

The rights of the accused to a fair trial are guaranteed under Section 33 of the Constitution. The accused must be presumed innocent until proven guilty (S. 33[5]), is guaranteed the right to a speedy and public trial (S. 33[3, 4]), to a notice of charge, to counsel, to confrontation and examination of sworn testimony, to cross-examination, to personal witnesses (S. 33[6]), and protection against double jeopardy and self-incrimination (S. 33[8-11]). To protect against abuse or arbitrariness, Section 78(1) of the Criminal Procedure Code defines conditions for search and seizure. Similarly, the rights to bail and the conditions are specified under Section 118(1) of the Criminal Procedure Act and Section 341(1) of the Criminal Procedure Code.

Pretrial Detention

Under Section 32(lc) of the 1979 Constitution, where there is reasonable suspicion of a criminal violation, or where it is necessary to restrain or prevent the accused from committing a criminal violence, the accused may be submitted to pretrial custody. Except where there is reasonable suspicion of a capital offense having been committed (S. 32[4]), the Constitution establishes that detention is unlawful unless the suspect is arraigned or tried within a reasonable time. Section 32(4) provides that a suspect must be brought before the court within one day from detention if there is a court of competent jurisdiction within a radius of 40 kilometers from the place of detention. Where the latter is lacking, detention may be extended to two days or longer depending on the judgment of the court. Any detention in excess of these provisions is unlawful.

Section 32(4) further demands the unconditional or conditional release of a detainee whose trial is delayed beyond two months from detention or arrest or three months for suspects already released on bail. Unless otherwise demanded by the severity of the violation, or the nature of the evidence available, a person charged with a felony may be admitted to bail at the discretion of the court. In any event, Section 120 of the Criminal Procedure Act protects against excessive bail.

Under Section 32(lc) of the Constitution, a person may be submitted to preventive detention where it is necessary to inhibit his or her commission of acts that are criminal offenses. Preventive detention is a pretrial measure, yet there are no legal grounds for a subsequent trial. Similarly, prevention is directed at a possible criminal violation, yet no reasonable suspicion exists as to an actual involvement in a criminal violation. The Preventive Detention Provision violates the individual's constitutional rights because it denies the right to bail, release, or trial within a reasonable time frame since detention is not accompanied by a criminal charge.

Lay Participation in Criminal Proceedings

In the absence of trial by jury, lay participation in criminal proceedings is confined to the preliminary phases. By law, any member of the public may initiate proceedings by making a complaint to a magistrate's court. Similarly, any information may be referred by a private person to a High Court with the endorsement of a law officer.

The power of a private person to arrest on warrant is limited to exceptional cases. Under the Criminal Procedure Act (S. 10, 12, 13) and the Criminal Procedure Code (S. 26-28) a private citizen is empowered to arrest anyone who commits an indictable offense in his or her presence or against whom there is probable and reasonable cause to suspect a misdemeanor offense at night or a felony, or anyone committing an offense injurious to the person's property.

Customary courts may be presided over by legal practitioners, but this is by no means the rule. By law, the president and other members of a customary court may also be appointed members of the public who are learned in customary law.

Juvenile Court Proceedings

Juvenile court trials are regulated by the provisions of the Children and Young Persons Act. In recognition of the broader social correlates of delinquency, a social welfare and rehabilitative approach has been elected for handling young offenders. Statutory provisions for the determination of guilt, and for hearing and deciding juvenile cases are contained in the specific Children and Young Persons Acts in the state of the children (under 14 years of age) and young persons (between 14 and 17 years of age).

Generally, juvenile proceedings differ from adult proceedings in many respects. Certain terms of criminal connotation are not used to avert the stigmatizing consequences. Thus children may be found guilty and an order may be made upon the guilt finding. Words such as *conviction* and *sentence* are avoided.

Juvenile cases are heard by a juvenile court. Any magistrate's court may be a juvenile court with a magistrate sitting alone or with other persons appointed by the chief judge of the state. Juvenile hearings are to be conducted in a room or a building different from that in which sittings of regular courts are held. The times and days may not coincide with those of other court proceedings.

Juvenile hearings must be held in camera. Other than the members and officers of the court, the parties and their respective counsel, the parents and/or guardians of the young person, the public is barred from juvenile hearings. No identifying information with respect to name, school, place of residence, photograph, or the like may be released on the youth, unless with the leave of the court or in accordance with statutory provisions.

A special feature of juvenile proceedings is the heavy reliance on social welfare reports on the youth's background, family, and social circumstances. Measures to be adopted in cases involving children are based on their special needs and problems. Juvenile courts, in fact, do not only handle offending youth. Children in need of care, protection, and supervision, orphans or destitutes by reason of parental institutional confinement, parental neglect, abuse, desertion, criminal or drinking habits, may become wards of the juvenile court. Similarly, those found or known to be in company of a prostitute, reputed thief, or otherwise with persons of disreputable character and dubious morality, children found mendicating, vagrant, or idling or lacking any means of sustenance or shelter may be handed over to the court. In such cases, a recognizance may be issued to the parent or guardian, or the child may be committed to the care of any fit person or to an approved school.

A guilty finding against a juvenile may be disposed of through a custodial or noncustodial measure depending on the offense, the domestic circumstances of the youth, and what seems appropriate for the youth's timely rehabilitation. A youth may be released on probation under a social welfare officer or to the care of any fit person. A restitution order, fine, or the payment of damages may be preferred against the parent or guardian or they may be required to guarantee the youth's good behavior. In other cases, corporal punishment may be administered.

The law prohibits that a child be sentenced to death or even to imprisonment. In the case of a young person, detention may be in an approved school, or other similar juvenile institution. Where a young person must be detained in an adult penal facility, the law prohibits any contact between the youth and the adult inmates.

Execution of Penal Measures
(Corrections)

Following the 1966 Prisons (Control) Decree and the 1968 Unification of Prisons, local prisons have been absorbed into one federal system. The Nigerian Prison Service, a Department of the Ministry of Internal Affairs, is the central control for prisons. The Service is under the direction of a director of prisons with the office in Lagos. The director's responsibilities cover management, financial planning, administration, statistics, internal organization, and monitoring the welfare of prison inmates. An assistant director administers prison operations in each state. The daily direction and running of the prisons are handled by a chief superintendent, superintendent, or assistant superintendent depending on the size, location, and prison population.

The classification of inmates in Nigerian prisons is the product of a statutory requirement necessitated more by security considerations than by any rehabilitative rationale. Ideally, inmates are grouped and segregated in terms of gender, age, convicted/unconvicted, criminal/ noncriminal criteria. By law, convicted offenders must be classified according to whether the prison term will be with or without hard labor. The distinction is hardly called for in light of the provision contained in Section 39(1) of the Prisons Act that established compulsory prison labor. The accommodation of inmates in a facility has not always adhered strictly to this classification system. Most prisons house all groups. The segregation policy is most often implemented by instituting different outside labor hours, or by the use of dividing fences to separate juveniles from adults or females and males.

In the absence of maximum security facilities, most prisons isolate and secure areas under maximum conditions within the regular facility. Recently, there has been a move in the direction of establishing facilities specifically for different security needs. Usually, first time or minimum security prisoners are under less restrictions and are eligible to open prisons or prison camps. The decision lies with the prison administration rather than with the sentencing court.

Overcrowding is a serious problem in Nigerian prisons. The bulk of inmates are those remanded pending trial. Inmates in federal prisons have increased from 20,980 in 1970, to 35,706 in 1979 and 36,069 in 1980 according to prison statistics. In 1979 alone, of a total of 129,618 prison admissions, 84,270 were unconvicted individuals, 178 were on death row, 25 were serving life, 9,580 were on long-term determinate sentences and 35,755 were short-term offenders. Caution must be taken with regard to the accuracy of these figures.

Though an exact count of facilities in the system is unavailable, the overcrowding problem, the inadequacy of facilities, the poverty of training programs, and general living conditions within these institutions may not be underestimated. The deteriorating status of the Nigerian prisons is further compounded by understaffing, and the low caliber of the prison personnel, most of whom have poor educational backgrounds and lack the qualifications appropriate for working with prisoners.

Rights and Responsibilities
of Incarcerated Offenders

Prison life is not without certain rights that are available to the inmates. Generally, despite the punishment and deterrence goals, the reform or correction of the inmate through educational programs, vocational training, productive and remunerated prison labor constitutes part of the prison responsibilities toward its wards. Often these have come short of adequate implementation.

Early release from prison occurs in several ways in Nigeria. Although used as a reward for proper conduct and industry, the practice of remission is intended more as a right than a reward. Except where an inmate violates some prison rules, maximum remission is generally automatic. Under an old prison law, parole or license could be granted to an inmate by the governor and in accordance with conditions established by him or her. At present, parole provisions are unavailable. A sick prisoner is entitled to a warrant of early release if there is medical evidence that release is feasible, will be beneficial to his or her health and life, although it will not facilitate more violations.

All inmates are expected to comply with prison regulations that include participation in any productive labor and training programs that are available. Prisoners are entitled to remuneration in recognition of the need to provide some form of after care to discharged prisoners beyond transportation assistance. In some localities, the Discharged Prisoners' Aid Society has provided some assistance, mainly by arranging tests for trade certification at the completion of trade training programs in prison or during release.

Execution of Noncustodial Measures

Noncustodial measures or, generally, alternatives to incarceration can hardly be included in the repertoire of penal measures in Nigeria. As indicated, provisions for early release through parole have never gone beyond the rhetoric or planning stage.

Probation services are of recent introduction and their use is largely confined to the more welfare- and rehabilitation-oriented juvenile arena. Adult probation services have been affected by the lack of personnel, policy guidelines, and legislative regulation. The juvenile court rules, on the other hand, have laid sufficiently specific guidelines and conditions for granting and supervising juvenile probation.

On the Issue of Policy

In their various messages to the nation, the civilian and military governments have expressed strong concern over the nation's crime epidemic. The leading causes have been associated with the mania for personal aggrandizement, moral decadence, decline or laxity of traditional and parental social control and vigilance, greed, indiscriminate importation of Western values, corruption, and ostentation. Kibuka (1979) has aptly remarked that in African official circles such public denunciations and expressions of concern do not necessarily mean that the war against crime is a priority given the myriad of issues competing for financial resources.

Official response to the alarming criminality has been a get-tough stance, evidenced by intimidating public sermons and increasingly severe penalties. So far, none of these measures has been the expected panacea to crime. In its national social rehabilitation and economic reconstruction agenda, the Federal Military Government of Major-General Guhari declared a nationwide "War Against Indiscipline" (WAI). With obvious historical antecedents, WAI was an inherited cliche, yet a misnomer given the potpourri of targeted social unorthodoxies under that umbrella term. It was a deja vu of erratic response to the spiraling rate of white collar and street crimes.

The official response to crime has always ignored the needed rational explanations, as well as the need to develop an indigenous penological philosophy and penal policy. The criminal justice system, the entire judicial network, and the principles on which they are erected are crying for a thorough reexamination. The easy culprits have been poor moral attitude, indiscipline, and the alleged materialistic fanaticism of the Nigerian people. Both Gowon (1970) and Murtala (1975) embarked on a program of moral rehabilitation in the attempt to fight the problem. Obasanjo (1978) advocated a program of national rehabilitation. Shagari (1983) called for the establishment of a Ministry of National Guidance to promote a national "ethical reorganization program." To sustain the lame duck anticrime strategy, since political demagoguery had proven a total failure, severe penalties in the name of deterrence were invoked. Capital punishment was extended to an ever increasing number of offenses. The sound of public execution bullets has prevailed over rational planning, global policy development, and financial investment in the development and implementation of an empirically and theoretically promising control and prevention policy.

It is a criminological truism that deterrence penology suffers from serious theoretical and empirical uncertainties. The Nigerian official penological orientation ignores this basic fact and the need for a more scientific and empirically grounded insight into the root causes of crime, the appropriate remedies and the most effective way of administering criminal justice. It also ignores the fact that the often litanized causal themes of greed, indiscipline, and corruption may well be symptoms, not causes, or at best correlates, of some exogenous forces including the very antiquated and lethargic criminal justice system. The decision-making circles seem impervious to the fact that a meaningful and effective criminal justice system needs a rational and theoretically sound penal policy. The fact that deterrence emerges as the overriding penal principle does not necessarily mean that its adoption has any theoretical or empirical legitimacy. Rather, it means that deterrence appears to be the quick "scared straight" response to crime regardless of its empirical status and effectiveness.

PART II

Civil Law Systems

Civil law, also referred to as continental law or Romano-Germanic law, developed in Europe and is primarily centered there, although through colonial expansion and adoption it has spread to most large areas of the world. The Federal Republic of Germany, Sweden, and Japan are the criminal justice systems described in this part. Sweden and West Germany are representative of the systems found throughout Western Europe. Japan may be viewed as a mixture of civil law with regard to substantive criminal law yet with elements of the common law in the field of criminal procedure. The Japanese criminal justice system was greatly influenced by the occupation following World War II when an attempt was made to inculcate American legal concepts.

Compared with other parts of the developed world, Western Europe has advanced further toward the concept of rehabilitation of offenders and the use of noncustodial measures. The day-fine, work release, relatively short terms of incarceration, and elimination of the death penalty have been incorporated into the criminal justice systems of Sweden and the Federal Republic of Germany as means to achieve these goals. The problems of political terrorism and criminality among guestworkers have affected European countries during the past decade, and steps have been taken to deal with these situations.

In each of the chapters students should make comparisons among the countries and especially among the two European countries and Japan. To what extent are there characteristics that are held in common?

4

The Federal Republic of Germany

JOACHIM HERRMANN

General Information

Characteristics of the Country

The Federal Republic of Germany originated after World War II when the German Reich was divided into a western part—the Federal Republic—and an eastern part—the German Democratic Republic. The city of Berlin, which lies in the eastern section, is an independent entity under the control of the four powers who were victorious in 1945.

The Federal Republic is a country in the center of Europe at the frontier between the Western and the Communist world. In the east it is bordered by the German Democratic Republic and Czechoslovakia, in the west by France and the Benelux States. In the north-south direction it stretches from the North Sea, Denmark, and the Baltic Sea to the Alps, Austria, and Switzerland.

The Federal Republic has a population of approximately 61 million. It covers an area of some 96,000 square miles. The population that is about one-fourth of the American, lives in a territory that is equivalent to only 3% of the United States in area.

Some 4 million of the 61 million are foreign "guestworkers" who mostly come from South European countries. Officially, they reside in

West Germany on a temporary basis, but a considerable number have stayed for many years. They and their families have started to blend into West German society.

The political order of the Federal Republic is based on the Constitution of 1949 which provides for a democratic and social federal state under the rule of law. The Constitution includes a bill of rights that affords a comprehensive protection of human rights and that plays an important role in public life. The ten West German states—Laender—exercise much less political power than do the states in the United States. Communities and counties are mainly administrative units with relatively limited autonomy.

Different from other West European states, the Federal Republic is not centered in a national capital. It rather is an association of regions and big cities, such as Northrhine-Westfalia with its heavy industry and the mostly agrarian Bavaria, the banking center of Frankfurt and Hamburg, the city of merchants and seafaring people. Balancing the different interests of the regions and cities makes for a great deal of political stability.

The Federal Republic is a highly industrialized state that, since its founding, has gone through periods of rapid economic growth. In terms of gross national product, it is ranked third among Western nations, after the United States and Japan. The output of industrial goods is much higher than the domestic market can absorb. Therefore, West Germany is heavily dependent on exports of its goods such as machinery and technical equipment, motor vehicles, chemicals, and precision tools.

West German economic life follows the principle of "social market economy" which provides for economic freedom and, at the same time, for a fair distribution of profits among the management and the worker. The income of West German workers is, by and large, comparable to that of their American counterparts. They work about 40 hours per week. Their fringe benefits, such as social insurance, old age pensions, and vacation bonuses, are extensive. Their annual vacations are more than three times as long as those of the American worker.

**General Description
of the Legal System**

Since the Federal Republic of Germany is part of the civil law system, German law is primarily codified. Many of its codes date back to the times of the German Reich. The Penal Code became effective in 1871, the Code of Criminal Procedure in 1879. Over the years, both have undergone numerous changes and thorough revisions.

When talking about peculiarities of civil law one cannot overlook that today the United States—a common law country—also relies on codes and statutes rather than solely on precedents. Yet different from most legislative acts in the United States, codes and statutes that are typical of a civil law system tend to be carefully integrated bodies of general principles arranged in a highly systematized manner and phrased in abstract language. These characteristics call for liberal rather than narrow interpretation. Traditionally, West German lawyers engage in a great deal of liberal statutory construction. They emphasize abstractions rather than particulars and concrete cases.

In the Federal Republic, as in other civil law systems, court decisions are not taken as sources of law but only used in interpreting the legal text. The common law doctrine, that precedent is binding, is unknown in West Germany. Judges of lower courts, however, quite readily follow prior decisions of higher courts, since they know that otherwise they are likely to be reversed on appeal.

West Germany is a federal state, but, unlike in the United States, almost all substantive and procedural criminal law is subject to federal legislation. On the other hand, all courts hearing criminal cases are state courts except the federal appellate court of last resort and the Federal Constitutional Court which hears cases only involving questions of federal constitutional law. Thus federal law is regularly applied by the state courts. This does not mean, however, that federal law is applied differently in each state. The general willingness of state courts to construe the law in the same way, as well as the wide reviewing powers of the federal appellate court, have proved effective in maintaining the uniformity of the law.

Amount, Structure, and Dynamics of Criminality

Crime rates have been rising in the Federal Republic for many years, but since 1984 there has been a downward movement. For example, in 1963 about 1.7 million offenses were known to the police; this figure increased to some 4.3 million in 1983. Road traffic offenses are not included in this count. Crime rates per 100,000 population were 2,914 in 1963 and 7,074 in 1983. This amounts to a 140% increase within 20 years, or to an annual increase of about 7%. In most recent years, however, the annual increase has slowed down, and in 1984 the crime rate seems to have decreased for the first time.

Figures of violent crimes (i.e., willful killing, rape, robbery, and aggravated assault) are substantially smaller in the Federal Republic than in the United States. Table 4.1 gives crime rates per 100,000 in 1983. The comparison is somewhat distorted, since the West German—but not the American—figures include complaints of crimes that police investigations later disclosed had not been committed. The figures seem to confirm the general assumption that there is much more violence in America than in other societies. Some reasons for this may be that West German society is more homogeneous, that it tends to heed traditional moral values, that the problems of juvenile delinquency and of drug-related crimes are less severe than in the United States, and that there is nothing in West German cities that could be compared to the American slums.

Larceny, aggravated larceny, and burglary amount to about two-thirds of all offenses, road traffic offenses not being included. This contradicts the idea that economic prosperity and high personal income reduce crimes against property.

Since World War II, criminality of juveniles and adolescents has risen faster than offense rates of adults. Some 25% of the identified offenders are between 14 and 21 years of age; 5% are even younger than 14. About one-third of all male persons are convicted at least once before they reach the age of 25.

The crime rate of guestworkers is somewhat higher than that of the West German citizens. Yet most guestworkers are male and belong to younger age groups where crime rates are generally high.

Scope of Criminal Law

General statements about the scope of criminal law are difficult to make. An example may illustrate this.

American criminal law requires a high degree of negligence for criminal responsibility, while in West Germany ordinary negligence is sufficient. It would be a mistake, however, to believe that because of this difference criminal law is more lenient in the United States than in the Federal Republic. American legislatures frequently have enacted strict liability statutes that impose criminal responsibility for conduct unaccompanied by fault. In addition, payment of damages may serve a

TABLE 4.1

	Federal Republic	United States
Willful Killing		
Not including attempt	1.4	8.3
Rape	11.0	33.7
Robbery	48.1	213.8
Aggravated assault	110.6	273.3

punitive function in American law. Both strict responsibility and punitive or exemplary damages do not exist in West German law.

During the last twenty years, the criminal law of the Federal Republic has undergone far-reaching changes. On the one hand, new provisions were added to the Penal Code to cope with newly arising crime problems, such as new forms of terrorism, kidnapping, hijacking, and environmental pollution, as well as the steady increase in white-collar crime.

On the other hand, there was a strong movement toward decriminalization, which was accomplished in two ways. First, offenses against morality, such as adultery, bestiality, and homosexuality among consenting adults, were stricken from the Penal Code. Second, petty misdemeanors (violations of traffic laws as well as of business and trade regulations) were relabeled petty infractions and removed from the criminal process. The sanctions provided for petty infractions are regulatory fines instead of the harsher penalties of the Penal Code involving moral blame. The prosecution of petty infractions and the imposition of sanctions are the province of administrative authorities, primarily the police. The judiciary becomes involved only if an accused files a complaint against an administrative order imposing a regulatory fine.

Abortion was liberalized in the middle of the 1970s, but, unlike in the United States, the woman's right to decide whether or not to terminate her pregnancy is still considerably restricted.[1] She may have an abortion only if it is required by medical or genetic reasons, if pregnancy is the consequence of a sexual assault, or if there is a case of "social necessity." The social necessity clause is based on the consideration that, under the totality of circumstances, giving birth to the child would be more than could be expected from the woman. To date, this clause has been liberally applied, four out of five abortions are based on it. Before a pregnancy may be terminated, the woman must, however, undergo medical counseling by a doctor and, in addition, social counseling by an authorized counseling center. Abortions may be procured only in hospitals; they are covered by medical insurance.

West German law on abortion is obviously based on considerations of social responsibility and solidarity. The pregnant woman receives all kinds of help but, at the same time, she is restrained in several ways. In the United States, on the other hand, an individualistic approach has been taken to the abortion problem. The woman is considered to be an independent person who knows what is best for her and the fetus. Even financial help to procure an abortion is not always considered necessary.

Structure and Functioning of Law Enforcement Agencies

Judges in the Federal Republic of Germany are career judges who enter the judiciary as soon as they have finished their legal education. After a probationary period of three or four years they are appointed for life. Judges who are best qualified are promoted to higher office—for example, to an appellate court.

There is a uniform court system with two tiers of trial courts for criminal cases in each state.[2] Local courts, having jurisdiction over less serious cases, sit with either a single professional judge or with a panel of one or sometimes two professional judges and two lay judges. District courts hearing serious cases are composed of panels of three professional judges and two lay judges.

Appeals *de novo* from local courts are heard by district courts. In addition there are state appellate courts and the High Federal Court of Appeals that hear appeals for error. After an accused has exhausted the possibilities of appeal he or she may enter a complaint with the Federal Constitutional Court if the accused can claim that his or her conviction was based on a violation of the Constitution.[3] The function of this court may be compared to that of the United States Supreme Court. The Federal Constitutional Court has handed down numerous decisions concerning the criminal justice system, but, on the whole, it plays a less important role than its American counterpart.

Petitions contending that the European Convention for the Protection of Human Rights and Fundamental Freedoms has been violated may be brought before the European Commission of Human Rights and the European Court of Human Rights. Thus international institutions have jurisdiction to review domestic cases.

West German prosecutors also work in a career system.[4] Some of the states provide for transfers between the prosecutor's office and the judiciary in order to make prosecutors familiar with the judge's business, and vice versa.

The prosecutor's office is hierarchically organized on a statewide basis, with an attorney general at the top who is responsible to the minister of justice. Whatever the single prosecutor does is supervised by his or her superiors. This results in considerable uniformity of law enforcement.

As everywhere, the police serve two purposes: to maintain law and order and to detect and investigate crime. As regards the latter function, they work together with the prosecutor, though police officers are not his or her subordinates.

West German attorneys, before being admitted to the bar, have to go through the same legal education as judges and prosecutors.[5] Any practicing attorney may defend any criminal case. There is no special criminal bar, though a few attorneys have specialized in defending criminal cases.

Substantive Criminal Law

General Principles
of Responsibility

The Constitution of the Federal Republic provides that no one shall be punished for anything that is not expressly forbidden by law. Since in civil law countries all criminal law is contained in the penal code and statutes, the problem of common law crimes does not exist.

Problems arise, however, with regard to the interpretation of penal provisions. Following civil law tradition, the West German Penal Code defines offenses in more general and abstract terms than typical American criminal codes. The common law method of strict construction of penal provisions would be incompatible with the general and abstract definitions. Therefore, West German judges construe penal provisions liberally in order not to defeat the intention of the legislature. On the other hand, judges are not permitted to resort to interpretation by "analogy" and apply penal provisions to conduct not proscribed by them.

Often it is not easy to distinguish between liberal interpretation and illegal analogy. Generally, West German judges do not hesitate to broaden the definition of an offense if they consider it necessary in the interests of justice. For instance, in the provision on dangerous assault, "by means of a weapon" was interpreted to include the throwing of hydrochloric acid in the victim's face and ordering a dog to attack. In the definition of robbery, "by force" was construed to include nonviolent narcotization of the victim.

A void-for-vagueness doctrine exists in West German criminal law. It plays a minor role, however, because general and abstract definitions of the penal code tend to make penal provisions less precise.

A provision forbidding retroactive application of criminal law is embodied in the West German Constitution. Like in the United States, there is some controversy among West German lawyers whether the ex post facto prohibitions apply also to laws of procedure and to judicial decisions. Generally, the view is taken that both may be changed retroactively, but in recent years it was suggested that exceptions should be made to protect the interests of the accused.

Grades of Offenses

The West German Penal Code places criminal offenses into two categories: felonies punishable by imprisonment for at least one year and misdemeanors punishable by imprisonment for a shorter minimum period or a fine. The category of misdemeanors includes many crimes that would be considered felonies under American law, such as larceny, fraud, extortion, abortion, and negligent homicide.

The classification serves practical purposes. For example, only a conspiracy to commit a felony is a crime. Jurisdiction of local courts and district courts depends mainly on the classification of offenses. Only an accused who is convicted of a felony may be disqualified from holding public office or from practicing as an attorney.

Age of Criminal Responsibility

Juveniles of less than 14 years of age are not criminally responsible at all. There is an irrefutable presumption of their criminal incapacity. Offenses they have committed are dealt with by guardianship courts.

Juveniles between 14 and 18 are criminally responsible if they are sufficiently mature to understand the wrongfulness of their conduct and to act in accordance with such understanding. Sanctions provided for juveniles are educational and disciplinary measures. Punishment is to be inflicted only as a last resort.

Adolescents between the ages of 18 and 21 are fully responsible. If the adolescent has a juvenile personality or if the offense he or she has committed was typical of a juvenile, one of the special sanctions provided for juveniles will be imposed; otherwise the adolescent will be punished as an adult.

Criminal Responsibility
of Corporations

Since West German criminal law is based on the principle that punishment presupposes personal guilt, criminal responsibility of corporations does not exist. Officers and agents of a corporation are individually responsible for what they have done in its behalf. Their individual guilt is to be the basis for fixing punishment. When imposing punishment upon an officer or agent, the court may, however, order the corporation to pay a regulatory fine and to forfeit the profits from the illegal enterprise. Thus, from a practical point of view, West German law may not be very different from that of the United States, where corporations are held criminally responsible.

The Mental Element, Strict
Responsibility, Mistake
of Fact and Law

All criminal laws have to face the difficulty of defining various mental elements of criminal conduct that in some way reflect actual states of mind and that, at the same time, can be used as manageable tools for attributing criminal responsibility. West German criminal law tries to solve this problem by distinguishing two main categories of culpability: intent and negligence. Intent is subdivided into three kinds. Offenders act intentionally when it is their purpose to accomplish a certain consequence, when they know that the consequence will result from their conduct, or when they consider such consequence possible and do not mind it.

Differing from American tradition, ordinary negligence is a sufficient basis for criminal responsibility in West German law. Only some modern statutes limit responsibility to gross negligence. Recklessness is unknown as a separate category of responsibility.

West German criminal law does not distinguish between conscious negligence where offenders are aware of the possibility that they may cause a harm, and inadvertent negligence where offenders are not aware of that possibility. From a psychological point of view, it may make a difference whether or not offenders foresee a possible damage. Yet in practice it is often impossible to ascertain offenders' actual state of mind. In addition, one must keep in mind that conscious negligence is not necessarily a more serious form of culpability than inadvertence. People who trust their own competence to such an extent that they are not aware of a great risk they create may deserve as much blame as ones who foresee the possibility of a damage they may cause but try to avoid.

The distinction between conscious negligence and intent is generally drawn in the following way: Offenders act with conscious negligence when they foresee that a certain consequence will possibly result from their conduct but trust that they will not effectuate it. They act intentionally when they foresee a possible consequence but do not mind it.

As mentioned above, strict responsibility is unknown in West German criminal law. Responsibility without fault would be irreconcilable with the principle that punishment presupposes guilt. It may be argued, however, that West German criminal law does not need to rely on strict responsibility because the concept of ordinary negligence is broad enough to cover all conduct deserving punishment.

West German criminal law recognizes in roughly the same way as American law that offenders who act under a mistake of fact negativing their intent may not be punished for an offense requiring such state of mind. As regards mistakes of law, however, both laws are in sharp contrast. While in the United States a mistake of law is generally no excuse, West German law distinguishes between unavoidable and avoidable mistakes of law.[6] The Penal Code provides: "If the offender in committing the act lacks the appreciation that he is acting unlawfully, he acts without guilt provided the mistake was unavoidable to him. If he could have avoided the mistake, the punishment may be mitigated." The practical impact of the concept that an unavoidable mistake of law serves as an excuse is, however, comparatively limited. In cases involving traditional criminal law—that is, *mala in se*—West German courts usually hold mistakes of law to be avoidable, since anyone knows or is expected to know the central prohibitions of the law. Only in cases involving exceptional legal questions do courts, to some extent, consider a mistake unavoidable.

Preparation—Attempt, Complicity (Conspiracy)

Attempts to commit a felony are always punishable; attempts to commit a misdemeanor only if expressly provided for. Punishment may be mitigated in cases of an attempt. Mitigation is not obligatory because the missing harm may be counterbalanced by the gravity of the offender's conduct.

The Penal Code defines "attempt" as an act by which the offender, according to his plan, directly begins to carry out the intended crime. The requirements of the offender's plan and of the direct beginning are devised to distinguish attempt from preparation. Courts, however, often have tended to include preparatory acts in the concept of attempt.

The impossibility of committing an attempted offense excludes or mitigates punishment only if, because of gross misjudgment of the law of causation, the offender fails to realize that the intended crime could not possibly be completed. An example would be a woman who tries to procure an abortion by drinking camomile tea.

Unlike in most American jurisdictions, voluntary abandonment is a defense in West German law. Exemption from punishment is based on different considerations: Offenders, so to speak, have rehabilitated themselves; they should be encouraged to desist from committing the planned crime; they deserve leniency.

Parties to a crime are divided into three categories: principals, instigators, and accessories. Principals are offenders who commit the crime in person, through another, or together with another principal. The instigator intentionally incites another to commit an intentional crime. The instigator is punished in the same manner as the principal. Accessories are persons who intentionally aid a principal before or while he or she is committing the crime. Punishment of the accessory is to be mitigated.

Because of this mitigation there is considerable controversy as to the proper distinction between accessories and principals. Courts ordinarily take a subjective approach by asking whether the offender intended to act as a principal or as an accessory. Consequently, the Federal Court of Appeals held in a widely publicized case that a secret agent of a foreign nation who had killed two persons with his own hands was to be considered an accessory to murder since he had totally subjected himself to the authority and plans of his employer. Scholars have criticized this approach for being arbitrary and for relying on an utterly vague criterion. They suggest asking who was in charge of committing the offense and of what importance was the individual contribution.

Conspiracy is a crime only if two or more persons agree to commit a felony. In addition, the Penal Code proscribes the forming of and joining in societies whose purpose or activities are directed toward committing crimes or acts of terrorism.

Defenses (Insanity, Self-Defense, and so on)

While American lawyers tend to treat criminal law problems in a procedural context, West Germans follow the civil law tradition and clearly differentiate between substantive law and procedural law. They do not talk about "defenses" but rather about justification and excuse.[7] Defenses, especially affirmative defenses, that first place a burden of producing some evidence and sometimes even a burden of persuasion on the defendant, would be irreconcilable with the presumption of innocence, which in West German law requires the state to carry these burdens without any exceptions.

Justification and excuse are concepts that are strictly separated in West German criminal law. An act that violates the literal terms of the criminal law is justified when it serves to protect a superior interest—for example, in cases of self-defense—or when protection of an interest is waived—as in cases of consent. An act may be illegal but offenders may not deserve personal blame, that is, they may be excused, since they acted under extraordinary psychological pressure, as in a case of duress.

The concept of necessity may help to explain the difference between justification and excuse because West German criminal law distinguishes between "justifying necessity" and "excusing necessity." If, for example, the cashier of a supermarket who is held up at gunpoint hands the robber a sum of money, the cashier acts in a state of "justifying necessity": the loss of his or her life, which was in imminent danger, would have been a greater harm than the loss of the money. If, however, after a shipwreck two sailors are reaching for the only life jacket and the stronger one pushes the other man away in order to save his own life, he is not justified since his life is not worth more than the life of the other sailor. He acts, however, under extreme psychological pressure and thus in a state of "excusing necessity."

The distinction between justification and excuse is of considerable practical importance. If, for example, an insane person points a gun and threatens to kill, the person is excused and thus not guilty of attempted homicide. His or her attack on the intended victim is, however, unlawful and, therefore, the intended victim is justified in wounding or even killing the insane person in self-defense.

As regards self-defense, there are two striking differences between West German and American law. First, American criminal law distinguishes among defense of persons, dwellings, and other property as well as between the use of deadly and nondeadly force. In West German law these distinctions are not made. The West German Penal Code defines self-defense in a very brief way as "the defense which is necessary to avert an immediate and unlawful attack from oneself or from another." This again may be taken as a typical example of the civil law method of legislation. It also may be argued that in an emergency situation the attacked person should not be hampered in his or her defense by detailed and complex provisions.

Second, the West German concept of self-defense does not require some kind of proportionality between the interests to be protected against the aggressor and the damage caused by the defense. The limits of justified defense are determined solely by the severity of the attack. Self-defense is based on the idea that the law does not have to yield to lawlessness. Thus deadly force may generally be applied to defend property even in the case of simple theft. There is a tendency, however, to restrict self-defense when the aggressor is a young, drunk, or insane person; when the attack is not carried out intentionally; when the interest to be protected is disproportionately less valuable than the interest damaged by the defense.

To define insanity, West German criminal law takes a two step approach. The Penal Code provides that the offender must suffer from "a morbid emotional disturbance, a profound interruption of consciousness, mental deficiency or another serious emotional deviancy." As a consequence, the offender must be "incapable of appreciating the wrongfulness of his conduct or of acting in accordance with such appreciation." West German law on insanity obviously comes close to the modern American approaches that have been developed in more or less strict conformity with the Model Penal Code. In one respect, however, the German concept of insanity is wider than the modern American definitions, for the clause of "serious emotional deviancy" is interpreted to include extreme cases of neurosis, psychopathy, and sexual perversion.

In addition to incapacity because of insanity, West German law recognizes diminished capacity. If the psychiatric or psychological conditions just listed substantially impair the offender's capacity of appreciating the wrongfulness of his or her conduct or of acting in accordance with such appreciation, punishment may be mitigated.

Philosophy of Penal Measures

To understand the West German philosophy of penal measures one has to keep in mind that it distinguishes between two types of sanctions: penalties and measures of rehabilitation and safety.

Penalties are, in the first place, considered means of retribution for the offender's guilt, but in addition they serve rehabilitative and deterrent purposes.[8] The Penal Code provides: "The offender's guilt shall be the basis for fixing punishment. The expected effects of punishment on the future life of the offender in society shall be taken into consideration." It remains an open question, however, what sentence, in a given case, will be required for retribution and for rehabilitation and how these heterogeneous objectives can be reconciled with each other.

Measures of rehabilitation and safety, such as commitment to a psychiatric hospital or revocation of a driver's license, serve solely preventive purposes. Their aim is to treat the offender with therapeutic and pedagogic means and to protect the public. Thus such, measures are imposed independent of the offender's guilt. For example, a defendant who is found not guilty by reason of insanity can be committed to a psychiatric hospital.

West German penal policy is guided by four main principles. The principle that guilt is to be the basis of punishment limits the penalizing power of the legislature as well as of the courts and thus helps to avoid penalties that would be out of proportion to the gravity of the offense. The indeterminate prison sentence, a sanction once often used in the United States, has always been considered irreconcilable with this principle.

The principle of legality that prohibits punishment without a statutory basis has already been mentioned above. It further is interpreted to require sentencing by the judge. Since the judge has ascertained the defendant's guilt, the judge, rather than a parole board, is considered the proper authority to determine the length of a sentence and to decide upon the suspension of a sentence.

A third principle guiding West German penal policy is the protection of human dignity. It forbids cruel and inhuman punishment and serves to limit criminal law in order to protect individual freedom and the development of a pluralistic society.

The principle of social justice requires that criminals not be simply incarcerated and thus expelled from society. They rather must be offered all kinds of help favoring their rehabilitation. This principle, above all, must guide the execution of penal measures.

Kinds of Penal Measures

Capital punishment has been abolished by the West German Constitution. It may not even be inflicted under military law or in times of war or revolution. Criminal lawyers and criminologists are of the opinion that it would be irreconcilable with human dignity and that it cannot be regarded as a better deterrent than life imprisonment.

The Penal Code prescribes a uniform type of imprisonment. Penal servitude was abolished in 1970, since it stigmatized the offender and thus impeded his or her rehabilitation. Imprisonment may be for a fixed term with a maximum of 15 years or for life. Life imprisonment, which is mandatory in cases of murder and genocide, means that the prisoner normally must serve 15 years before he or she may be paroled. Some years ago, life imprisonment was criticized as destructive of the prisoner's personality, but the Federal Constitutional Court held it constitutional.

There is general agreement in the Federal Republic that short-term imprisonment is more harmful than useful. It is too short for rehabilitation but long enough to alienate prisoners from their families and jobs. Therefore, short-term imprisonment, to a great extent, has been replaced by fines. According to the Penal Code, a prison sentence of less than six months may be imposed only "if special circumstances concerning the offense or the personality of the offender render confinement indispensable to influence the offender or to protect the legal order."

The West German equivalent to probation in American law is the suspension of a prison term for a fixed period, placement of the defendant under the supervision of a probation officer, and issuance of probation directives. The upper limit for sentences that may be suspended is two years.

Since the combined problem of crime and poverty does not exist in the Federal Republic in the same measure as in the United States, fines play an important role in the West German law of sanctions. In recent years, West German courts have imposed fines in more than 80% of all cases. Fines are fixed according to a day-fine scheme that was imported from Sweden.[9] First, the court determines the number of day-fines proportionate to the defendant's guilt and takes into consideration aspects of rehabilitation and deterrence. Second, the amount of a single day-fine is specified in proportion to the defendant's daily net income after deducting necessary expenses. For example, a defendant is sentenced to 20 day-fines; a day-fine is set at 50 West German marks.

As mentioned above, the Penal Code provides not only for penalties but also for measures of rehabilitation and safety. While guilt serves as a limitation of punishment, measures of rehabilitation and safety are limited by the principle of proportionality.

There are some measures that involve a deprivation of liberty: protective custody, commitment to a psychiatric hospital, and commitment to an institution for withdrawal treatment. Other measures do not restrict the offender's liberty: revocation of driver's license, prohibition against practicing a profession, and probationary surveillance. Revocation of driver's license plays by far the most important role.

**Distribution of Penal
Measures in Practice**

As a consequence of a strong reform movement that swept the West German criminal justice system some twenty years ago, prison sentences have to a considerable extent been replaced by suspended sentences and fines. This drastic change is evidenced in Table 4.2. The table does not include juveniles and adolescent offenders who were sentenced according to juvenile law. On the other hand, the table indicates that in most recent times there seems to be a slight tendency to place again more emphasis on the more severe sanction. But fines are still the ordinary sanctions in the field of light and medium criminality.

**Special Treatment of Juveniles,
Recidivists, and Other Offenders**

If a juvenile, or an adolescent who is to be ranked as a juvenile, has committed a crime, educational or disciplinary measures such as

TABLE 4.2

Year	Total of Sentenced Offenders	Percentage of Fines	Percentage of Suspended Prison Sentences	Percentage of Prison Sentences Not Suspended
1965	505,441	65.4	11.6	23.0
1970	553,962	83.9	8.5	7.6
1975	567,605	83.4	10.2	6.4
1980	599,832	82.4	11.6	6.0
1983	636,105	81.3	12.1	6.6

warnings, directives, correctional education, or short-period detention may be imposed. For serious crimes, the juvenile or adolescent may be punished by imprisonment in an institution for juveniles.

No increased sentences are provided for recidivists: the statutory maximum sentences are considered high enough. The Penal Code sets the minimum term at six months for third convictions when the defendant already has been imprisoned for at least three months and "fails to heed the warning of the prior sentences." Thus habitual offenders who tend to commit more or less insignificant crimes may be sentenced to a prison term that is not too short for therapeutic and pedagogic effects.

Parole

Prisoners must be paroled after having served two-thirds of their term if they consent and if they are not likely to commit new offenses. In exceptional cases parole may be granted after half the term has been served.

Diversion from the Criminal Justice System

As in the United States, diversion has become an important tool in the administration of criminal justice, but West German authorities have developed their own methods of removing criminals from the ordinary course of proceedings.[10]

According to West German law the police are obligated to investigate every crime that comes to their notice. In cases involving trivial offenses, however, they employ a kind of informal diversion. They simply refrain from initiating investigations. Instead, they sometimes consider it their duty to calm down and caution disturbers and to exercise a conciliatory function.

In proceedings against adults, prosecutors and judges may drop a case if a misdemeanor is involved, if the offender's guilt is minor, and if prosecution is not required in the public interest. Dropping a case may be conditioned upon the offender making restitution, paying a sum of money to the public treasury or to a charitable organization, or performing some other act in the public interest. In practice, the offender is almost without exception asked to contribute to a charity. The difference between this kind of payment and the payment of a fine can be discerned only from a theoretical point of view.

In proceedings against juveniles and adolescents, prosecutors and judges have a wide scope of diversion possibilities. Due to the fact that the young person's education is the predominant consideration, cases are usually dropped only after some educational measures have been taken.

Criminal Procedure

General Principles

Some principles of criminal procedure in the Federal Republic are similar to those in the United States. For example, in both countries formal accusations to the courts are made by prosecutors. In the Federal Republic some crimes can be prosecuted only after the victim has filed a motion for prosecution. In cases involving a breach of domestic peace, an insult, or other offenses directed against predominantly personal interests, the victim may press a private charge.

The trial must be public. The principles of orality and immediacy require that witnesses who have observed the alleged crime must be examined at the trial. As different from some other European countries, the examination may not be replaced by reading the record of a previous examination or of a written declaration. The accused has a right to be heard by the court and to confront the witnesses against him or her.

The accused is presumed to be innocent until the court is convinced of his or her guilt. As pointed out above, West German law never places a burden of producing evidence or a burden of persuasion on the accused. In courts sitting with more than one judge, a two-thirds majority is necessary to find the accused guilty. After a decision has become final, the principle of *res judicata* forbids a retrial for the same offense.

Other principles of West German procedure demonstrate major differences from the American criminal justice system.

According to the principle of compulsory prosecution, the West German prosecutor is required—except in certain situations specified in the Code of Criminal Procedure—to prosecute all charges for which there is sufficient evidence.[11] Equal enforcement of the criminal law and protection against prosecutorial arbitrariness are predominant values.

The West German trial follows the inquisitorial principle.[12] It is not the parties but the judge who calls and interrogates the witnesses and who decides upon the order in which the evidence is taken. The distinction between examination-in-chief and cross-examination is unknown. Questions to test the reliability of a witness and the accuracy of his or her statements are put by the judge in the course of the comprehensive interrogation. The judicial inquiry into the facts also includes the questioning of the accused at the beginning of the trial.

In advance of the trial, the judge studies the file of the case that was assembled by the police and the prosecutor and that was given to the judge with the written accusation. Without being thoroughly informed about the facts as they appear in the file of the case the judge could not effectively interrogate the witnesses and the defendant.

Prosecutor and defense counsel play comparatively minor roles at the trial. After the judge has finished the examination of a witness, or of the accused, they may ask additional questions. They also may move that the judge take further evidence. Defense counsel in West German criminal procedure has a right to pretrial inspection of the prosecutor's file. Experience has proved that pretrial inspection does not lead to a tainting of the evidence or to fabricating defenses.

Following European tradition, West German courts do not exclude hearsay evidence. Exclusion of evidence would be considered irreconcilable with the trial judge's duty to find the facts. At the same time, professional judges are trusted that they can properly evaluate the probative value of hearsay evidence.

The West German criminal trial thus evidences striking differences from American proceedings. Since it is bureaucratically organized and placed under tight judicial control, it may be considered an authoritarian search for the truth. The American trial is based on the idea of individualism. Fact finding by the parties may be called competitive and experimental. Procedural fairness and protection of individual rights are esteemed very highly. American criminal proceedings display the general conviction that, above all, the individual has to be protected against an abuse of power. West German criminal procedure is influenced by the European heritage that accepts tight official control if it is necessary to protect public order.

Phases of Criminal Proceedings

Three phases may be distinguished in West German criminal proceedings: proceedings before trial, the trial, and appellate proceedings. Proceedings before trial are the province of the prosecutor and the police. According to the law, the prosecutor is in charge of the investigative proceedings. In fact, however, it is the police that in almost all cases carry out investigations. The prosecutor's function ordinarily is reduced to deciding whether a formal charge is to be filed with the court.

The trial begins with the judicial interrogation of the accused as to his or her personal circumstances. Thereupon the prosecutor reads the accusation. The presiding judge advises the accused that the accused may decline to speak about the case. If the accused is willing to speak, he or she is interrogated by the presiding judge. To hear the accused at the beginning of the trial is considered a privilege, since the accused is offered an opportunity to present his or her version of the case before other evidence is taken.

After the accused has been heard, the presiding judge calls and interrogates the witnesses. The other professional judges, the lay judges, the prosecutor, the accused, and the defense counsel may ask additional questions. The presiding judge also reads documents and other written matter serving as evidence. After the interrogation of each witness, as well as after the reading of each piece of written matter, the presiding judge asks the accused whether he or she wishes to comment. The prosecutor and the defense counsel also have a right to comment.

After all evidence is taken, the prosecutor and the defense counsel present their closing arguments. The accused is entitled to a last word.

Thereupon the judges retire to deliberate and decide on innocence or guilt and, if the accused is found guilty, on a sentence. Separate sentencing procedures are unknown in the Federal Republic. Evidence necessary for sentencing is gathered in the course of the trial.

As opposed to American law, the prosecutor and the defense have equal rights to appeal.[13] This means that the prosecutor may appeal from an acquittal. Since the presecutor is under a duty to see that justice is done, he or she even may, and sometimes does, appeal in favor of the accused.

If an appeal *de novo* has been filed by the defendant or the prosecutor, a second trial will be held before the court of the next higher instance. An appeal *de novo* may attack both the verdict and the sentence. It may also be limited to attacking the sentence if the verdict is accepted. In this case, the second trial is concerned only with issues of sentencing.

Appeals for error have to be justified by a statement that the trial court has committed legal error. In former times, a sentencing decision was rarely ever overruled by an appellate court since it was considered to be based on the trial judge's discretion. Today, however, the idea of uncontrolled discretion is no longer accepted. Consequently, appellate courts have shown an increasing readiness to review sentencing decisions.

Rights of an Accused

Defense counsel is admitted at the trial as well as during the proceedings before trial. In a number of cases, for example, if a serious offense is involved or if the accused suffers from a serious mental impairment, no trial may be held without defense counsel. Whenever an accused does not have counsel, the judge will appoint one for the accused. If the accused should wish to have no counsel, the judge will appoint one despite his or her objection. The accused's right to self-determination is considered less decisive than the protection of his or her procedural rights and the accuracy of fact finding. In American law a less authoritarian and more individualistic approach is taken, for an accused who does not wish to have counsel may appear unrepresented at his or her trial.

Before the accused is interrogated by a police officer, a prosecutor, or a judge in the course of pretrial investigations, the accused must be advised that he or she need not answer questions; that the accused may, even before the examination, consult with an attorney of his or her choice, and that the accused may move for the taking of particular evidence. The similarity of West German law to the Miranda warnings is obvious. Yet no lawyer is appointed to represent the accused during interrogation before trial, nor is a lawyer the accused has chosen entitled to attend an interrogation by the police.

If an accused who has not been properly advised of his or her rights makes a confession, it will nevertheless be admitted at the trial. Exclusion of illegally received evidence that has become an important instrument for protecting individual rights in the United States, plays a much less decisive role in West German criminal proceedings.[14] For example, statements obtained by coercion, fatigue, hypnosis, or deception are to be excluded. Likewise, evidence that was received by an undue invasion into the right of privacy, for example, by an illegal recording of a private conversation or by an illegal seizure of an intimate diary, may not be admitted. In general, however, exclusion of illegally received evidence is considered neither an efficient means nor necessary to deter police misconduct. It is argued that the West German police, hierarchically organized on state level, is efficiently controlled through inner office supervision.

Arrest, Bail, and Pretrial Detention

A judge may issue an arrest warrant if a person is suspected of an offense and if, in addition, the person is likely to flee, to tamper with the evidence, or to commit certain further offenses that are listed in the Code of Criminal Procedure. Prosecutors and police officers may arrest without a warrant, if applying for a warrant would cause unreasonable delay. Even a private citizen can arrest without a warrant if a person who is caught "red-handed" is likely to flee of if he or she cannot be identified.

An arrested person is to be brought before a judge without delay. The judge may release the person if the latter, for example, agrees to report periodically to the police, remain within his or her residence, not contact certain persons, or furnish bail. In practice, conditional release is granted in only a small percentage of cases. An accused who is detained prior to his or her trial has the right to communicate with his or her lawyer. Their oral communication may not be supervised; letters they exchange may be inspected only if the accused is charged with terrorism.

A detainee may, at any time, move for a judicial hearing to determine whether the arrest warrant should be vacated or its execution be suspended. There is no upper limit for the period of detention. It may, however, be extended beyond a six month period only if continued detention is justified by the peculiar difficulties of the investigations or by some other important reason.

Special Modes of Criminal Proceedings

The guilty plea is unknown in West German criminal procedure.[15] It is generally argued that a guilty plea might be entered by an innocent person and that accepting such plea would be irreconcilable with the duty of the judge to ascertain the facts of the case. Individual control of the case would be improper in proceedings that are to be considered an authoritarian search for the truth.

On the other hand, the criminal justice system of the Federal Republic cannot afford a trial for every case. Therefore, the Code of Criminal Procedure provides for a less formal, written procedure to process the bulk of less serious cases. In cases involving misdemeanors the prosecutor may, instead of taking the case to trial, apply to the judge for a "penal order." The prosecutor prepares the draft of the proposed penal order. The judge decides whether to issue the order solely on the basis of the prosecutor's draft and the file of the case. Usually, the judge's review of the proposed order and of the file is perfunctory. To some extent, the penal order is comparable to the guilty plea in American procedure. It is a written offer by the judge to the accused to accept the prosecutor's charge and admit his or her guilt.

Lay Participation
in Criminal Proceedings

In former times, two types of courts with lay participation existed in the German criminal justice system: jury courts and mixed courts where lay judges sat together with the professional judges in a single panel.[16] In German jury courts the functions of the judges and the jury were different from what they typically are in the United States. Jurors were asked not to decide on the issue of guilt as such but only on single questions of fact. Since jurors did not always comply with this restriction, they were looked upon with suspicion. They also did not conform to the idea of uniform and bureaucratically organized justice. General distrust of the jury was one of the main reasons why it was abolished in 1924.

The mixed system of lay judges and professional judges still operates today.[17] As was pointed out, lay judges sit together with professional judges in local courts and in district courts. They deliberate and decide together on guilt, punishment, and procedural questions. It goes without saying that professional judges exercise great influence during the common deliberations.

Since decisions on guilt and punishment require a two-thirds majority, the two lay judges who in local courts sit with a single professional judge can outvote the professional judge and find the accused guilty over the judge's objection. If the two lay judges who in district courts sit with three professional judges vote for acquittal, the accused cannot be found guilty. In practice, however, it rarely happens that lay judges affect the determination of guilt. Likewise, their influence on sentencing is to be considered very moderate.

Special Procedures
for Juveniles

Cases involving juveniles and adolescents are heard by juvenile courts, which are special branches of the criminal courts. Depending on the seriousness of the case, juvenile courts sit with a single judge, with a professional judge and two lay judges, or with three professional judges and two lay judges. Professional judges and lay judges as well as prosecutors should have pedagogic qualifications.

Since education is the predominant consideration, proceedings against juveniles and adolescents follow their own rules. The prosecutor and judge cooperate with the local youth authorities, which supervise the offender and prepare a report on his or her personality. The public is excluded from trials against juveniles. The judge may summon the juvenile's parents to attend his or her trial.

Execution of Penal Measures
(Corrections)

Aims and Basic Principles
of the Execution of Penal Measures

According to the Code on the Execution of Prison Sentences and of Measures Involving a Deprivation of Liberty, imprisonment in the first place should serve rehabilitation. As explained in the section on the philosophy of penal measures, retribution is the basis for fixing punishment. This is not a contradiction to the rehabilitative purpose of imprisonment, for different aims may be followed in meting out punishment and in the execution of a prison sentence.

The extent to which the rehabilitative ideal is achieved in practice is difficult to evaluate. So far any optimism seems to be unfounded. On the other hand, the new American attitude that rehabilitation does not work is not endorsed in the Federal Republic. It is argued instead that carefully planned treatment in prisons may offer possibilities for rehabilitation.

Execution of Deprivation
of Liberty and
Other Custodial Measures

Penal institutions are administered by prison authorities on the state level under the supervision of the state ministries of justice. The Code on the Execution of Prison Sentences provides that expert advice has to be solicited for the administration of prison labor, social help, professional training, health care, and other treatment of inmates.

Supervision over prison authorities is exercised by special courts that are organized on the district court level in districts that have penal institutions. These courts hear inmate complaints against prison authorities. In addition, they hear cases dealing with the execution of penal sanctions, such as revocation of probation or parole.

The prosecutor supervises the legal formalities of the execution of penal sanctions and sets the date when offenders have to begin serving their prison terms or when they have to pay a fine. The prosecutor is, however, not authorized to interfere with the administration of penal institutions.

Total numbers of prisoners have changed considerably in recent years. In the late 1960s and also the early 1970s they decreased as a consequence of the already mentioned reform movement to replace prison sentences by noncustodial sanctions. Starting with the middle of the 1970s, however, the figures have been going up again, mainly because of a general increase of serious crimes. Table 4.3 gives figures of this development and compares them with American statistics.

Ordinarily, offenders are classified according to age, sex, type of offense, length of sentence, and prior convictions. Different types of offenders are assigned to different penal institutions. Prison experts have criticized this classification system because it is not primarily based on individual treatment. In addition, offenders with prior convictions who turn out to be high recidivist risks may be unnecessarily stigmatized.

When entering a penal institution, inmates who have to serve a term of more than one year are assigned to an observation unit for a detailed classification procedure. Their personality is examined and a treatment plan is worked out to cover the following: placement in a closed, an open, or a half-open institution; assignment to a special residential unit or to a treatment group; assignment to work, professional training, and continued education; special privileges, such as supervised or unsupervised work outside the institution; and preparations for release.

Formerly, inmates at the beginning of their sentence had to serve

TABLE 4.3

| | Federal Republic | | United States | |
Year	Total Number of Prisoners	Per 100,000 Population	Total Number of Prisoners	Per 100,000 Population
1965	49,573	84.0	210,895	108
1968	48,501	80.6		
1970	35,927	59.2	196,429	96
1972	33,314	54.2		
1975	34,608	55.3	240,593	111
1977	39,918	65.0		
1980	42,235	68.6	315,974	138
1983	48,243	78.5	438,830	179

NOTE: German figures refer to March 31 of respective years.

some months with hardly any privileges. This retributive phase of imprisonment was abolished long ago, since it was considered irreconcilable with the rehabilitative ideal.

It was pointed out above that the West German Penal Code prescribes a uniform type of imprisonment to aid rehabilitation. At the same time, the rehabilitation goal requires different types of penal institutions. Therefore, a considerable variety of institutions exists in the Federal Republic. Closed institutions are distinguished from half-open and open institutions where security measures are reduced or virtually nonexistent. Closed institutions by far outnumber the other types.

Many penal institutions are still located in old-fashioned, large, star-shaped buildings designed to isolate inmates and improve control. These antiquated buildings seriously hamper rehabilitative efforts. Today, modern institutions for rehabilitative treatment mostly are built in pavilion style and designed for between 200 and 300 inmates. Some penal institutions are especially equipped for professional training and continuing education. Separate institutions exist for juveniles.

Psychiatric hospitals and institutions for withdrawal treatment are outside the administration of penal institutions. Institutions of social therapy are deemed penal institutions but are under the management of physicians. No separate institutions of protective custody exist. Since only a few recidivists are sentenced to protective custody, they are committed to top security prisons.

Inmates are obliged to work and are paid a few marks per day. An increase of payments is provided for by the Code on the Execution of Prison Sentences, but the effective date of the relevant provision was postponed by the legislature for financial reasons. To encourage professional training, inmates in training programs are paid as if they were working.

Disciplinary measures to control inmates are limited to those listed in the Code on the Execution of Prison Sentences. They include warnings, denial of entertainment such as television or sports programs, visitor limitations, or placement in solitary confinement for up to four weeks.

The Code on the Execution of Prison Sentences also makes detailed provisions for a variety of privileges and rights of inmates, such as mail, telephone calls, visitors, and permission to leave the institution for up to 21 days per year.

In the past, decisions concerning inmates were left to the uncontrolled discretion of prison authorities. Today inmates are entitled to file complaints whenever they believe their rights have been violated. Complaints are heard by the courts that supervise prisons. The inmate's right to formal complaint is considered essential to the rule of law, though prison authorities sometimes argue that inmates take irrelevant cases to court and impede prison administration. Yet an allegedly irrelevant case may be important if looked upon from an inmate's point of view. To the inmate it will make a difference whether his or her complaint is decided upon by prison authorities or by a court.

NOTES

1. Horton, Abortion Law Reform in the German Federal Republic, 28 Int. & Comp. L.Q. 288 (1979); Sealy Abortion Law Reform in Europe: The European Commission on Human Rights Upholds German Restrictions on Abortions, 15 Texas Int. L.J. 162 (1980).

2. Details are listed in the table by Casper and Zeisel, Lay Judges in German Criminal Courts, 1, J. Legal Studies 135, 142 (1972). See also Meador, Appellate Subject Matter Organization: The German Design from an American Perspective, 5 Hastings Int. & Comp. L. Rev. 27 (1981).

3. Rupp, The Federal Constitutional Court and the Constitution of the Federal Republic of Germany, 16 St. Louis U.L.J. 359 (1972); Singer, The Constitutional Court of the German Federal Republic: Jurisdiction over Individual Complaints, 31 Int. & Comp. L.Q. 331 (1982).

4. As to details, see Langbein, Comparative Criminal Procedure: Germany, 91 (1977).

5. For a comparison between the West German and the American system of legal education see Casper, Two Models of Legal Education, 41 Tenn. L. Rev. 13 (1973); Schluter and Morris, A Comparison of Legal Education in the United States and West Germany, 72 W. Va. L. Rev. 317 (1970).

6. For a careful analysis of the West German law see Fletcher, Rethinking Criminal Law, 737 ff. (1978); Arzt, Ignorance or Mistake of Law, 24 Am. J. Comp. L. 646 (1976).

7. Eser, Justification and Excuse, 24 Am. J. Comp. L. 621 (1971).

8. Herrmann, Sanctions: German Law and Theory, 24 Am. J. Comp. L. 718, 719 ff. (1976); Weigend, Sentencing in West Germany, 42 Md. L. Rev. 37, 70 ff. (1983).

9. Herrmann, supra note 8, at 730 f.; Comment, The West German Day-Fine System: A Possibility for the United States?, 50 U. Chi. L. Rev. 281 (1983).

10. Herrmann, Federal Republic of Germany: Diversion and Mediation, 54 Rev. Int. Dr. Pen. 1043 (1983).

11. Herrmann, The Rule of Compulsory Prosecution and Prosecutorial Discretion in Germany, 41 U. Chi. L. Rev. 468 (1974).

12. Herrmann, The German Criminal Justice System: The Trial Phase—Appellate and Review Proceedings, in: Association Internationale de Droit Penal. The Criminal Justice System of the Federal Republic of Germany, 65 (1981); id., The Philosophy of Criminal Justice and the Administration of Criminal Justice, 53 Rev. Int. Dr. Pen. 841, 846 ff. (1982).

13. As to details of appellate proceedings see Herrmann, supra note 12, at 86 ff.; Weigend, supra note 8, at 68 ff.

14. As to details see Bradley, The Exclusionary Rule in Germany, 96 Harv. L. Rev. 1032 (1983); Volkmann-Schluck, Continental European Criminal Procedures: True or Illusive Model?, 9 Am. J. Crim. L. 1, 13 ff. (1981).

15. Langbein, Land Without Plea Bargaining: How the Germans Do It, 78 Mich. L. Rev. 204 (1979).

16. Casper and Zeisel, supra note 2, at 136 ff.

17. Casper and Zeisel, supra note 2, at a44 ff.; Langbein, Mixed Court and Jury Court: Could the Continental Alternative Fill the American Need?, 1981 A.B.F. Res.J. 195.

18. Total number of sentenced prisoners in state and federal institutions. Sources: Department of Justice, Bureau of Justice Statistics, Prison 1925-1981, Washington, D.C. 1981; Criminal Justice Newsletter, 19(9), May 1984—Jail population is not included in these figures.

5

Sweden

ALVAR NELSON

General Information

Sweden is situated in the northern part of Europe and has land frontiers with Norway and Finland and sea boundaries with Denmark, West and East Germany, Poland, and the USSR. The total area is approximately 175,000 square miles, of which less than one-tenth consists of cultivated land. Sweden has a population of approximately 8,360,000 (48 persons per square mile), which is rather unevenly distributed. During and after the two world wars immigration has been considerable. The former Nordic ethnic unity is gradually disappearing as a result of the influx of 600,000 immigrants, refugees, and, after World II, guestworkers, and, again, in the last few years, refugees.

Sweden is a kingdom, although the royal power has been gradually diminishing and the king is now primarily a symbol of national unity. Political power has been taken over by Riksdagen (the parliament) and Regeringen (the government). The Parliament is responsible for legislation and economy while the government is responsible for administration. The political parties form two blocks of almost equal strength: the bourgeois and the socialist. Although in principle apolitical, the main organizations of the employees—in particular the Confederation of Trade Unions and the Central Organization of Salaried Employees—take part in the debate on nearly all political matters.

The Swedish economy is mainly based on industrial production and on the export of iron and wood products. The standard of living is among the highest in Europe. Living costs are high due to the high standard of living, the climate, and the taxes. On the other hand, social, educational, vocational, and health benefits are unsurpassed in the world.

Survey of the Legal System

The Swedish legal system is based on meticulous legislation, independent courts, and public control of the administration. Although the system, in principle, is derived from the early Middle Ages, it has been reviewed, revised, and improved over time in order to protect the citizens and other residents from arbitrary and unjust actions by the rulers, once the king and the army, now the politicians and the civil servants. The present Constitution of 1974 gives the legislative power to the Parliament alone and empowers the government to issue ordinances within that legislation. Additional directives are issued by the central administration boards. County and municipal authorities, however, have gained partial independence with regard to health and social services, public schools, and vocational training centers.

All the ordinary courts hear both civil and criminal cases; with rare exception, sessions are open to the public. Judges and justices are appointed by the government and may not be removed. Lay assessors, serving in the local courts and the courts of appeal, are elected by the municipal and county councils, respectively. Administrative matters were once handled by the civil servants but are now, to an increasingly greater extent, heard by administrative courts. Thus the county administrative court decides matters concerning mandatory treatment of children and young persons and of abusers of alcohol or drugs.

Public control is exercised not only by the man on the street and the mass media but also by the lay members of the administrative boards and the lay assessors in the courts. Moreover, the Parliamentary Ombudsmen supervise all parts of the administration. All documents in the courts as well as in the central and local administration, in principle, are available to everyone.

Structure and Functioning
of the Law Enforcement Agencies

The Ministry of Justice has a staff of 135 persons and is divided into 11 units, of which six work within the field of criminal justice: prison, probation and parole, courts, police, pardons, procedure, penal law, and "law and order" regulations. The Ministry considers applications for pardons and prepares the governmental bills on criminal justice to be presented to Parliament.

The central administration of criminal justice under the Ministry is entrusted to five independent boards and two offices: the Council for Crime Prevention; the National Police Board, the Prosecutor General and his office; the Courts' Administration Board, the Central Board of Corrections and Local Boards for Probation and Parole; the Attorney General and his office; and, finally, the National Prison and Probation Board. There are lay members on all the boards, with the exception of the officers of the chief prosecutor (who has an advisory board of laymen) and of the attorney general.

The police (including the National Security Police) have a total staff of 20,000 persons, of whom approximately 550 work in the National Police Board and the others in 118 local districts. Modern equipment and an efficient computer system have been added since 1965, when the municipal police forces were transferred to the national organization under the Ministry of Justice. The police have a strictly limited authority not to refer some reports involving petty offenses to the prosecutor provided the offender is advised or admonished. They are also empowered to impose fines for breaches of regulatory prohibitions.

Prosecution is almost entirely in the hands of public prosecutors. There is a total staff of 1,400 persons. The head of the prosecution function is the prosecutor general who is also, by virtue of his office, prosecutor at the Supreme Court. The state prosecutors are in charge of the three largest cities and of 13 regions, which are subdivided into 83 districts, each having several district and assistant prosecutors. Moreover, a special state prosecutors' office in Stockholm handles widespread or complicated cases. All prosecutors are professionally trained. The prosecutors have the authority to impose day fines for minor offenses and to dismiss prosecution for certain groups of offenses in general, without limitations for youthful offenders and, to a restricted extent, for mentally deviant persons and abusers of drugs or alcohol under care in institutions.

All the courts hear both civil and criminal cases. The total staff exceeds 4,300 persons working in the 97 district courts, the six courts of appeal, and the Supreme Court. In the district court, petty offenses are tried by a professional judge sitting alone (in 1984, 12,000 cases) while the more serious cases are heard by a professional judge and three (or, in very serious cases, five) lay assessors (in 1984, 63,000 cases). In the court of appeal, criminal cases are heard by three justices and two lay assessors. Only 6,150 cases were appealed in 1984. Criminal cases can be brought to the Supreme Court only with the consent of the court or, without limitation, upon the request of the prosecutor general. Three justices hear applications for review (in 1984, 1,241 applications were heard) and review is granted if at least one of the justices agrees to take the case (in 1984, 39 approvals were granted).

The judges and justices are appointed by the government on purely professional merits and retain their jobs until retirement. Lay assessors are elected by the municipal and county councils on proposal from the political parties. They are paid $50 per day in service. They vote individually and the most lenient opinion of two (in serious cases three) members of the court becomes the judgment of the court.

The Prison and Probation Administration has a total staff of 5,760 persons, of whom 370 work at the central administration, 4,620 in the penal institutions, and 770 with probation and aftercare. Probation and aftercare work is directed by a central board and local boards, and supervision of the clients is carried out by 2,000 professional and 4,000 lay supervisors.

The country is divided into 13 regions, each including local prisons and probation districts. There are 20 national and 57 local penal institutions with a total capacity of 4,100 (2,400 in closed institutions and 1,700 in open) and a few halfway houses. Pretrial detention institutions are also administered by the prison service. But it must be emphasized that probation and aftercare are the core of the correctional system and incarceration today is used as a last resort, mainly for deterrent purposes. Currently, there are almost four times as many people under supervision as there are in prison. In 1984, there were 11,832 probationers and conditionally released (including 1,340 women) and an average prison population of 3,371 (including 122 women).

The Crime Prevention Council was established in 1974 to coordinate responses to crime and to conduct research on crime problems. The Council has published approximately 100 reports, has given economic support to various conferences, and has provided economic support for research outside the Council. Efforts to reduce crime are also undertaken by the National Police Board throughout the country as well as in specific regions or districts and by local social welfare agencies.

Scope of Criminal Law

When the Penal Code of 1864 was being prepared, the leading principles were that the Code could include only infringements of human rights (innate or granted) and be restricted to intentional acts. Neither principle was fully observed, as the Code punished cruelty to animals as well as causing another's death through carelessness. Although the present Penal Code of 1962 (PC) follows the same lines, the arrangement of its content has been completely changed. It is divided into three parts:

(1) general provisions concerning offenses and sanctions (Chapter 1) and the competence of Swedish courts with regard to offenses committed outside the realm (Chapter 2)
(2) specific types of offenses (Chapters 3-22) and provisions regarding preparation, attempt, conspiracy and complicity (Chapter 23), and excuses, for example, self-defense (Chapter 24)
(3) the different sanctions (Chapters 25-36) and provisions regarding the central and the local boards (Chapter 37) and a few administrative provisions (Chapter 38)

The specific offenses are subdivided into four categories, mentioned below together with information concerning the number of persons found guilty in 1984 (including those who had obtained dismissal of prosecution or agreed to pay fines imposed by the prosecutors):

(a) offenses against persons (Chapters 3-7; 10,717 persons of whom 2,158 sentenced to imprisonment)
(b) offenses against property (Chapters 8-12; 51,453 persons convicted, of whom 4,362 sentenced to imprisonment)
(c) offenses against the public (Chapters 13-15; 1,593 persons convicted of whom 191 sentenced to imprisonment)
(d) offenses against the state (Chapters 16-22; 6,493 persons convicted of whom 1,023 sentenced to imprisonment)

Mainly due to the inability to incorporate many types of modern offenses in the Code, a great number of offenses are regulated in other acts or in ordinances. The most important acts shall be mentioned here with the statistical data for 1984:

(1) The Road Traffic Offenses Act of 1951 (36,464 persons convicted of whom 5,008 persons sentenced to imprisonment). The most important offense is drunken driving (7,833 persons convicted, of whom 4,529 sentenced to imprisonment).
(2) The Smuggling of Products Act of 1960 (10,149 persons convicted, of whom 928 sentenced to imprisonment).

(3) The Narcotic Drugs Penal Act of 1968 (4,311 persons convicted, of whom 928 sentenced to imprisonment).

(4) The Revenue Offenses Act of 1971 (1,072 persons convicted of whom 329 sentenced to imprisonment).

In all, 107,924 persons have been found guilty of offenses outside the Penal Code (of whom 6,980 sentenced to imprisonment). It has already been indicated that the prosecution is empowered to dismiss the charges or to impose day fines. Thus, in 1984, prosecution was dismissed with respect to 20,867 persons (of whom 14,954 were convicted of offenses against PC) and 83,744 persons (of whom 69,268 were convicted of offenses against PC) agreed to pay fines imposed by the prosecutors. Additionally, 200,875 persons paid monetary fines imposed by the police for petty offenses, mainly outside PC. In this way the courts have been relieved from a great number of trivial cases. Nevertheless, the courts in 1984 heard 78,464 suspects. Only 4,895 (6.2%) were found not guilty while 73,569 were convicted and 14,714 were sentenced to imprisonment. The figures given indicate that the Penal Code today applies only to a minority of the total number of criminal acts. Nevertheless, the majority of those sentenced to imprisonment have committed offenses proscribed by the Penal Code (52.6%). Another 200,875 persons paid fines, imposed by the police for petty offenses.

Considerable technical changes were made in the legislation within the category "offenses against the person." With regard to offenses against life and health, the complicated old-fashioned provisions were simplified. Among the sexual offenses, adultery and prostitution were decriminalized in 1918, and bestiality in 1937. Homosexual acts were partially decriminalized in 1944 and totally in 1978; and incest, with the exception of carnal knowledge of parents-children and brother-sister, in 1973. Within "offenses against property," the provisions for receiving stolen goods, extortion, and usury were broadened. Among offenses against the public and the state, important innovations occurred as well. The Military Penal Code was abolished and members of the defense forces are subject to the same punishments as civil servants for minor offenses punishable according to the (military) Disciplinary Act, 1986. Offenses committed in office by public servants were restricted in PC and further restricted in 1975, but broadened with regard to bribery in 1977 to include staff members of private enterprises. The punishment for public drunkenness was abolished in 1976. In 1981, offenses against the environment were included in the Code and in 1986 several offenses against property were reformulated.

As can be seen, modern offenses are to a large extent kept outside the Code partly due to technical problems, but mainly due to an inability to incorporate them within the old structure.

Decriminalization is the slogan of today, but very little has happened. When the punishment for public drunkenness was abolished, a statute on temporary care was introduced. The provision on disorderly conduct (Chapter 16, Section 16) is still in force but rarely used as such behavior may result in short time detention according to the Police Act, 1984. Persons committing petty offenses (such as shoplifting) are rarely brought to the courts, but rather are either remitted or administratively fined and in both cases registered.

In the last few years efforts have been made to reduce the mass of minor offenses through the extensive use of surcharges instead of fines. Infringement of local parking regulations is thus no longer an offense but simply an act leading to surcharge in accordance with a statute. A similar solution can be found in the use of public transport without a ticket. The same legislative technique applies to minor mistakes in income-tax reports and the like. Surcharge is applied without regard to *mens rea* and may be imposed on corporations as well as individuals.

Today, criminal policy with regard to criminalization-decriminalization is characterized, on the one hand, by attempts to find a new value system as a basis for legislation and, on the other hand, by attempts to coordinate administrative regulations (e.g., on consumers' protection and protection of the environment) with the main body of penal legislation where criminal sanctions seem to be appropriate. The results are not impressive. In other fields of criminal justice new trends have been established and the development is still in progress. The rigid system of bringing offenders to court is gradually being abandoned by wider power to use discretion, more frequent use of administrative imposition of fines, and by the introduction of surcharges instead of fines.

In 1982, the social-democratic government launched two projects: one for the fight against organized and economic crime, one for combatting the use of narcotics. While the second project gained general support, the bourgeois parties were strongly against the former. The task force on drugs produced a vague program with a few new statutory provisions and substantial economic resources to be used for this purpose. The commission on organized and economic crime presented an extensive program with draft regulations in many fields of legislation. These projects were adopted by the Parliament and are already in force.

Their impact on society cannot be properly evaluated after such a short time. The fact that only legal actions have been taken may be attributed either to an increase in law obedience or to expected inefficiency of other measures. It is unlikely that any future bourgeois government will engage in a political fight in order to have the laws revoked.

Philosophy of Penal Measures

In comparison with the European continent, Sweden has based its penal reforms more upon pragmatism than on abstract philosophy. Nevertheless, it would be fair to mention that during the last two centuries the constant aim has been to combine humanity with efficiency. The manner in which this has been carried out can be seen in the approach to different types of penal sanctions.

Death penalty. This punishment was rarely used in the nineteenth century, and the last execution took place in 1910. The death penalty was abolished in 1928 for peacetime offenses and in 1973 for wartime offenses. The Constitution of 1974 bans the death penalty entirely (Chapter 2, Section 4).

Incarceration. The present prison system dates back to 1825 when the central administration of the prisons was established. The Code of 1864 knew penal servitude (for life or from three months to ten years) and imprisonment (from one month to two years or, according to a scale, as a penalty for failure to pay a fine). These two types of incarceration were amalgamated into one, referred to as imprisonment, by the Code of 1962. Imprisonment may be imposed for a period of 14 days to 10 years (or in certain cases to 16 years) or life. Specific time limits for each offense are provided for in the law describing the offense. The use of imprisonment is restricted with regard to young offenders.

(1) *Imprisonment.* In 1984, 14,087 men and 560 women began to serve their terms of imprisonment. Only 18 (all men) were under 18 years of age. For 9,589 of the convicts the term was 14 days-3 months, and for another 3,316, between 4 and 11 months. Only 68 were sentenced from 6 to 12 years and just 4 to life imprisonment. Of the convicts, 18% were aliens, the majority of them from Finland. It should be noted that 26% of the convicts were found guilty of drunken driving, 27% of offenses against property, and 15% for crimes of violence. Less than 1% were sexual offenders. Conditional release is regularly granted after half time (or a

minimum of two months in prison). It has just been proposed that the minimum period of imprisonment be one month and that two-thirds of the sentence should have been served before release. Those sentenced to life imprisonment are regularly pardoned and have the sentence converted into a definite period and are then in due time conditionally released. Supervision for one year follows regularly upon release.

(2) *Youth imprisonment* was introduced in 1935 (in force since 1938) for young offenders, but was abolished in 1980.

(3) *Internment* was introduced by the Code of 1962 as a substitute for earlier indeterminate sanctions for mentally disturbed offenders and mainly for recidivists. This sanction was abolished in 1981, but there are still a few convicts left serving this penalty.

Probation. Different forms for probation and conditional sentence were introduced in 1906 and expanded in 1918 and 1939 (in force since 1944). The Code of 1962 makes a clear distinction between conditional sentence and probation as only probation is combined with supervision.

(1) *Conditional sentence* is a court order by which sentencing is postponed during a trial period of two years. It may be combined with day-fines. In 1984, 11,043 persons were sentenced (of whom 7,062 in combination with day-fines).

(2) *Probation* with a trial period of three years and supervision for one year. It may be combined with day-fines and even with imprisonment for a maximum of three months. In 1984, the courts imposed probation orders on 5,946 offenders (for 1,504 in combination with day-fines and for 818 with imprisonment).

Fines. While monetary fines were used for petty offenses, the introduction in 1931 of day-fines allowed the use of fines in the field of more serious offenses, sometimes in combination with other sanctions. Fines calculated in a different manner are rarely used and will probably disappear in the near future. Today, monetary fines are regularly used as a penalty imposed by the police, while day-fines are imposed by the prosecutors or the courts. The current trend is to widen the use of fines and to limit the use of imprisonment and probation. The exaction of fines is efficient so that 90% are finally paid.

(1) It has already been mentioned that surcharges to a large extent have replaced fines although such monetary sanctions are kept outside the criminal justice system and are imposed by central or local authorities on

the basis of strict responsibility and in this way are applicable to corporations as well as individuals.

(2) With regard to drunkenness in a public place or other disorderly conduct, the responses are kept outside the criminal justice system. Here the police are empowered to use detention for a short period, in principle not exceeding six hours (in 1984 around 110,000 detained).

(3) Since 1983 no conversion of fines to imprisonment can be ordered in default of payment of fines. However, if the offender contumaciously neglects or refuses to pay the imposed fine, the court may order him or her to suffer imprisonment for a fixed period of a minimum of 14 days to a maximum of three months. There are around 50 cases a year.

Surrender for special care. This sanction was introduced by the Code of 1962. Where the prosecutor has refrained, for special reasons, from prosecuting a young person, an addict, or a mentally deviant person, the court is empowered to surrender such a person for special care as a penal sanction if no other penal sanction is applicable or found appropriate. Such an order generally implies mandatory institutional care of an addict or mentally deviant offender, while a young offender might be handed over to the social authorities for care—optional or mandatory— at their discretion. In 1984, court orders for special care were used as a sanction with respect to 322 mentally deviant persons, 657 young persons, and 36 addicts.

Legal consequences of an offense. An offense may lead to many different legal consequences, for example, revocation of a driver's license by order of an administrative court or disqualification of a doctor or nurse by the National Board for Social Welfare. The Code of 1962 mentions only the obligation to pay damages and to suffer a court order of confiscation. Here just a few remarks should be added concerning confiscation.

(1) *Forfeiture* of goods or money may be directed toward a physical or legal person in order to deprive the defendant of unlawful gain or unlawful evasion of costs. Special provisions concern business activities.

(2) *Punitive confiscation* was introduced in 1986 and is directed only toward business activities within limits of $2,000-$500,000 in order to obliterate possible gains obtained by unlawful transactions.

(3) All types of confiscation within or outside the Code have been made discretionary in order to avoid unnecessary hardship or double burdens (e.g., fines or surcharge and confiscation).

In the last decade a vivid debate has arisen on the principles governing the choice of sanctions and the assessment of punishment. Lack of confidence in the possibilities of care and treatment within the criminal justice system has lead to a demand for just sentencing based on the qualities of the offense in the particular case. In April 1986, a Parliamentary Commission in their extensive report recommended the use of sentencing guidelines and at the same time stressed the necessity of more lenient sentencing.

Substantive Criminal Law

The Principle of Legality

The rule observed in Sweden is—no crime, no punishment without law. An explicit provision based on this principle, however, was not given until the present Constitution of 1974, according to which no penal sanction or legal consequence could be imposed for an act that was not unlawful when committed, and no more serious sanction could be imposed for a punishable act than the sanction stipulated at that time. This implies that penal provisions can never be retroactive to the detriment of the offender.

With regard to the assessment of punishment, one could scarcely carry the principle of legality so far as to say that punishment should be enforced in the same way against every offender. The power given to the police and to the prosecutor to drop a case, as well as the liberty of the court to choose the appropriate sanction in a particular case with regard to the offender's personal characteristics and situation, show the boundaries for the principle of equality before the law.

Grades of Offenses

According to the Penal Code, all violations for which punishment is stated are called offenses regardless of the gravity of the act. The penalty for an offense may range from a monetary fine to life imprisonment. Further differentiation takes place in the field of the administration of criminal justice. The police have the discretionary power not to report petty offenses to the prosecutor. The prosecutors are empowered to dismiss prosecution for less serious offenses.

Age of Criminal Responsibility

Since 1864, the age of criminal responsibility has been 15 years. While the Penal Code of 1864 had been based on the ideology of personal responsibility, the present Penal Code replaced it with restrictions concerning the use of different sanctions. As no sanction is applicable to anyone for an offense committed before reaching 15 years of age, no prosecution is undertaken. The police may investigate the case and report the child to his or her parents or to the social board for appropriate measures.

Criminal Responsibility
of Corporations

The criminal justice system in Sweden is based entirely on individual responsibility not only for the one who has committed the act but also for anyone who has furthered it by advice or deed. Thus a corporation as such cannot be found guilty of an offense. However, the responsible decision makers may be found to be individually responsible. In recent years there has been discussion regarding the introduction of some form of responsibility for corporations and similar juridical entities for certain types of offenses—such as those against the environment—but no final decision as yet has been made. In the meantime surcharges have been introduced and the provisions on confiscation extended.

Mens Rea

A violation of law does not constitute an offense unless individual guilt exists at the moment of the act. No definition of guilt is given in the Code, although intention or negligence is mentioned in the Code as well as in many other penal regulations. The conceptual definition of *mens rea* has been left to jurisprudence and the practice of the courts. The legislative method adopted by the Code has been to assume that intent is required unless the contrary is specifically stated. However, where special penal regulations are involved outside the Code, negligence is often considered sufficient.

Swedish jurisprudence recognizes three forms of intent: direct intent if the consequence of the act is desired; indirect intent if the consequence is necessary but not desired; oblique intent if the offender realized the possibility of the consequences and still undertook the act with the risk that the consequence might occur.

The concept of negligence in Swedish criminal law includes both conscious (advertent) and unconscious negligence. Criminal liability arises only when the negligence reaches higher degrees of carelessness, foolishness, or thoughtlessness than in the law of torts.

Within the Code, intent is the general requirement for an offense, although it is sometimes limited to purpose (direct intent). For some acts, negligence is enough to constitute an offense, such as causing another's death. Outside the Code, negligence is often sufficient—for example, in the case of dangerous driving.

Swedish criminal law has never accepted strict liability. However, in several statutes there are presumptions according to which the accused is liable for omitting to prevent acts committed by other persons; for example, an innkeeper for not having had such control of his staff that violations of the liquor regulations were not prevented.

Where intent is required for criminal responsibility, mistake of fact excludes liability if the fact is an essential part of the offense. In regard to ignorance of criminal law, the practice of the courts has leaned toward a reluctance to accept such a defense unless the ignorance is due to:

(a) improper publication of the statute;
(b) ambiguity of the statute; or
(c) erroneous information from an authority.

The belief that the act is right from a religious or moral standpoint does not constitute a defense. The legislators have tried to avoid conflicts between the interests of society and the conscience of the individual by offering alternatives to governmentally mandated activities or laws (such as civilian work instead of armed service) or by construing statutes narrowly as to avoid the undesirable criminalization of an activity (for example, by accepting participation in a strike organized by a union). With regard to intoxication by alcohol or drugs, the Code states that such a state of mind does not per se exclude intent.

Attempt, Preparation, Conspiracy, and Complicity

With regard to attempt and preparation, Swedish criminal law has chosen a different approach than most continental systems. Attempt and preparation are only punishable where express provision is made and where special requirements for attempt or preparation are met. The same applies to conspiracy.

Although the Code, in conformity with common usage, makes distinctions among the actor, the instigator, and the accessory, all offenses are punishable for all three categories, each according to the offender's intent or carelessness. Outside the Code the same principle is applied *per analogiam* for serious offenses (such as drunken driving). The penalty for an accessory can be set below the punishment stated for the offense.

Defenses

In Swedish jurisprudence a distinction is usually made between cases where the object to be protected is missing and cases where the act is justifiable by reference to other interests. Exceptions amount to defenses either by express legal provision or by court decisions.

Attack on one's own interests. People can abuse their body or their health, or even attempt to take their own life as long as they do not thereby incapacitate themselves for completion of a public obligation (for example, military service). They can damage their property as long as no creditor's right is injured or the act does not prejudice another's right or involve jeopardy to another's life or health or destruction of another's property.

Consent. It is sometimes expressly required that the act be committed without consent. Usually the courts decide the extent to which lack of consent may be an essential part of the offense. They have taken a cautious approach toward implied consent.

Obedience of orders. Exclusion of responsibility takes place only if an offense that a person commits was performed in the execution of an order from a person to whom one owes obedience, and only in cases where one had to comply with the order.

Lawful authority. When people acting in the course of their official duty (a policeman on duty, a serviceman on sentry duty, and the like) are confronted with violence or the threat of violence, they are permitted to exercise such force as can be regarded as justifiable in view of the circumstances in order to accomplish their task. Any person who comes to their assistance has the same right to use force as the person they assist.

Self-defense. Self-defense against an attack upon one's person or property has traditionally been considered permissible but is now considerably restricted by the Code.

Acts of necessity. A provision regarding the exclusion of responsibility in such a case is included in the Code.

A person who uses more force than required when exercising lawful authority or acting in self-defense or in situations of necessity is, in principle, responsible for the excess force used but can be freed from responsibility or subjected to a lesser penalty.

Kinds of Penal Measures

Part Three of the Penal Code regulates the application of the various sanctions and the form they may take. There are also provisions for forfeiture of property. Other legal consequences of crime (such as revocation of a driver's license and forfeiture of inheritance) are regulated elsewhere. The sanctions include fines, imprisonment, conditional sentence, probation, and surrender for special care.

When fines are imposed for more serious offenses, the system of *day-fines* is used. The number of day-fines imposed varies to a maximum of 120 depending upon the gravity of the offense. Each day-fine has a value of $2 to $200, depending on the economic situation of the offender. For petty offenses and breaches of regulations, fines take the form of a fixed sum ($200 maximum) and are known as *monetary fines.* A few types of offenses lead to fines calculated on another basis and are referred to as *standardized fines.* The vast majority of fines are imposed by the police or the prosecutor.

For *imprisonment* the latitude in sentencing ranges from 14 days to 10 years or life. The court makes the assessment within the terms set forth for the offense (for theft, at most 6 years). The convict is usually released on parole (conditional release) after having served half of the sentence (at least 2 months). Under certain conditions, release may follow only after two-thirds of the sentence has been served. The very few persons who are sentenced to life imprisonment may, by grant of pardon (mercy), have their sentences converted to a fixed period of imprisonment and are released after 7-14 years of imprisonment on the same conditions as others. It has just been proposed that conditional release should be allowed to occur only after two-thirds of the sentence has been served. At the same time it has been argued that preterm release should be totally abolished and determinate sentencing with shorter terms of deprivation of liberty introduced.

If an offense is punishable by imprisonment, the court may impose a *conditional sentence* (without a fixed term of punishment) on an occasional offender. This implies that no further sanction will be imposed provided the convicted person does not commit any other offenses within two years (trial period). The sentence is not combined with supervision or any special obligations but may be coupled with day-fines (up to 180) if this measure is considered necessary for the rehabilitation of the offender or from the point of view of general prevention.

Probation may be applied where an offense is punishable by imprisonment. Probation implies that no further sanction will be imposed if the convicted person does not commit any other offense within three years (trial period). During the first year probationers are under supervision and have to obey instructions that may be given concerning their residence, work, and treatment. As in the case of conditional sentences, probation may be combined with day-fines. It may be decided that the probation order should include institutional care for at least 14 days but not more than 3 months. The courts sometimes use the institution order as additional sanction upon reconviction of a probationer for a new offense.

Surrender for special care is a sanction that may be imposed in accordance with social and medical welfare statutes on offenders in need of care and treatment outside the criminal justice system:

(a) care and treatment under the Social Welfare Act of 1980 or the Act of 1980 on Mandatory Care for Persons under 20 years of Age (the sanction may be combined with day-fines)
(b) mandatory care and treatment in an institution for inebriates under the Act of 1981 on Mandatory Care of Alcoholics or Drug Addicts (the sanction is mainly used for minor offenses)
(c) mandatory care under the Insanity Act of 1966 (this sanction may in exceptional cases be used even when the mental disturbance has occurred after the offense was committed)
(d) open psychiatric care for cases where such care is deemed appropriate and institutional treatment is not considered necessary

Such court orders correspond to a great extent to decisions rendered in similar situations by the prosecutor. Nevertheless, many cases still reach the court.

Special Categories of Offenders

Under this heading information is given concerning different categories of offenders: youthful offenders, mentally deviant offenders, addict offenders, persistent offenders, female offenders, and non-Swedish offenders.

Since 1865 the age of criminal responsibility has been 15 years. According to the Code, even children may legally commit offenses, but such offenders may not be sentenced to any sanction within the criminal justice system for an offense committed before they have reached 15 years of age. Depending on the gravity of the offense, the police may, after investigation, hand them over to their parents or report the case to the Social Welfare Board. It is then the responsibility of the board to find appropriate measures for the child within the Social Services Act of 1980 or the Mandatory Care of Young Persons Act of 1980.

Offenders aged 15-17 at the time of the offense fall, in principle, under the Social Welfare System. However, the prosecutor is given a decisive role. The prosecutor may drop the case and merely notify young offenders of the decision. In cases where the prosecutor finds social welfare measures appropriate, prosecution is dismissed in accordance with the Social Welfare Act of 1980 or the Act of 1980 on Mandatory Care of Persons Under 20 Years of Age. Fines may be imposed administratively. The remaining cases are brought before the court. If the court finds the young offender guilty, the choice of sanctions is restricted with regard to probation, imprisonment, and youth imprisonment. Probation can be used only as an alternative to surrender for social welfare if probation is deemed more appropriate. Probation may be combined with fines and even with deprivation of liberty for a period of 14 days to three months, ordered by the court. Imprisonment may be used only in exceptional cases, for a specified term but never for life. Milder punishment than that which is provided for the offense may be imposed. In 1984, 6,001 young persons were granted prosecution remission and only 9 were sentenced to imprisonment.

There are few limitations with regard to sanctions for offenses committed by youthful offenders after 18 years of age: imprisonment may be imposed on offenders between the ages 18-20 only when deprivation of liberty is particularly called for in deference to public law obedience or when imprisonment is found to be more appropriate than another sanction (in 1984, 992 persons in this age bracket were sentenced to imprisonment).

While rejecting the concept of criminal responsibility based on the offender's maturity and sanity, the legislators in Sweden have made such personal characteristics prerequisites for the use of all or of some sanctions. Although such limitations can easily be specified with regard to the age factor, problems arise in defining the borderline between mental health and illness. Psychiatry has now established generally accepted criteria for insanity and debility, but there is still uncertainty concerning abnormality (especially psychopathy) and temporary insanity. In addition, psychiatrists sometimes have difficulty deciding whether the mental defect existed at the time of the offense or whether it requires mandatory care, while the courts may have difficulty determining whether the offense was committed under the influence of such mental conditions.

The Penal Code limits the sanctions that may be imposed on offenders who committed crimes while suffering from insanity, debility, or higher degrees of abnormality. Such sanctions include surrender for special care, fines (if they serve the purpose of deterrence), and probation, if such a sanction is considered more appropriate. Such an offender should never be sent to a correctional institution and probation may never be combined with institutional care. If none of these sanctions is found appropriate, the offender shall be convicted but no sanction will be imposed.

For those offenders who suffer from psychopathy of a lesser degree, all sanctions are applicable. A milder punishment than that provided for the offense may, however, be imposed for an offense committed under the influence of such mental abnormality.

In order to avoid suffering by the mentally deviant offenders and unnecessary court proceedings, the prosecutors are empowered to dismiss prosecution of such offenders given the condition that it is obvious that the offense was committed under influence of insanity, debility, or a higher degree of abnormality and that some provision for institutional care is made. In 1984, prosecution was dismissed with respect to 419 persons.

The decisions and convictions concerning mentally deviant offenders are based on medical reports ordered by the court. These reports are of two types: a brief report by a doctor (in most cases a psychiatrist) and an exhaustive report by a psychiatrist connected with a clinic or station within the state forensic organization. In rare instances, the offender requests that a doctor make a report. The court may ask an expert panel to give its opinion on a doubtful report. The Ministry of Justice in 1986 prepared a bill on mentally deviant offenders with regard to the applicability of penal sanctions. At the same time the (state) psychiatric clinics are going to be transferred to the counties and prepared to receive deviant offenders for care.

Offenders with Alcohol or Drug Problems

Research has confirmed that drunkenness and alcoholism are very important factors in the crime pattern of Sweden. For this reason, in 1964 drunkenness in a public place was made a penal code offense punishable by a monetary fine. Offenders were seized by the police, placed in custody for a few hours to sober up before signing an agreement to pay the fines ordered by the court (or by the prosecutor). The fines were rarely paid and as a result were converted to imprisonment.

It was not until 1916 that society began to take responsibility for the inebriates on the basis of the Temperance Act of 1913. The local communities and the counties were empowered to control alcohol consumption and to take care of the alcoholics through supervision or controlled care. The Temperance Act of 1954 followed the same lines as the older statutes. By that act, prosecutors became empowered to dismiss prosecution for minor offenses committed by persons under controlled care. Despite the preventive and mandatory measures taken to care for alcoholics through supervision, the results were very limited and often a failure. In 1976, 22,034 persons were subject to various measures of the Act. Of this number, 8,170 were admitted to institutions, (4,232 to private institutions and 3,938 to public ones). Only 527 men and 37 women were received in accordance with an order for mandatory care.

Since 1977, drunkenness in a public place has not been a punishable offense. However, persons who are found unable to take care of themselves are taken into temporary custody, or, rarely, to hospitals for treatment and social assistance.

Treatment and care of alcoholics and drug abusers are now, as mentioned above, placed under the Social Welfare Act of 1980 and the Act of 1981 on Mandatory Care for Addicts of Alcohol or Drugs. Most admissions to institutional care are now voluntary (17,312 in 1983) but sometimes ordered by the administrative courts (827 in 1983), rarely on the initiative of the prosecutor as a prerequisite for dismissal of the prosecution.

Since 1960 the use of narcotics has become an increasingly serious social problem inducing many persons to commit crimes in order to obtain money for drugs on the black market. This has caused an increase in the crime rate, especially for robbery and burglary. Numerous persons have become involved in the illegal traffic of drugs and stolen goods. To the public, drug addicts seem to be a greater threat to society than inebriates. Nevertheless, alcoholism is still a much more widespread and destructive factor than drug addiction. The state liquor shops collect larger sums in taxes than those used for the total criminal justice system (police, prosecution, courts, and prison and probation administration).

The prison and probation administration has estimated that, in 1985, 25% of the probationers and 28% of all inmates were drug addicts. No estimates have been published with regard to the percentage of alcoholics. Mixed abuse of alcohol and drugs is common in the clientele.

Dangerous and Persistent Offenders

Until the end of World War II, Sweden had very few offenders who had committed dangerous crimes or had been a serious threat to the prison staff. Many of those who had committed serious offenses—for example, homicide or rape—were certified insane and put into mental hospitals for mandatory care. The rest served long sentences without conflicts with the staff. The rather peaceful atmosphere in the institutions seemed to depend on their small size and the authority of the staff.

Today the situation is different. Bank and post office robberies are frequent, terrorism has come to Sweden, as well as smuggling and the sale of hard drugs. Police and prosecutors have concentrated their efforts on fighting crime that is dangerous to society and they have been fairly successful. However, riots occur in the penal institutions and the narcotic traffic does not stop at the prison walls. The authority of the prison staff is declining and staff members are uncertain about their roles. Prison conditions have become more difficult for inmates and staff. Although this situation has not called for maximum security prisons, a few sections of existing closed institutions have been fortified in order to meet the demands from the public and the staff. An increasing number of inmates are requesting isolation for their own security and restrictions have been ordered concerning furloughs for certain groups of offenders.

The traditional division of offenders into first-time offenders, recidivists, and persistent offenders does not fit into the system of

Swedish criminal justice. It is easy to follow the persistent offenders through their careers, beginning with the child welfare system long before reaching criminal age, finding them some years later loaded with prosecution dismissals prior to their first appearance in court, then sentenced to probation several times and, at last, sentenced to imprisonment. This pattern seems frustrating, but at the same time it is deceptive. The machinery of the criminal justice system sorts many more out of the system at every step, and those who do follow the line to the bitter end (long-term imprisonment) are certainly persistent but often rather harmless.

Female Offenders

Although women are the majority of the total population, they are a small and often neglected group among offenders. Female criminality is less frequent and less serious than male criminality. In 1984, females constituted 17.5% of the total number of cases dismissed by the prosecution and 11.1% of all persons sentenced to imprisonment. The proportion of female offenders differs from offense to offense: homicide, 5.2%; theft, 15.1%; petty theft, 40.1%; robbery, 4.9%; unauthorized use of a motor vehicle, 3.8%; arson, 16.7%; driving under the influence, 6.7%; and narcotic offenses, 15.3%. During 1984, the prison and probation administration received 14.9% female probationers and the penal institutions only 3.8%. Of those sentenced to two years imprisonment or more, 32 out of 628 were women.

Offenders from Abroad

The increase of immigration by refugees and guestworkers in conjunction with the swelling stream of foreigners coming over the borders for shorter visits has caused an upward trend in the crime rate along with a corresponding increase in pressure on the criminal justice agencies. The variations in cultural patterns and the multitude of spoken languages have increased the difficulties for the staff in handling cases where aliens are involved.

The Nordic countries allow their citizens to pass from one Nordic country to another without a passport and to take a job without residence and work permits. Due to the economic situation in their own country, many Finnish citizens live and work in Sweden. Other immigrants try to stay in Sweden with or without required permits.

Most guestworkers are men in their active years living away from their families. During the present period of economic depression, the public is less tolerant of aliens, especially those causing trouble. Only a few realize that the national prosperity, to a considerable extent, was created by the inflow of foreign manpower.

In 1984, Sweden had 7,952,056 Swedish citizens (of whom around 400,000 were naturalized foreigners) and 390,561 alien residents, registered in the local community where they lived. Of those, 143,928 came from Finland, 38,253 from Yugoslavia, 8,980 from Great Britain, 15,414 from Poland, 21,159 from Turkey, and 8,086 from the United States. Although the registered foreigners constituted 4.7% of the total population, their participation in crime was almost twice as high.

According to the 1984 statistics prepared by the prison administration, 2,469 (16.9%) foreigners out of 14,647 (in 1961, 687 out of 10,040) were admitted to the Swedish prisons to serve sentences. Foreign female inmates accounted for 18.2% of the female prison population (102 out of 560). For 404 of the total 2,469 foreign males, the sentence was combined with expulsion after execution of the sentence.

Diversion from the
Criminal Justice System

Diversion has never been clearly recognized in the Swedish criminal justice system. The Swedish ideology has been that all cases should be brought to court and all offenders punished. Even today, Swedish procedure is based on the concept of an absolute duty to institute public prosecution in all such cases. This principle has been replaced in many areas by a relative duty giving prosecutors the power to exercise discretion under conditions stipulated in the legislation. Sometimes the crime is viewed as being so trivial that prosecution would be unnecessary or cause more trouble than would be merited. In other instances, the criminality of a given kind is so widespread that it would be impossible to prosecute every case. There are also instances where legal proceedings would result in the interruption of care, education, or upbringing already in progress, or where social or medical care seem more urgent than the imposition of a sentence.

Furthermore, the Penal Code empowers the prosecution to exercise discretion on conditions specified for particular offenses. The chief prosecutor and lower-level prosecutors carefully supervise the administration of diversion.

Criminal Procedure

Criminal procedure in Sweden can be described briefly as follows. A preliminary investigation is undertaken by the police or the prosecutor. Inquiries are made concerning the person who reasonably may be suspected of the commission of the offense. Any person may be questioned who is thought to possess information of importance to the investigation. Suspects are entitled to have their defense counsel and a witness commissioned by the community council present at the examinations. Suspects and their counsel may put questions to the person conducting the inquiry. If suspects have no private defense counsel, the court designates, upon request, a member of the bar association to assist them in the capacity of public defense counsel, if the court finds it expedient for the protection of the suspect's rights. All decisions concerning pretrial detention and measures taken to secure evidence are made by the court. Seizure, however, may take place without court order if it is not possible to wait for such an order. As soon as the decision to prosecute has been made, the accused or their defense counsel may receive a copy of the record or notes of the investigation. All cases are heard by an ordinary court. If penalties are administratively imposed but not accepted by the offender, the case may be reviewed by the court. The courts are presided over by judges who have been appointed by the government strictly on professional merit. Lay assessors are a part of the district court and the court of appeal in all criminal cases, except in those cases where the maximum penalty is a fine. The accused is presumed to be innocent until he or she is found guilty and the conviction has obtained legal force. The procedure is adversary, and the court is bound to follow the description of the act as presented in the summons. The accused is protected against double jeopardy. The procedure is in principle free of charge for the offender. A public defense counsel is paid in advance from public funds. Other costs are paid by the offender. Most offenders' costs are covered in accordance with the 1972 Legal Aid Act. If offenders are incapable of understanding Swedish or if their speech or hearing is seriously damaged, the court may designate an interpreter to assist them in court. The costs are paid from public funds. The judgment of the court is given in writing and specifies the reasoning in support of the judgment, including a statement of what has been proven, the conviction, and the sentence. All criminal cases may be appealed from the district court to a court of appeal. The judgment of the court of appeal is generally final.

Phases of Criminal Proceedings

Most criminal cases begin with the police investigation. Its purpose is to ascertain whether an offense has been committed and, if so, who the offender might be. The police officers in charge of the investigation keep the prosecutor continually informed about the progress of their work. In order to obtain evidence the police may question any person who is thought to possess relevant information and request anyone found at the scene of the offense to accompany them to the police station where the person may be kept for up to six hours.

A suspect person will be subject to a process involving three stages:

(1) Apprehension. Any policeman may apprehend a person when there is cause for arrest. Anyone may apprehend a person who has committed an offense punishable by imprisonment, if the suspect is caught in the act of committing the offense or running away from the scene.
(2) Arrest. The investigating authority (police or prosecutor) may issue a warrant of arrest for a suspect person. The suspect must be released within 24 hours unless detention is initiated by the prosecutor.
(3) Detention must be ordered by the court within 4 days. The court then decides when the suspect shall be released. The detention order details the offense of which the detained person is suspected and states the cause for the detention.

In 1984, 26,388 persons were arrested and 8,855 applications for detention orders were issued. Of those arrested or detained, 10% were women. Any period exceeding 24 hours during which a person has been arrested or detained leads to a corresponding reduction of the penalty to which he or she is sentenced. If acquitted, the detainee may claim compensation.

The prerequisites for arrest and detention, travel prohibition, and temporary attachment of property, as well as for seizure, are carefully specified by the law. Bail is unknown in Swedish law.

Persons who are detained in accordance with court order are generally kept in a remand prison under the prison administration. Their cases have priority in the courts. The detention period varies, but two-thirds of the cases are heard within 1 month. Offenders under 18 are rarely detained.

When the investigation has proceeded to a point at which a person is reasonably suspected of the offense, he or she is informed of the suspicion. The person and his or her defense counsel are provided with the opportunity to be informed of what has taken place at the investigation. Prosecution may not continue until they have been given such an opportunity. After the conclusion of the investigation, the prosecutor must decide whether or not to proceed to trial. Plea-bargaining is not used.

Prior to the trial, the prosecutor or the accused may ask for a personal case study. The court may not order such a study to be carried out unless the accused has pleaded guilty or the court is satisfied that the evidence against the accused is reasonably strong. No person may be sentenced to imprisonment for 6 months or more, conditional sentence, probation, or surrendered for special care unless a personal case study is undertaken or equivalent information is made available to the court. The study is carried out by a competent person, selected by the local chief probation officer. The court may also order that a medical examination of the accused be conducted. In 1984, 12,171 persons underwent a personal case study, and 1,848 of them a medical examination. Even stronger restrictions limit the court from ordering a forensic psychiatric examination of the accused. Such a report concerns the offenders' mental state when the crime was committed and the conditions under which they may be surrendered for mandatory care under the Insanity Act. In 1984, 511 persons were examined and 227 of them were found to be in need of mandatory care.

At the main hearing, the prosecutor states the charge and the accused is asked whether or not he or she admits the offense. The plea of guilty or not guilty is not used in the same way as in England or the United States. To the astonishment of many foreign visitors, the accused rarely denies the act as such but the accused or the defense counsel more often raise objections to the legal implications of it. The objections may concern a defense or the applicability of the provisions upon which the charge is based. Cross-examination as it is known in the Anglo-Saxon system is not practiced. After the pleadings of the prosecutor and the accused have been completed, the court must decide on guilt and sanctions. The verdict is usually given the same day, but in complicated cases it may be postponed for a couple of weeks. The verdict is given in writing and includes information concerning steps for appeal.

When the sentence is pronounced, the accused and the prosecutor are asked whether they accept the judgment. A declaration from the sentenced person can be given at any time before the elapse of the term for appeal. The execution of the sanction commences when an affirmative declaration is given. Such a declaration is irrevocable. The court may decide that a sentence to probation with imprisonment shall take effect even though it has not acquired legal force.

In principle, the execution of the sentence takes place when it has acquired legal force or an affirmative declaration of acceptance has been given. An order of summary punishment by fines, consented to by the suspect, has the same effect as a final verdict. If the offenders are detained in a remand prison after being sentenced to imprisonment, they are immediately transferred to serve their sentence.

From the time of the Middle Ages, the King had the prerogative of granting a pardon and used it frequently either in the form of total pardon or more often of commutation of the sentence. Today, pardon is granted by the Council of Ministers, following a recommendation from the Minister of Justice. An application for pardon may be made by the offender or by anyone else. It is reviewed in the Ministry of Justice and supplemented by relevant information before being considered by the minister. Applications for pardon, to some extent, have become an alternative to appeal in regard to the assessment of the punishment. The procedure is quick and free. In 1984, the Council rendered decisions on 1,892 applications, of which 283 led to pardon or commutation. Almost all favorably decided cases concerned commutation of the sentence to a milder sentence or postponement of the execution of the sentence. Pardon is also granted an applicant when the type of offense he or she had committed is changed or repealed resulting in unjust incarceration of the applicant. Thus, in 1977, over 500 conscientious objectors were granted pardons.

Execution of Penal Measures (Corrections)

Criminal justice in Sweden in based on humanity, fairness, and efficiency. Efficiency is achieved by means of selection, training, and continuing education of the staff within the criminal justice agencies and by classifying the clients with regard to their personalities, social situation, criminal record, and served sentences. Fairness is built into the total criminal justice system and is under the control of the Ministry of Justice, the central authorities, the Ombudsman, and the mass media. The humanitarian tradition is kept alive by current public debate and the resistance of the politicians and the civil servants to demands for harsher methods in fighting crime through the use of more severe measures against offenders.

There is no statement in the Code of the philosophy on which it is based, but it is clear from the views expressed during its preparation that it has as its foundation the idea of rehabilitation and prevention and not retaliation. It is stipulated that in the choice of sanction in the individual case the court shall, without ignoring the need for general deterrence, keep in mind that the sanction should serve to foster the offender's adaptation to society (Chapter 1, Section 7).

Fines

The execution of fines is regulated in the statutes of 1964 and supplementary ordinances. Imprisonment in default of payment is carefully restricted and may be ordered only by the courts. It is now under consideration to abolish the conversion of fines to deprivation of liberty.

Probation and Parole

Probation and parole are based on the idea of supervision of the offender in liberty. The supervision includes support and control by lay supervisors (for a nominal fee) or social workers (in all, approximately 6,000 persons, mainly laymen) under the guidance of the local chief probation officer and his or her staff (in 1985 there were 65 such offices in the entire country) and under the control of the local probation and parole boards (in 1985, 29 boards). As the control is based on cooperation of the offender with the supervisor, failing to cooperate may lead to intervention by the chief probation officer or the board through the use of constructive and disciplinary measures. Thus, in 1984, the boards decided to warn 486 clients, to take 1,997 into temporary custody, and to issue special directives for 918 clients with regard to residence and lodging, work or participation in educational or vocational training, or submittance to social or medical care. In 1984, the boards revoked the conditional release of 92 persons and requested the prosecutor to raise with the court the question of revocation of the probation order and of a new order to undergo imprisonment for 64 probationers.

A probationer or a person conditionally released may appeal against some of such decisions by a local board to the central board of corrections.

The supervision is usually restricted to a period of one year and may be terminated prior to that. The board may decide to resume the supervision during the trial period. In 1985, the clientele was composed of 8,276 probationers and 3,556 conditionally released (in all, 11,832 clients, of whom 1,340 were female).

Prisons and
Prison Administration

The National Board of Prison and Probation Administration governs both probation and aftercare and remand prisons and local and national penal institutions. The country is divided into 13 administrative regions and a central administration to which the local probation and parole boards and the central board of corrections are attached, though their decisions are independent. The central board of corrections decides on the release of a small number of dangerous offenders and tries appeals against decisions taken by prison governors and local boards.

The prisons are divided into two groups: the national (20 prisons), the local (57 prisons), and 26 remand prisons (for pretrial detainees). The national prisons consist altogether of 1,300 closed and 488 open accommodations and the local prisons 1,100 closed and 1,200 open. Inmates who are sentenced to imprisonment for two years or more are regularly placed in a closed part of a national prison but are later transferred to an open part and, finally, to a local prison in preparation for their release. To some extent, the national prisons also receive troublesome inmates from local prisons and accept short timers and inmates who do not fit into the local prisons.

Sweden never fully adopted the principles for classification of offenders and at present there are very few provisions concerning placement of the inmates according to age, sex, risk of escape, previous convictions, dangerousness, or mental deviance. However, division of the prisons into national and regional, closed and open institutions allows a certain margin for variations. With regard to security arrangements, some prisons are more likely to care for dangerous offenders or offenders likely to escape. However, there are no maximum security institutions per se.

Treatment and Care

The basic ideas behind the present correctional system can be summarized as follows:

(1) A minimum of intervention; noninstitutional care is the principal form of correctional care.
(2) Institutional care should be closely related and coordinated with noninstitutional care.
(3) Institutional care should be carried out near the offender's home unless the public safety requires otherwise.
(4) Outward-oriented activity—society's service organs (such as social service, medical and dental service, the educational and vocational training facilities, and the leisure-time activities) should be used to the greatest possible extent.

The guideline for correctional care is that it should make full use of the services that are offered by the community to all inhabitants and should restrict and supplement them only when it is necessary with regard to the purpose of punishment. The probation and aftercare service offered to offenders is restricted to use as a supplement to ordinary social service while at the same time serving as a control instrument.

The objectives of correctional care in institutions are (1) to promote the inmate's adjustment to society and (2) to counteract the injurious effects of deprivation of freedom. A treatment plan is established for every inmate. It includes preparation for life outside the institution as well as work and studies within the institution.

During their stay in the institution, inmates are placed on a time schedule that includes 40 hours of work or studies per week. Since the average period for inmates sentenced to imprisonment is very short, vocational training is mainly restricted to long timers. In 1984, of prisoners admitted to serve sentences of imprisonment, 9,569 had a sentence of 3 months or less, another 1,919 of less than 6 months, another 1,397 of less than a year, another 1,144 less than 2 years, and only 628, 2 years or more, the periods of conditional release not included. The majority of the clientele usually participate in work training—that is, training for work in a factory or the outdoors. The educational program is primarily directed toward basic school subjects and social subjects and social adaptation. The teaching program as well as the training program is carried out by the local and county authorities or in collaboration with them.

Many countries use grades, marks, and rewards as instruments to maintain peace and order in their institutions and further the prison work. This is no longer accepted in Sweden. The methods of "whip and carrot," which were formerly advocated by many, have been abolished.

In earlier times, the prisoner's conduct during his or her stay in the institution and his or her mental attitude at the time of parole were taken into consideration by the probation and parole board.

Prisoners' rights are carefully regulated by statutes. The inmate is entitled to freedom of worship and to uncontrolled written communication with Swedish authorities and members of the bar association. Control of other correspondence and of telephone calls is restricted but shall, in principle, be available to the inmate. Prison visits are generally allowed and rarely controlled.

Extramural Activities

Many inmates in local and some in national institutions are granted "town passes" for participation in schooling (including university studies), vocational training, and leisure activities, such as in study groups or sports associations. Some of the inmates are accompanied by staff members while on these "passes."

Inmates may be granted permission to leave the institution for a brief period in order to facilitate their adjustment to society and maintain their contact with their families. For long timers the board of corrections may allow a longer period prior to the date of release in order to make arrangements for working and living. Altogether, 40,066 short furloughs were granted in 1984. Of these, 3% were abused by late returns and 1% due to other misconduct, such as misuse of alcohol or drugs or criminal activities.

In the case of some offenders sentenced to institutional care, such care may prove detrimental to their readaptation to society. In such instances the court is empowered to place these inmates in a school with a boarding establishment, a treatment home for addicts, a suitable private home, or in military service. In 1984, 555 inmates were given this opportunity, some within a few days after their admission to a prison. Approximately 30% of them misused the privilege.

Disciplinary Measures
Within the Institutional Care

The relative freedom given to the inmates has, in many respects, made prison life more tolerable in comparison with earlier regimes. Nevertheless, many inmates, particularly long timers and recidivists, point out that the incarceration still involves a lot of suffering due to the time schedule and types of prison activities and to their total submissions to the discretion of the staff. Prison strikes are not uncommon and some riots have occurred. However, the small size of the institutions as well as the large staff has diminished these occurrences. There were 995 escapes from prisons in 1984.

The statutory provisions for breaches of prison discipline (not including offenses) are rather limited. Interruption of the term of imprisonment due to abuse of furlough or escape leads to a prolongation of the time to be served by the number of days of unlawful absence. The purely disciplinary measures are a warning (in 1984, 2,371 cases) and prolongation of the time to be served is limited to a period of at most ten days (in 1984, 1,711 cases). Such prolongation may be repeated for new breaches but may never exceed 45 days in total. Other disciplinary measures used are restrictions of extramural activities, delay of furlough, and transfer to another prison. In 1984, such transfers occurred in 1,578 cases, most frequently due to escape or abuse of furlough.

Concluding Remarks on
Swedish Criminal Policy

Criminal policy in Sweden has always been a mixture of pragmatism and ideology with a few drops of experience and research. The near future seems to follow the same lines.

The firm belief in the possibilities of using penal measures as instruments for controlling citizens has lead to extensive legislation against "economic and organized crime." Wide mandates have been granted to the public agencies to investigate private economy and private life by access to public documents and balances in banks and companies. The burden of taxes and charges on individuals as well as those having the status of legal persons is heavy and at the same time has the backing of the welfare state.

The protracted debate on penal policy, in particular, on the question whether punishment should be past or future oriented, has resulted in the abolition of indeterminate sentences of youth imprisonment and internment as penal sanctions. The wide discretion of the courts to impose what they find to be an adequate punishment for the offender is going to be hampered by the introduction of modern sentencing guidelines based on an assessment of the offense under review. At the same time, the demand for a reduction of imprisonment sentences has given rise to overrating the merits of probation and a wish to introduce new methods of control of the probationers and the use of community work as a sanction alternative to short-time imprisonment. The efficiency in exacting fines has encouraged the policymakers to propose a more frequent use of fines as a sanction even for rather serious offenses.

With regard to the use of imprisonment as a sanction for serious crimes, many had expected proposals leading to the abolishment of conditional release. Instead, a special commission recommended a return to previous provisions on obligatory conditional release after two-thirds of the sentence served. This did not satisfy those who wished to introduce strict sentencing or those who wished to have conditional release as an instrument to encourage good behavior in prison.

The mental capacity of the offender at the time of the crime has always been a precondition for criminal responsibility in Europe. Only Sweden in the Code of 1962 rejected this standpoint and provided that the act or omission should be regarded as a crime even when committed by a child or a mentally disturbed or defective person but restricted the use of sanctions for such offenders. Thus no sanction is applicable to a person under 15 years of age and surrender for care is the only sanction to be used as deprivation of liberty for the insane or defective offenders. In this way the use of the prerequisites of criminal intent or criminal negligence have been obscured and the safeguards against misuse of the criminal justice system with regard to them weakened. Despite protests, the government seems to be reluctant to abandon the present standpoint and unwilling to reintroduce the continental approach. Instead, the government tries to find new ways to indicate which categories of mentally disturbed persons are to undergo sanctions inside or outside the present criminal justice system.

Looking back to my contribution in the first edition of this textbook, I find rapid and profound changes in Swedish criminal policy within the last decade and a few fields where reforms have been opposed. The method of trial and error is generally accepted but to some extent hampered by ideological arguments or economic realities.

**International Collaboration
Within Criminal Law
and Criminal Procedure**

Since World War II, Sweden has actively supported international collaboration in the fight against crime, particularly by agreements within the Nordic countries (Denmark, Finland, Iceland, Norway, and Sweden, often referred to as Scandinavia). After the formation of the Council of Europe many such agreements were merged in the European conventions. Still the Nordic countries have kept their tradition to carry out their negotiations in this field by the ordinary countries' authorities and not in the diplomatic way. International conventions, agreements, and treaties are transformed in Swedish law by legislation in as far as the undertakings are not already covered by existing provisions. Such legislation is marked after the conventions by year and number in the statute book.

Extradition of offenders:

(1) Memorandum of 1956 on Extradition by delegates from the Nordic States (1959: 254)
(2) European (Paris) Convention of 1957 on Extradition (1957: 668)
(3) Bilateral treaties, for example, with Great Britain and United States

Transfer of criminal proceedings:

(1) European (Strasbourg) Convention of 1959 on Mutual Assistance in Criminal Matters
(2) European (Strasbourg) Convention 1964 on the Punishment of Road Traffic Offenses (1971: 965)
(3) Agreement of 1970 on the Transfer of Proceedings within the Nordic countries
(4) European (Strasbourg) Convention of 1972 on the Transfer of Proceedings in Criminal Matters (1976: 19)

Execution of sentences:

(1) Recommendation of 1962 by the Interparliamentary Nordic Council (1963: 193)
(2) European (Strasbourg) Convention 1964 on the Supervision of Conditionally Sentenced and Conditionally Released Offenders (1978: 901)
(3) European (Hague) Convention of 1970 on the International Validity of Criminal Judgments (1972: 260, below)
(4) European (Strasbourg) Convention of 1983 on the Transfer of Convicted Persons (1972: 260, as amended 1984: 876)

While the inter-European collaboration in the fields of transfer proceeding and of sentenced persons have had little importance to Sweden (20-50 cases a year), the inter-Nordic negotiations have reached considerable dimensions and work smoothly. However, the statistical information is poor and irregular. With regard to the execution of

TABLE 5.1

Persons undergoing		1968	1973	1980	1982	1985
imprisonment to	Denmark	27	25	25	15	33
	Finland	109	227	76	104	52
	Norway	33	22	30	19	26
imprisonment from	Denmark	32	39	63	59	51
	Finland	39	42	115	77	106
	Norway	25	25	33	30	37
supervision from	Denmark	7	6	1	1	1
	Finland	20	72	83	58	47
	Norway	–	–		–	1

sentences to imprisonment and probation (including supervision following conditional release), the figures in Table 5.1 are available concerning the collaboration with Denmark, Finland, and Norway.

The figures may seem surprisingly low taking into account the close connections, the free labor market, and the unconditioned right to take residence in another Nordic country. However, it should be noted that most imprisonment sentences are very short and that transfer is rarely carried out against the offender's wish unless an expulsion order is included in the sentence.

6

Japan

KENICHI NAKAYAMA

General Information

Japan consists of four main islands and thousands of smaller islands and islets. The archipelago, lying off the eastern coast of the Asian continent, stretches in an arc 2,362 miles long. It covers an area of 234,577 square miles, which is about one-twenty-fifth that of the United States.

Between 1872 and 1978, the population of Japan more than tripled, from 34,800,000 to 120,240,000. Japan now ranks sixth in the world in terms of population and is one of the most densely populated nations in the world.

The new constitution, which was promulgated just after World War II in 1946, differs in many important respects from the Meiji Constitution of 1889. Some of its key provisions are these: The Emperor is a symbol of the states, and sovereign power now rests with the people; Japan renounces war and the threat of force to settle international disputes; fundamental human rights are guaranteed as eternal and inviolable; the bicameral Diet consisting of the House of Representatives and the House of Councilors is the highest organ of state power and is elected by the people; executive power is vested in the Cabinet, which is collectively responsible to the Diet; and local self-government is established on an extensive scale. Besides the ruling conservative party (liberal-democratic), there are currently four major opposition parties (middle and left). The former conservative party, although narrowly and with relatively weakened influence, still has long maintained an absolute majority in the Diet.

The legal system of Japan was modernized mainly by introducing the model of continental Europe, French, and German law. But after World War II, Anglo-American law exerted a strong influence. Furthermore, the old traditions of the Orient Japanese law are still maintained, especially in its way of operation. Japanese law is characterized as a kind of special mixture of these three elements. But, as a whole, it still belongs to the continental Civil Law system.

Japan has adopted, like almost all European countries, the statutory law principle. In criminal law this principle has been carried through without exception: Only statutory law, neither custom nor judicial decisions, may define crimes and punishments. In practice, judicial decisions play an important role in the legal system. Although their primary purpose is to decide cases, the principles or theories behind the decisions create precedents for future cases with identical or similar facts. Supreme Court decisions have binding force for the future, but strictly speaking, they are not recognized as a source of law under the Japanese legal system.

Amount, Structure, and Dynamics of Criminality

For the last 100 years, the number of persons arrested annually by the police for Penal Code offenses on the whole has risen, as has the nation's population. Some fluctuations of criminality are worth mentioning. The figure of registered crimes rose in 1890, when inflated rice prices led to riots and Japan's immature capitalist system suffered its first panic. A rather steady increase followed, amid fluctuations. A long economic depression in 1919 brought about a continued increase in crime. The worldwide depression of the 1930s, with a high rate of unemployment, resulted in the unprecedented growth of criminality. It reached its peak in 1934 but abated thereafter, probably due to economic recovery, international tensions, and war. These events, in turn, strengthened society's cohesiveness.

Just after the war, in 1946, the crime figure almost doubled that of the previous year. It increased steadily until 1950, but then declined until 1956. This may be attributed to the economic and social recovery from the postwar devastation. The number of recorded crimes started to rise again in 1957, mainly due to the increase in traffic offenses. It reached a peak in 1970, but then underwent a steady decline until 1974. However, the figure of so-called Penal Code offenses has shown an upward trend since 1975, reaching over two million in 1984, the largest figure since World War II.

This increase is mainly due to the considerable increase of larceny (usually minor) among juveniles. The number of heinous offenses is rather stable; sexual offenses are, on the whole, showing a downward trend. Recently, quite a few dangerous phenomena, such as robberies of financial institutions, murder, and other violent offenses committed by "Boryokudan" (a Mafia-type organization) members and drug offenses have occurred. However, the crime rate in Japan is still estimated as considerably lower than other Western civilized countries and is becoming a matter of great interest to Western criminologists.

Scope of Criminalization

The Penal Code of 1907 covers crimes and criminal punishments. The catalog of Penal Code offenses is fairly stable and fixed in regard to traditional crimes such as homicide, theft, and rape. But sometimes the ambit of criminal sanctions changes drastically by some alteration of the existing social and political order. It is very characteristic that just after World War II the Penal Code dropped such crimes as those against the Emperor, espionage, and adultery. On the other hand, newly introduced after the War were such offenses as illegal possession of real property, intimidation of witnesses, armed assembly, and so on. The Revised Draft Code of 1974, which is definitely geared toward further criminalization, was criticized for this tendency. However, the necessity of having criminal laws on so-called computer crimes has recently been discussed. Homosexuality is not criminalized, and abortion, practically speaking, is not punishable by virtue of the special law of eugenics.

Besides the Penal Code, special laws regulate various offenses such as hijackings. A separate body of law is the law of violations dealing with minor breaches of the legal order. There are also many special laws of administrative character that carry punishments.

Structure and Functioning
of Law Enforcement Agencies

The National Police Agency now belongs directly to the Prime Minister's Office. Before the war, it belonged to the Ministry of Internal

Affairs, which is no longer in existence. Moreover, to secure the political independence of the police, the National Police Public Safety Commission was created. The Agency comes under its control. The regular police force was 253,625 in 1984, 1 policeman per 553 persons.

The Public Prosecutor's Office belongs to the Ministry of Justice. The office consists of the Supreme, high, district, and local levels in accordance with court hierarchy. Public prosecutors, who are accountable to the minister of justice, initiate prosecution of criminal cases, request the proper application of law by courts, and supervise the execution of judgments. The minister of justice exercises general supervision and control over their activities. The number of prosecutors in 1985 was 2,092, the same number as existed in 1980.

Defense attorneys are not public officials, but, because of the public nature of their responsibilities, they are regulated by law. They are organized in collectives of lawyers, possessing wide autonomy in their activities. The number of defense attorneys has increased gradually to 12,944 in 1985, but the ratio is still about 10,000 persons per 1 defense attorney.

According to the Court Organization Law (1947), the five courts are the Supreme Court, high courts, district courts, family courts, and summary courts. The Supreme Court, with 15 judges, is the highest court in Japan and has appellate jurisdiction only. High courts are located in eight major cities and as a rule hear appeals filed against judgments of the lower courts. District courts hear cases primarily of original jurisdiction. Family courts exclusively handle domestic and juvenile cases. Summary courts have the power to try minor civil and criminal cases by summary procedure, where the claims and punishments are relatively limited. There were 2,792 judges in 1985, representing a small increase from year to year, but not enough to cover the increasing number of cases.

Judicial power is vested exclusively in a Supreme Court and other courts established by law, and the executive has no final judicial power. The court organization is completely separate from the Ministry of Justice, and the authority of judicial administration is also given to the Supreme Court. The Constitution has empowered the courts to determine the constitutionality of any law, order regulation, or official act, and has also guaranteed the independence of judges, who are bound only by the Constitution and the laws.

However, in practice, the Japanese Supreme Court has been reluctant to declare laws unconstitutional. This has happened only in very rare cases, for example, where the provision of parricide was declared unconstitutional. And also in the field of judicial administration the Supreme Court authority was sometimes suspected of discriminative nomination of new judges and the refusal of reappointment to the full judges for political reasons. The principle of the independence of judges and the judiciary as a whole must be protected from being potentially undermined inside as well as outside.

Substantive Criminal Law

The present Penal Code of Japan was enacted in 1907. Although partial reforms and additions have been made several times, one-fourth of the Code is still in its original form. Overall, reform of this Code has been urged and the Revised Draft Code was made public in 1974, but the movement is still under way.

General Principles
of Responsibility

In the present Penal Code of Japan there is no specific provision proclaiming the principle of "no crime, no punishment without law." However, the Constitution says no person shall be deprived of life or liberty, nor shall any other criminal penalty be imposed, except according to law. The Constitution furthermore forbids double jeopardy and says criminal laws shall not be imposed retroactively. Specifically, no person shall be held criminally responsible for an act that was lawful at the time of its commission. According to the Penal Code, when a punishment is changed by law after the commission of a crime, the lesser punishment is to be applied. Charges must be dropped when the punishment has been abolished by a law or ordinance subsequent to commission of the offense. In theory, it is also recognized that customary law is not the source of criminal law and that absolutely indeterminate punishments are prohibited. Interpretation by analogy is also not accepted, although in practice the boundary between analogy and acceptable extensive interpretation is sometimes difficult to fix with precision.

The Penal Code has no formal gradation of offenses into felonies and misdemeanors, although the Code of 1882 had such gradation. Violations—that is, minor breaches of the legal order—are regulated almost fully by the Law of Violation of 1948. They are now subject only to penal detention or minor fines. Punishments provided for in Penal Code offenses are much more diversified.

According to the Code, the age of criminal responsibility is 14 years and under no circumstances may anyone younger be held criminally responsible. Under the Juvenile Law, 16 is the age of regular prosecution. Anyone who is younger may be sentenced to educational measures by the family court. Until a juvenile is 20 years old he or she may be criminally prosecuted or educational measures may be applied to him or her by the family court.

For a long time, the concept of criminal responsibility of corporations was rejected by scholars and practitioners. Recently, however, opinions in favor of criminal responsibility of corporations have been heard. Some special administrative-type laws already provide for the imposition of fines on corporations. Nevertheless, the punishment of the corporation is still exceptional. Caution regarding this matter seems well recommended.

The Penal Code recognizes the importance of the mental element of crimes. Intent and negligence are two basic forms of *mens rea*. An act committed without criminal intent is not criminal except as otherwise specially provided for by law. This exception has been interpreted to introduce crimes due to negligence. This means, consequently, that the principle "no crime, no punishment without *mens rea*" has been fully implemented. Unfortunately, there exist some exceptions to this rule. For example, some special administrative-type laws provide for punishment of negligent crimes despite the fact that the laws are silent on this issue. Some deviations from the principle of guilt can also be seen in the case of the crime aggravated by the result. In practice, even negligence is not required regarding the result aggravating responsibility. The Revised Draft of the Penal Code in this instance is clearly progressive: It tries to improve the situation by saying that if it is impossible to foresee such results, aggravated punishment cannot be imposed.

Theory and practice recognize the mistake of fact as a defense. An offender may be held responsible for an intentional offense only if he or she was aware of all definitional elements of the offense. The mistake regarding the existence of self-defense is regarded in practice as the mistake of fact, excluding intent.

Ignorance of the criminal law is not considered a defense. Knowledge that the act is prohibited is not a necessary element of intent. Ignorance of law may not exclude but only mitigate criminal responsibility for intentional offense. The Revised Draft of the Penal Code also, in this instance, is more progressive: If lack of awareness of the law is excusable, the responsibility is excluded. This solution has been supported by scholars.

Preparation is punishable only in a few serious crimes, such as insurrection, arson, homicide, and robbery.

Attempt is punishable in about 20 crimes. In addition to those mentioned above, the following may be listed: rape, abortion, theft, and extortion. The punishment for attempt may be mitigated. This optional, not mandatory, mitigation of punishment for attempt has been said to reflect the subjective approach to criminal responsibility favored by the Code.

Attempt has been defined, following the German law, as the commencement of the execution of the offense. This objective element differentiates attempt from mere preparation. In practice, the boundaries of attempt have been drawn rather narrowly.

Complicity is divided into three forms: coprincipals who act jointly in the commission of crime, instigator of another's crime, and accessory to a crime. Instigators and principals are to be punished within the same limit, while the punishment of accessory is reduced. Each of the coprincipals acts, as a rule, for himself or herself, but court practice has long recognized another category of coprincipals where two or more persons conspire to commit a crime and any one conspirator commits the crime pursuant to the common design. Despite strong theoretical criticism, this concept of conspirator-principals is fixed in court practice. The Revised Draft Code has certified it legislatively.

Insanity is one of the permitted defenses. According to the Penal Code, the act of an insane person is not punishable, and in case of diminished responsibility punishment is reduced. Theory and practice say insanity exists when the perpetrators lack the mental capacity to evaluate their conduct properly or to act in accordance with such evaluation. In the case of diminished responsibility, this capacity is seriously limited. Japanese courts are rather reluctant to accept the defense of insanity, fearing that dangerous persons are released without any effective measure of control.

Theory and practice recognize the so-called self-induced insanity. The defense of insanity will not be available to a person who, with intent of negligence, has induced himself or herself to the state of insanity and committed the act prohibited by law. This will mainly apply to criminal acts committed while intoxicated.

Self-defense and the state of necessity are also defenses. They are both urgent, spontaneous acts. Self-defense is characterized as a kind of defense-right against unjust, illegal attack, while in the dire necessity one aims at shifting the danger onto another's shoulders. Therefore, especially in the latter case, injury should not exceed the harm sought to be averted.

Penal Measures

The Penal Code of Japan, despite its age (1907), has been sufficiently modernized to meet the growing demands of contemporary penal policy. The Code is characterized by simple and abstract descriptions of crimes and by a great variety of penal measures at the judge's disposal, leaving ample room for judicial discretion. The Code allows for modern criminological means of social defense and individualized treatment of offenders. As long ago as 1907, the widely framed suspended sentence with supervision during the trial period as well as parole with relatively early possibility of release were introduced. Both institutions are motivated by the spirit of special prevention and rehabilitation of offenders. At the same time, it cannot be denied that the spirit of general prevention and retribution is deeply rooted in the penal policy. Its function is conservative, aiming at the irrational threat of severe punishment in the interest of securing public order.

According to the Penal Code, the kinds of penal measures are as follows: death, imprisonment with labor, imprisonment without labor, fine, penal detention, minor fine, and confiscation as a supplemental punishment.

The death penalty is still retained as the most severe punishment for certain crimes, such as insurrection, arson, sabotage of trains, homicide, and death resulting from robbery. Influential arguments for abolishing the death penalty have recently been offered by scholars in connection with some cases of *de novo* proceeding for the convicted criminals. But the Revised Draft Code does not abolish the death penalty but diminishes the number of capital crimes. In practice, the death penalty is imposed only in the rare case of aggravated homicide or homicide resulting from robbery.

Imprisonment with labor is the most typical punishment and is imposed for either life or a specific term. The minimum length of imprisonment is 1 month, the maximum, 15 years, but under special aggravating or mitigating circumstances, the term may be extended to

20 years or reduced to less than 1 month. Even a life term is, in fact, not indefinite as one can be paroled after 10 years.

Imprisonment without labor is provided for in such instances as political, official, and negligent crimes. These offenders are not obliged to work but may work upon request. Since they do exercise this right in practice, there remains hardly any substantive distinction between them. Recently, scholars have argued in favor of rejecting the distinction based on work. They asked for unification of imprisonment as a correct step from the point of modernizing penal policy. But the Revised Draft Code still maintains this distinction.

Penal detention means a short (1-30 days) deprivation of liberty in a penal detention house and is limited to a few offenses, such as insult or public indecency. Scholars are critical of this type of punishment because of the negative effect inherent in a short-term imprisonment. But the Revised Draft Code retains this punishment with an even wider scope of application.

Fines (4,000 yen or $20 and up) and minor fines (up to 4,000 yen) are the monetary punishments. Those who cannot pay are detained in a work house for 1 day to 2 years. In cases of minor fines, the period of detention is up to 30 days. The so-called day-fine system has not been introduced in Japan.

According to the official statistics, the distribution of penal measures applied by courts in 1984 was as follows: death, 3 (0%); imprisonment with labor, 73,984 (2.9%); imprisonment without labor, 4,947 (0.1%); fine, 2,374,394 (95.5%); penal detention, 41 (0%); minor fine, 29,138 (1.1%). However, as far as the Penal Code offenses are concerned, the situation is quite different: imprisonment ranks first, while fines account for only about 5%.

One of the special correctional measures other than criminal punishment is educational measures for juveniles, mainly probation and committal to Juvenile Training School. The latter is a custodial measure. Although it is not considered punishment and is to be applied for the protection and education of the juveniles, it still cannot help having, in fact, an aspect similar to the imprisonment as punishment. That is the reason why the due process requirements should be met also in juvenile cases. When a juvenile is to be sentenced to criminal punishments, special rules govern. For example, the death penalty must not be applied to a juvenile under 18; life imprisonment is replaced by a determined term; a juvenile is given an indeterminate sentence.

The provisions of the present Penal Code relating to recidivism are simple. Punishment for a second offense shall not exceed twice the maximum term of imprisonment with labor provided for the crime committed. A third or subsequent conviction is treated in the same way as the second. The Revised Draft Code introduced a category of habitual recidivists. An indeterminate sentence could be imposed (with the minimum term of 1 year) on such a recidivist. But, this idea also has been criticized by scholars for its ineffectiveness as well as the imposition of punishment beyond the limit of culpability.

The Penal Code has no provision for security measures concerning insane, drug, and alcohol offenders. These categories of offenders have been treated partly as within the mental health law system. The Revised Draft Code has tried to introduce a system of security measures as a kind of judicial treatment of these offenders. Two kinds of security measures were proposed: medical measures for mentally disordered offenders and abstinence measures for addicts. These measures were meant not only to protect society but also to treat the offenders. But more than a few lawyers doubt the effectiveness of these measures and claim that the only real effect would be long and indeterminate terms of isolation of these offenders from society. But, it is also true that whenever so-called phantom-killer cases happened and were sensationally reported by the press, people demanded more protection and supported the new security measures. It might be fair to say that the country's social and medical policy must be improved first. The issue of security measures is one of the problems hotly debated in Japan within the context of criminal law reform.

Probation under the Japanese system takes the form of suspension of execution of sentence—with or without probationary supervision—and may be applied to a person who was sentenced for not more than three years or a fine of not more than 200,000 yen ($1,000), providing he or she has not been previously sentenced to imprisonment or that five years have passed since the last sentence. It should be noted that in adult probation no presentence report prepared by the investigator is required; in the case of a juvenile, such a report is absolutely necessary. The sentence is suspended for a trial period (from one to five years). If an offender is convicted of another crime during this period, the suspension may (in some cases must) be revoked and the sentence executed. In 1984, 55.5% of the sentences were suspended regarding imprisonment with labor and 92.0% regarding imprisonment without labor. Of all suspensions, 14.0% were with supervision; 14.3% of suspensions were revoked.

One of the characteristics of Japan's probation concept is the fact that besides the government probation officers who are responsible for the cases as caseworkers (about 800 in total) there are also many volunteer probation officers who act as their assistants and directly carry out probation works (about 47,000). The participation of voluntary probation officers may be seen as an enrichment of the system; some claim, though, that the voluntary probation officer was introduced to alleviate the constant shortage of the professional probation officers.

Those serving the penalty of imprisonment may be released and put on parole by the parole board after they have served one-third of the sentence for a specific term or ten years of a life sentence. The board must be of the opinion that the convict has been genuinely rehabilitated. If a parolee violates the conditions of the parole, the parolee may be sent back to prison to serve the remaining part of his or her sentence. In 1974, 4.0% of all applications for parole were rejected. Of the prisoners released from prison, 54.4% were released on parole. About 80% of the parolees were discharged from prisons after having served more than 80% of their sentences, so the probation periods for parolees are generally very short (the majority are for two months). Only 5.8% of the parolees had their paroles revoked.

According to the prevailing scholarly opinion, the classical approach, emphasizing retribution, was headed after World War II to set a reasonable limitation on the criminal responsibility and punishment. Later on, the need for modernization was felt. Penal policy moved toward individualization of punishment and rehabilitation of the offender. In the last period, some scholars have returned to the idea of just punishment; most practitioners, though, still favor the idea of rehabilitation and are fairly optimistic as to its feasibility.

Criminal Procedure

General Principles

The procedure followed in criminal cases is the same throughout Japan. There is only one nationwide jurisdiction. The Code of Penal Procedure (1948) and the Rules of Penal Procedure (1949) are the main sources of law governing criminal procedure.

The Japanese law of criminal procedure is a mixture of European and Anglo-American law. After the Meiji Restoration, the Japanese Code of Criminal Procedure was enacted, first on the basis of French law (1890), and then on that of German law (1922). The new Code of Penal Procedure (1948) was adopted under the influence of American law, although, in its general scheme, there still remain traces of the old law.

The Code declares that the purpose of criminal procedure is to clarify the facts in criminal cases and to implement criminal laws fairly and speedily. At the same time, public welfare and security must be maintained and fundamental human rights observed. The principal task, therefore, is to establish the facts of the case. According to the Constitution, this process must be fair, speedy, and performed in the manner provided by law, in particular with preservation of all the accused's rights guaranteed by the Constitution and other laws.

Another objective is that innocent persons must not be punished. The underlying principle is the presumption of innocence. The new Constitution provides for basic human rights in criminal procedure, including the guarantee of due process and the prohibition against double jeopardy.

The present law adopted to a great extent the adversary principle as it has been thoroughly applied in the Anglo-American legal system. Proceedings are usually conducted in the form of attack and defense by the parties, and the initiative of the courts has come to be auxiliary.

As far as the general principles of criminal procedure are concerned, the basic change from prewar to postwar systems seems obvious and characteristic. But, in spite of this drastic change, the old style of solving the case by obtaining a confession is widely in existence even now, which may weaken the constitutional rights of the accused in exchange for the effective and earnest pursuit of truth.

Phases of Criminal Proceedings

Criminal proceedings consist of the following phases: investigation, prosecution, trial appeal, and, finally, extraordinary remedies.

The principal investigating agencies are the police and public prosecutors. Usually the police conduct an investigation and refer the case to the public prosecutor, who directs the police to make a further inquiry and sometimes proceeds to conduct his or her own independent investigation. The public prosecutors, if they are convinced of the guilt of the suspect, may file an information with the court to open the prosecution; they may also decide to suspend prosecution. The rate of suspended prosecution in 1984 was 8.3% for all crimes, but for larceny 44.1%, and for fraud 30.3%.

Public trial consists of such stages as the introductory procedure, opening statement, introduction of evidence, closing argument, and judgment. The structure of proceedings can be said to be an adversary system, and judges have no information before trial except the fact of indictment, but in fact they come to know the dossier of the case as the written evidence is presented to the court. And, in the final analysis, the prosecutor's indictment is approved by the court with very few exceptions (acquittals amounted to 0.1% in 1984). The party may appeal to a high court or, under certain conditions, further to the Supreme Court. A decision of the Supreme Court, or that of a high court from which no appeal is made, is final. However, even the final judgment can be revised by means of extraordinary proceedings. The first is an extraordinary *de novo* proceeding for the benefit of the defendant, requested by a prosecutor or the defendant, and the second is an extraordinary appeal to the Supreme Court, requested by the prosecutor-general and couched in terms of the violation of law. These proceedings are very rare, but currently the gate to an extraordinary *de novo* proceeding seems to be opening a bit wider. Up to now, in 8 cases the defendant has been found innocent, including cases of condemned criminals in 1983 through 1984. It means that in these cases convictions (resulting in death penalties) were proved clearly erroneous. It proves that the value of defendant's confession has been overestimated.

Rights of the Accused

The Constitution contains detailed provisions for defendants' rights. The main rights of a suspect as well as an accused are that no person shall be arrested except upon warrant issued by a competent judicial officer unless caught in the act. No person shall be detained without being at once informed of the charge against him or her and without the immediate privilege of counsel. Each search or seizure shall be made upon a separate warrant issued for adequate cause by a competent judicial officer. Torture by any public officer and cruel punishments are absolutely forbidden. In all criminal cases, the accused shall enjoy the right to a speedy and public trial by an impartial tribunal. The accused shall have the assistance of competent counsel, who shall, if the accused is unable to secure counsel by his or her own efforts, be assigned by the state. No person shall be compelled to testify against himself or herself, and a confession made under duress, torture, or threat shall not be admitted in evidence. The Code of Penal Procedure also guarantees an accused awaiting trial in custody the right to request release on bail, although under certain circumstances granting of bail depends on the discretion of the court. Needless to say, the accused has the right to appeal to a higher court.

The problem is, of course, how and to what extent these rights and principles are realized in the practice of criminal procedure. The interest of maintaining public order and finding the true facts of cases sometimes runs counter to the realization of the rights. For example, although the confessions under duress, torture, or threat shall not be admitted in evidence, in practice most of the confession records taken by the investigator have been found as voluntary by the court. It is difficult to claim the involuntariness solely because the accused has no right to ask his or her defense attorney to attend the inquiry as a witness. The right of the accused under pretrial detention to communicate privately with his or her defense attorney has been also restricted in practice.

Pretrial Detention

Arrested suspects must be taken by police to a public prosecutor within 48 hours. The public prosecutor must inform suspects immediately of the charges against them and of their right to counsel, and if the detention of the suspects is necessary and supported by reasonable grounds, the prosecutor must, within 24 hours, request a judge to issue a warrant for pretrial detention.

When the judge is asked to issue a warrant for detention, the judge interrogates the suspects and gives them an opportunity to offer explanations and examines the evidence submitted by the prosecutor. This procedure is closed to the public, but if a warrant is issued, the suspects may request the judge to disclose the grounds for detention in open court. According to the statistical data in 1984, 82.1% of the detained suspects were requested to be detained by the prosecutors, and 99.8% of requests were approved by the court.

As a rule, the period of detention is 10 days, but it may be extended to 20 days. In certain serious cases, an additional extension for up to 5 days is possible. Public prosecutors are requested to carry out their investigations within the time limit and to decide whether or not there is sufficient evidence to prosecute the detained. If they are convinced of the guilt of the suspects, they may file an information with the court to open their prosecution. Otherwise, the suspects must be immediately released. The period of detention fixed by law shall be observed, so even if they need more time to investigate the case they may not keep the suspects in custody any longer. But, a method of detaining suspects on another charge in order to investigate the original case still remains; this practice, however, is doubtful from the point of the rule of law.

As far as the period of detention after indictment is concerned, it is 2 months with the possibility of monthly renewal, where the accused may be released on bail.

Special Modes of Criminal Proceedings

Public prosecutors may institute relatively informal criminal actions in the summary courts (without public hearing) involving minor crimes, provided that the defendant makes no objection. However, fines over 200,000 yen ($1,000) may not be imposed and the defendant may always demand a formal trial if not satisfied with the sentence.

The Traffic Violation Fine System is a special procedure under which an offender who commits a minor traffic offense receives a notice from the police requiring the payment of a fine. If the fine is paid, the matter is over. If the fine is not paid, the case is dealt with under regular criminal procedures. This system was introduced in 1968 in order to deal with the growing number of traffic violations. At present, about 85% of the traffic violations are handled through this system.

Lay Participation in Criminal Proceedings

Japan has no such system as a grand jury. Since 1948, however, the Prosecution Investigation Committee, or Inquest of Prosecution, consists of lay people chosen by lot who investigate and control the discretionary power of the public prosecutors. The function of this body is to examine the propriety of the nonprosecutive dispositions by public prosecutors. It represents the sense of lay people, and offers quite a few decisions against the prosecutor's dispositions, especially in the cases of officer's corruption or environmental pollution. But, they have only advisory powers without any binding force to the prosecutors.

Currently, Japan also has no such system as a jury trial. Trial is conducted only by the official professional judges without any lay assessors. But, for a period, before World War II, the Jury Trial Law was in force (1923-1943). Even prior to its suspension the right to jury trial was only seldom exercised, and the trend emerged to trust the professional judge rather than lay jury. Recently, however, interest in the jury system is growing again among scholars.

Special Proceedings
for Juveniles

Under the Juvenile Law (1948), persons under 20 years of age are classified as juveniles and are subject to special procedures designed for their protection, education, and treatment. Not only juvenile offenders but also predelinquent juveniles who are likely to commit offenses come under this procedure. All the cases must be sent first to the family court, which is staffed with presentence investigators who are social workers. The trial shall be conducted in a friendly atmosphere with warm sympathy to the delinquent juveniles. It is an informal procedure and closed to the public. The family court may impose only educative measures, such as probation, commitment to the Child Education Home, commitment to the Juvenile Training School, and so on. Those measures are not deemed punishments. If the court finds it reasonable to impose punitive measures, the case may be referred to the public prosecutor, who prosecutes the juveniles over 16 years in an ordinary court.

The reform movement of Juvenile Law has also been under way. The proposals of dealing with elder juveniles (18 and 19 years) as adults were criticized as too punitive. But, the necessity to introduce the due process requirements in juvenile proceedings are worthy of much attention. They might promote the protection of the juvenile by making it necessary for the court to make absolutely sure that the alleged conduct has really taken place. However, if this were to lead to the adversary system with the participation of public prosecutors, it might have a negative effect on the educational character of the Juvenile Law.

Execution of Penal Measures
(Corrections)

Aims and Basic Principles

The present Penal Code and the Prison Law (1908) do not spell out the aims and basic principles of penal measures. However, it has been claimed that in practice the principle of rehabilitation through individualized treatment is dominant. Although there still remains some thought of retribution, there seems to be no question of the dominance of the principle of rehabilitation. However, recently the thought of protection of human rights of prisoners and their legal status has been gaining recognition. This trend may result in the reevaluation of the ideas of retribution and rehabilitation. The reform movement of the Prison Law has been also under way. The necessity to convert the prison management law into the prisoner treatment law has become obvious.

Use and Implementation
of Death Penalty

The death penalty is implemented by an order from the minister of justice within six months from the day the death sentence becomes final, with an extension of time if the defendant appeals. If a person sentenced to death is insane, or a woman sentenced to death is pregnant, the execution is stayed by order of the minister of justice until the defendant is deemed sane or the pregnancy is concluded. Death is by hanging at a prison in the presence of a public prosecutor, the assistant officer, and a director of the prison, or his or her representatives, who attest to the execution.

The number of persons sentenced to the death penalty and eventually executed has been very small in recent times (1 in 1982), although there are still quite a few offenders awaiting execution in prisons (28 in 1982). They are trying to apply for the extraordinary *de novo* proceedings or pardon and, in fact, as was mentioned above, 3 of them were released by the *de novo* proceedings.

Execution of
Deprivation of Liberty

Penal administration and the treatment of prisoners are regulated by the Prison Law (1908), the Prison Law Enforcement Regulations (1908), the Ordinance for Prisoners' Progressive Treatment (1933), the Prisoners' Classification Regulation (1972), and other directives of the Ministry of Justice. The basic Prison Law is dated. The reform movement started in 1967 and is still under way.

Since the Meiji Restoration, penal administration has been under the authority of the Bureau of Corrections of the Ministry of Justice, although from 1874 to 1903 it was under the authority of the Ministry of

Internal Affairs. The Bureau of Corrections is now responsible for the administration not only of prisons, houses of detention, and juvenile prisons but also of juvenile training schools, juvenile classification homes, and women's guidance homes.

Treatment of convicted prisoners is based on the classification and progressive system. The classification system introduced in 1949 has been substantially revised by the new Prisoners' Classification Regulations (1972). A specially equipped and staffed institution was established as a classification center in each of eight correction regions. The examination of offenders for classification purposes takes about two months. Under the regulations, there are two prisoner groups: one for custodial considerations (sex, nationality, age, prison term, degree of criminal inclination, mental or physical defect) and the other for treatment considerations (types of treatment required, such as training, schooling, therapy, and protection). Prisoners are assigned to suitable penal institutions in accordance with this classification, and the specific treatment program is prescribed on the basis of classification.

The progressive system is conducted under the Ordinance for Prisoners' Progressive Treatment (1933). The system has four grades starting with the lowest, or fourth, grade for newcomers. In principle, those who are placed in the fourth and third grades are confined in communal cells and those in second and first grades are in single cells at night. In the highest grades they enjoy extensive self-government and privileges. This system has had the merit of arousing the prisoners' aspiration to advance themselves, but it has a tendency to be practiced in a formalistic way not reflecting the extent of the prisoners' social adaptability. It may also be used simply as a means of controlling prisoners by the authority that has discretion to bestow favors, depending upon the inmate's behavior in the institution.

Japan has 58 prisons, 9 juvenile prisons, 3 medical prisons, 7 detention houses, 56 juvenile training schools, 53 juvenile classification homes, and 3 women's guidance homes. Besides the traditional type of closed prisons, there are 39 prison labor camps attached to prisons or juvenile prisons throughout Japan, 19 of which are of open-type "living in" camps. There are also open institutions for traffic offenders. In other ordinary prisons, a kind of open institutional treatment has been tried since 1965 as a sort of intermediate prison for those whose release date is close.

According to the statistical data, the average daily population of penal institutions in 1984 was 54,508. Among them the number of sentenced prisoners amounted to 45,036, while that of unconvicted prisoners 9,278. The rate of "Boryokudan" members among prisoners amounted to 28.6% in 1984. Prison population was at its lowest in 1975 (45,690), but thereafter it has increased gradually year by year. Among the newly admitted prisoners in 1984, 96% were male, 4% were female. In terms of age, 36.9% were in their 30's, 26.7% were in their 40's, 24.3% were in their 20's. Larceny was the most common offense committed by male prisoners, while drug-related offenses the most common among female offenders.

The rights and duties of inmates of the penal institutions are specified by Prison Law. Labor is compulsory for prisoners sentenced to imprisonment with labor. Those sentenced to imprisonment without labor and penal detention may be employed at their own request. Token wages are paid for prison labor, not high enough to stimulate prisoners to work. Vocational training is offered to those who might be rehabilitated easily as well as to youth and juvenile offenders. Such training is offered in addition to regular labor and includes the repair of automobiles, barbering, dressmaking, and the like. School education is given four hours a day to juveniles and other inmates who need such education. For juveniles and adult inmates, correspondence courses are encouraged.

Basically, convicted prisoners receive food, clothing, and medical care, while those awaiting trial may purchase their own food if they so desire. An interview between a prisoner and a visitor is conducted in the presence of a prison official, except in the case of an interview between unconvicted prisoners and their attorneys. All mail to and from prisoners is censored. To prevent escape, violence, and suicide, restraining instruments, such as straight jackets, handcuffs, and arresting ropes, are used, but no chains. Revolvers, gas guns, and police sticks are used, but no swords. Japanese prisons are, as a whole, safe and well protected inside as well as outside. The number of accidents in penal institutions has not increased recently in spite of the increase in prison population and especially the growing number of "Boryokudan" members. In 1984, there were only 3 escapes from the penal institutions and 10 suicides.

Outstanding prisoner conduct is rewarded, and any inmate who violates prison rules is liable to receive disciplinary punishment, such as reprimand, suspension of privileges or physical exercise, reduction of food, or minor or major solitary confinement. Punishment is not regulated by the law, and reformers are proposing to introduce the guarantee of due process as well as to eliminate the punishment consisting in the reduction of food and major solitary confinement.

Under present law, inmates are entitled to submit petitions or complaints to either the minister of justice or to inspecting officers, but there is no regulation that obligates the authorities to answer promptly. The number of petitions by inmates has increased recently (792 in 1984), which seems to reflect the rising tendency of consciousness for rights among prisoners. The number of civil suits and criminal accusation is also on the increase.

The Japanese correctional system and its enforcement seem stable and well organized as a whole, but it still leaves wide room for further improvement, especially in the more open and liberal directions with more specific regulation of rights and duties of inmates. Much attention must be paid to the proposals that a social observation committee be introduced to soften the closed and secret character of the penal institution.

PART III

Socialist Law Systems

In this final portion are found descriptions of criminal justice of two socialist countries—the Union of Soviet Socialist Republics and the Polish People's Republic. These European socialist systems exhibit a level of apparent diversity that some may explain as being related to national characteristics, while others may suggest that even though they profess a common ideology, their criminal justice systems reflect the different paths of historical development in each country. In the USSR, the Revolution of 1917 seems to have caused a prompt rejection of the prerevolutionary system and by 1919 a new statement of principles of criminal law in the Russian Soviet Federative Socialist Republic. This statement argues that the proletariat should not adopt the ready-made bourgeois state machinery to its own aims, but abolish it and create its own system of justice. However, in those Eastern European countries that became socialist following World War II, there has been a greater tendency to maintain elements of the prior continental legal system.

When trying to understand these countries, the nonsocialist must realize that he or she is trying to study not only another legal system but one based on a totally opposite ideology. To understand properly socialist criminal justice, one must become well acquainted with a set of basic philosophical ideas of Marxist-Leninist thought. But it is also to recognize, as some scholars point out, that there are elements of the civil law tradition that are apparent in the socialist system of criminal justice. As pointed out in the introduction, some scholars continue to believe that there is not a separate legal family of socialist law. Finally, it is important to recognize that, to some extent, there are differences among the countries under review. When reading the chapters one must ask the question as to whether the particular phenomenon can be explained by the fact that we are dealing with the socialist family of law or simply because the individual element is part of the particular national heritage.

7

The Union of
Soviet Socialist Republics

VALERY M. SAVITSKY
VICTOR M. KOGAN

I. General Information

The Union of Soviet Socialist Republics *(USSR)* is a multi-national state formed on the principle of socialist federalism as a result of the free self-determination of nations and the voluntary association of equal Soviet Socialist Republics (Art. 70 of the 1977 Soviet Constitution). There are fifteen Union Republics in the USSR. Through their representatives, all of them take part in decision-making processes of the Supreme Soviet of the USSR, the Presidium of the Supreme Soviet of the USSR, the Council of Ministers of the USSR, the Supreme Court of the USSR, and other federal organs of power. As of January 1, 1984, the population of the Soviet Union was 274 million people, out of which 65 percent lived in cities and towns.

The highest body of state authority is the Supreme Soviet, which consists of two chambers: the Soviet of the Union and the Soviet of Nationalities. The two chambers have equal rights. Deputies to the Supreme Soviet are elected in universal, equal, secret, and direct suffrage for a five-year term of office. Laws of the USSR are enacted by the Supreme Soviet of the USSR or by a nationwide vote (referendum) held by its decision.

The Legal System

There is a uniform system of legislative regulation of social relations. The Supreme Soviet of the USSR promulgates Fundamentals of Legislation of the USSR and the Union Republics in each major branch of law in the area of criminal justice, (e.g., the Fundamentals of Criminal Legislation, the Fundamentals of Criminal Procedure, and the Fundamentals of Corrective Labor Legislation). The Fundamentals stipulate the basic provisions of law and the main legal institutions. Then, each Union republic adopts its own codes (the penal code, code of criminal procedure, and corrective-labor code), based on the essential provisions of the relevant Fundamentals. As regards detailed regulation, however, the codes reflect geographic, economic, national, and other characteristics of each republic.

For example, crimes which constitute relics of local customs are specified only in the Criminal Code of the Russian Soviet Republic. It must be explained that such relics as the payment of bride money, abduction of the bride or polygamy surface on rare occasions in Northern Caucasus. The right of the victim to participate in court proceedings is handled differently in each republic. For example, in Latvia and Estonia, this right is not restricted. In Lithuania and Uzbekistan, a victim has the right to speak in court if the procurator does not take part in the trial. In Moldavia, a victim has such right only in a certain category of cases. In other republics a victim has no right to participate in judicial proceedings.

Judicial decisions do not have the power of precedent and must be pronounced in strict conformity with the legislation in force. In practice, though, a major role is played by the so-called "guiding explanations," issued by Plenums of the Supreme Court of the USSR. Compliance with such explanations is obligatory for the courts, other bodies, and officials involved in the application of the laws subject of such explanations.

Amount, Structure, and
Dynamics of Criminality

In any consideration of the quantitative and qualitative aspect of criminality it should be borne in mind that crime is an act inseparably linked with its evaluation in criminal law. The amount of criminality, both in some definite period of time and in its dynamics, therefore, depends not only on the number of socially dangerous acts actually committed but also on the following factors: the expansion or reduction in the law itself of the number of categories of acts which are deemed to be criminal; the intensity of criminal justice bodies' involvement in combatting crime; and, finally, the characteristics of individual categories of crime, for the reaction of society to criminal acts differs from one category of crime to another, and, consequently, so does the detection rate. For example, following the promulgation of the USSR Supreme Soviet decree "On Increasing the Responsibility for Hooliganism" (July 26, 1966), the number of convictions for hooliganism in 1967 was twice as high as that in 1965. This, however, certainly does not mean that there were twice as many acts of hooliganism in 1967 as in 1965. Another factor to be taken into account is the victim's reaction to the crime. Selective survey data indicate that crimes reported by citizens accounted for 98 percent of registered murders and grievous bodily injuries, but 80 percent of women who had to be hospitalized after a criminal abortion denied that such abortions had taken place. The reliability of quantitative indicators, therefore, varies greatly from one category of crimes to another.

It may be assumed, though, that the longer the period under review, the more reliable are the quantitative indicators of criminality, and the more obvious their relationship with a given social system and with living conditions of the people. It is estimated that during 60 years of Soviet power the crime rate in the USSR has been reduced three and a half times.

At present, the distribution of the most frequently occurring crimes is as follows: hooliganism—eighteen to twenty-five percent; theft, embezzlement, and misappropriation of socialist property other than petty theft—fifteen to eighteen percent; crimes against personal property, including theft and robbery—fourteen to sixteen percent; crimes against the person—including murder, grievous bodily injuries, and rape—six to seven percent.

Crimes committed by juveniles account for eight to twelve percent of all crime. Theft and hooliganism predominate. They account for approximately 80 percent of juvenile delinquent acts.

Persons with previous criminal records commit one crime out of every three; special recidivism varies significantly: two percent of murderers have previously been convicted for homicide, seventy five percent of thieves have committed thefts previously.

At the present stage of the development of the Soviet society the causes of criminality are of a complex nature. The substantial rates of economic growth, combined with the need for the modernization of production processes place stringent demands on management. In some cases, this results in malfunctions in certain social institutions. Such malfunctions as the violation of the principle of distribution according to work performance, poor management, and insufficiency of consumer goods and services, have a definite impact on the structure and dynamics of profit-oriented crimes. As is known, human behavior is influenced not only by the material living standards of an individual but also by one's subjective evaluation of these standards. Selective survey data indicate that criminality is relatively higher in those areas where the differences in living standards are greater, compared to the areas where these standards are lower. While crimes for profit are rational in nature, i.e., they can be rationalized in terms of categories of "the end" and "the means," violent crimes represent usually irrational behavior which is incomprehensible without deeper psychological analysis. Selective survey data show that persons involved in simple manual work commit more than half of premeditated murders, grievous bodily injuries and acts of hooliganism. The lower the technological and organizational level of manual work, the smaller the degree of satisfaction of man's basic needs, and the more difficult it is for him to develop the needs associated with spiritual advancement. This analysis leads to the conclusion that anti-social behavior is motivated by both social and psychological factors. It is well-known that there is a relationship between a job with a lower intellectual content, on the one hand, and, on the other, a lower educational level, diminished participation in production management, a lower level of socio-political involvement, and, as a consequence, a relatively low level of social integration. Thus, the probability of these factors evolving into criminal behavior in the sphere of everyday life—where individualistic orientations fraught with personal conflicts and outmoded traditions which promote criminal ways of settling such conflicts, are most pronounced—and in the sphere of leisure, which is a natural area of compensation for lack of success in studies, work or in family life.

Recent Soviet criminological studies indicate that the contemporary criminality can be characterized as follows: (a) in general, crime in the Soviet Union is on the decline; there is a more pronounced differentiation among various categories of crime as regards the place and time of their commission; (b) there is a decline in the level of social dangerousness of registered crimes on the whole, while theft of personal property and crimes committed by officials in connection with the performance of their duties are on the increase; (c) certain categories of crime, which were associated with the period of transition from capitalism to socialism, are gradually disappearing.

Timely solution of the tasks faced by society, advancement along the path of social progress, improved well-being of the people, and more developed culture and conscientiousness of the broadest masses are all essential factors in the effort to combat crime. In addition, a system of crime prevention planning measures must also be mentioned. This system is an integral part of social planning which is closely linked with the socio-economic development plans of republics, regions, areas, cities and towns, and work collectives. A substantial decline in crime which has taken place during the years of Soviet power convincingly demonstrates that socialist societies have a major potential as regards crime prevention.

Criminal Justice Agencies

Soviet courts include the Supreme Court of the USSR; the Supreme Courts of Union Republics; the Supreme Courts of Autonomous Republics and Territories; regional and city courts, courts of autonomous Areas, district people's courts, and military tribunals in the Armed Forces.

District people's courts are the main element of the Soviet judicial system. These courts, which function only as courts of first instance, hear 98 percent of all civil and criminal cases. The higher courts function both as courts of first instance (in a limited number of more important and complicated cases) and as courts which supervise the propriety of lower court's decisions.

All judges and people's assessors (lay judges) of all courts, with no exception, are elected. The minimum age limit to be elected is 25.

Judges of district people's courts are elected by the population of the district in universal, equal, secret, and direct suffrage for a five-year term. People's assessors of people's courts are elected by a show of hands at meetings of citizens held at their places of work or residence for a term of two and a half years.

Higher courts are elected for five-year terms by the corresponding Soviet of People's Deputies. For instance, the judges and people's assessors of the Supreme Court of the USSR are elected by the Supreme Soviet of the USSR.

In 1982, the total number of elected judges was 10,303. Judges under forty years of age accounted for over fifty percent, women for thirty six percent. Among over seven hundred fifty thousand people's assessors of district courts elected in 1984, fifty five percent were Communist Party members and members of the Young Communist League (Komsomol);

twenty five percent of those elected were under thirty.

Judges and people's assessors are accountable to their constituencies and may be recalled by them in the manner prescribed by law. In recent years, some judges in the Azerbaijan and Turkmen Republics, in Chuvash Autonomous Republic, Krasnodar Territory, and Tula and Vitebsk Regions have been recalled because of their improper behavior which was incompatible with the high office of the judge.

The Procurator-General of the USSR and the procurators subordinate to him have the general power of supervision over the observance of laws by all ministries, state committees and departments, enterprises, institutions and organizations, executive-administrative bodies of local Soviets of People's Deputies, collective farms, co-operatives and other social organizations, officials, and citizens.

Procurator's offices are structured and function on the principle of centralization. The Procurator-General of the USSR is appointed by the Supreme Soviet of the USSR for a five-year term. All other procurators are appointed for the same term by the Procurator-General of the USSR or with the latter's approval.

Procurator's offices exercise their power independently of any local authorities and are subordinate only to the Procurator-General of the USSR.

Under the "Law of the USSR on the Procurator's Office of the USSR" (November 30, 1979), procurators possess broad powers as regards crime control. They exercise supervision over the observance of laws by the organs of inquiry and preliminary investigation; during the hearing of criminal cases in courts; in places of detention and preliminary confinement, during the execution of punishment and other measures of coercion applied pursuant to a court decision. The procurators' offices are entrusted with the task of working out, jointly with other state bodies, measures to prevent crime and other offenses, and coordinating the activities of all law enforcement agencies in the area of crime control. Directives issued by the Procurator-General of the USSR on questions of investigative work must be complied with by all investigative bodies.

The Ministry of the Interior of the USSR, and the Ministries of the Interior of the Union Republics are also part of the criminal justice system. One component of the Ministries of the Interior is the Militia, which protect public order, are involved in maintaining the safety of road traffic, pursue the investigation of crime and offenders, and conduct inquiry of certain, uncomplicated in nature, categories of crime. The investigators employed by the Ministry of the Interior investigate most crimes committed. The Ministry is in charge of places of pre-trial confinement of suspects, as well as prisons and corrective-labor colonies where the convicts serve their sentences.

The Ministry of Justice of the USSR and the Ministries of Justice of the Union Republics exercise organizational guidance with regard to courts. The ministries provide training and advanced training of judges, and are responsible for the holding of elections of judges and people's assessors, for the maintenance of court premises, etc.

II. Substantive Criminal Law

General Principles of Responsibility

Soviet criminal legislation has as its task the protection of the social system of the USSR, its political and economic systems, socialist property, the person, rights and freedoms of citizens and the whole of the socialist law and order. To carry out this task, criminal legislation of the USSR and the Union Republics determines which socially dangerous acts are criminal and establishes the penalties to be applied to persons who have committed offenses.

The current Fundamentals of Criminal Legislation of the USSR and the Union Republics, adopted on December 25, 1958 (hereinafter referred to as FCL); and criminal codes of the Union Republics constitute the main sources of the Soviet criminal law.

The criminality and punishability of an act are determined by the law in force at the time of the commission of the act. Laws decriminalizing an act previously deemed criminal, or mitigating a punishment, shall be applied retroactively. In turn, laws establishing the punishability of an act or increasing a punishment shall be applied only prospectively (Art. 6 of the Fundamentals). All-Union laws enter into force on the territory of the USSR ten days after their publication unless the statute provides otherwise.

All persons who have committed crimes on the territory of the USSR are subject to Soviet criminal laws; the question of the criminal responsibility of diplomatic representatives or other persons who are not subject to the jurisdiction of Soviet courts in criminal cases is resolved through diplomatic channels. Citizens of the USSR who have committed crimes abroad are subject to criminal responsibility under Soviet criminal laws. If those persons have served punishment abroad for the crimes they have committed, the Soviet court may mitigate the sentence or completely relieve the guilty person from serving the punishment. Foreign nationals are subject to responsibility under the Soviet criminal laws for crimes committed outside the boundaries of the USSR, in the instances provided for by international treaties (The Fundamentals, Articles 4 and 5). If the criminal act committed by a foreigner outside the boundaries of the Soviet Union is not covered by an international treaty (for instance, such a grave crime as an espionage against the Soviet Union), the foreigner is not liable under the Soviet law.

Only a person guilty of committing a crime, i.e., a person who has committed, intentionally or by recklessness, a socially dangerous act provided for by the criminal law may be brought to criminal responsibility.

A crime is deemed committed intentionally where the person who has committed it was conscious of the socially dangerous nature of his or her act or omission, anticipated its socially dangerous consequences and intended such consequences to ensue (direct intent) or consciously allowed such consequences to ensue (indirect intent). A crime is deemed committed by recklessness if the defendant anticipated the possibility of socially dangerous consequences ensuing from his or her action or omission, but recklessly relied on their being prevented, i.e., committed an act of carelessness, or failed to anticipate the possibility of socially dangerous consequences, although he or she could and should have anticipated them, i.e., committed an act of negligence (Articles 8 and 9 of the Fundamentals). An important addition to these All-Union rules is contained in the Criminal Code of the Georgian SSR: if the law provides for a more severe punishment in view of some grave consequences which were not part of the original design, such a punishment may only be imposed if this person should and could have anticipated such consequences.

Some studies indicate that the ratio between crimes committed intentionally and those committed by recklessness is seven to one; the predominant role in the structure of criminality based on recklessness is played by traffic offenses (approximately seventy five percent) and negligence by officials (approximately twenty percent).

Only physical persons who, as a rule, have attained 16 years of age when the crime was committed, are subject to criminal responsibility. Persons between 14 and 16 are subject to criminal responsibility only for murder; intentional bodily injuries causing serious harm; rape; robbery; theft; malicious or especially malicious hooliganism; intentional destruction of or damage to state, social, or personal property resulting in grave consequences; theft of firearms, munitions, or explosives; theft of narcotics; as well as intentional acts which can result in a train accident.

Soviet criminal law establishes criminal responsibility not only for completed crimes but also for the preparation of a crime and for attempted crime. According to one study, attempted crimes accounted for 17 percent of rape cases and 30 percent of homicide cases heard by the courts. Preparation is defined as the procurement or adaptation of means or instruments or any other intentional creation of conditions for the commission of a crime. An intentional action directed immediately toward the commission of a crime, where the crime has not been brought to completion for reasons not depending on the will of the guilty person, is deemed to constitute an attempt. In some cases the legislature has defined the offense in such a way that it is deemed completed already at the stage of attempt (for instance, the crime of false accusation of a person as an alleged perpetrator of a crime is completed whether or not criminal proceedings have been instituted as a result of such accusation) or even at the stage of preparation (for example, mere participation in a criminal band). To prevent the occurrence of serious consequences, the legislature made punishable a mere threat of homicide, or the infliction of grievous bodily injury, or of the destruction of property by arson, provided that there were grounds to believe that the threat would be put into effect. A person who has voluntarily abandoned the perpetration of a crime is not subject to criminal responsibility irrespective of the motivation of such abandonment unless the act actually committed by such person constitutes a separate offense.

Intentional joint participation of two or more persons in the commission of a crime constitutes complicity. The organizer, instigator and accessory is deemed to be an accomplice of the direct perpetrator. A person who has organized the commission of a crime or has directed its commission is deemed to be an organizer; a person who has incited the commission of a crime is an instigator; a person who has promoted the commission of a crime by advice, instructions, provision of means or removal of obstacles, and also a person who has promised beforehand to conceal the criminal, the instruments and means of commission of the crime, traces of the crime, or fruits of the crime, is deemed an accessory. Concealment, where not promised in advance, of a criminal, and also of instruments and means of commission of a crime, traces of a crime, or fruits of the crime, as well as failure to report the reliably known preparation or commission of a crime, do not constitute complicity and are punishable only in instances explicitly provided for by the criminal law. One study has shown that crimes committed in complicity constitute eighteen percent of all homicides, twenty percent of cases involving the infliction of grievous bodily injuries, thirty nine percent of rapes, forty three percent of malicious hooliganism, forty six percent of speculation (unauthorized sale of goods for profit), sixty three percent of thefts of state or social property (other than petty thefts), seventy five percent of acts of robbery and ninety nine percent of embezzlement of state or social property on an especially large scale.

A person who, at the time of the commission of a socially dangerous act, was *non compos mentis*, i.e., was unable to account for his or her actions or to govern them in consequence of a permanent mental illness, temporary mental derangement, mental deficiency or other pathological condition, is not subject to criminal responsibility (Art. 11 of the Fundamentals). Some studies indicate that fifteen to twenty percent of persons subjected to a psychiatric examination in connection with the institution of criminal proceedings were found to be *non compos mentis*.

If a formally prohibited act has been committed in a state of necessary defense, such an act is not criminal, provided that the necessary defense has not been excessive. Acts which would be allowed to make use of such a defense include protecting the interests of the Soviet state, social interests, or the person or rights of the defender or another person against a socially dangerous attack by causing harm to the aggressor. Clear disproportion between the defense and the nature and danger of the attack is deemed to be excessive. One study has established that 82 percent of persons present at the scene of the commission of a crime made use of self-defense.

An action by a citizen, aimed at apprehending a criminal, is legitimate and not criminal even if, as a result of such action, considerable harm was caused to the perpetrator of the crime. The Criminal Codes of the Ukrainian and Uzbek republics place the apprehension of a criminal within the scope of necessary defense. The Criminal Code of the Estonian SSR defines the right to the apprehension of a criminal as an independent institution of the criminal law.

An action which has been committed in a state of dire necessity, i.e., in order to eliminate a danger to the interests of the Soviet state, social interests, or the person or rights of the given person or other citizens, is not a crime, where in the given circumstances such danger could not have been averted by other means and where the harm caused is less substantial than the harm prevented.

The characteristic features of crimes provided for in the criminal codes of the Union Republics differ from one republic to another. For instance, ten republican codes provide a lesser penalty for a mother killing her newly-born child; in the Ukraine, Azerbaijan, Lithuania, Latvia, Tadzhikistan and Turkmenia, persons over the age of 14 at the time of the commission of the act are subject to criminal responsibility, while in Uzbekistan, Moldavia, Kirghizia, and Estonia, the minimum age limit is 16. The Criminal Code of the Armenian SSR provides for responsibility for red tape and foot-dragging in the consideration and introduction of inventions and innovators' proposals (Art. 188); the Criminal Code of the Kazakh SSR provides for responsibility for criminal mismanagement (Art. 150); the Criminal Code of the Uzbek SSR provides for responsibility for officials employed by enterprises, institutions, and organizations for failing, on a systematic basis, to take measures for the prevention of the embezzlement of state or social property, which failure has resulted in the spread of thefts (Art. 1142).

Selective survey data indicate that most judicial errors are associated with the application of those criminal law rules which require making a value-judgment. For instance, in the course of appeal proceedings, errors have been found in every fourth case involving necessary defense, and every third case of hooliganism.

Penal Measures

The substance or the essence of criminal punishment is a set of restrictions of rights which bring about suffering to the convicts (retribution). Under Soviet criminal law, the aim of punishment is the rehabilitation and re-education of the convict, as well as the prevention of new crime by the convict or by other persons, i.e., both general and special prevention (Art. 20 of the Fundamentals). In addition to political educational work, socially useful labor, general education and vocational training, retribution is one of the means used for attaining the goals of punishment.

The type and amount of punishment express its qualitative and quantitative characteristics.

The following types of punishment are known to Soviet criminal law: deprivation of liberty for terms ranging from three months to fifteen years (in cases when the death penalty is commuted to deprivation of liberty by way of pardon, the term of that punishment may be for more than fifteen years but for no more than twenty years); exile, restricted residence for a period ranging from two to five years; corrective labor without deprivation of liberty (two months to two years); deprivation of the right to hold specific positions or engage in specific activity (for a period from one to five years); a fine from 50 to 1,000 rubles (this measure is not known in the criminal codes of two republics); dismissal from office; deprivation of parental rights (not known in three republican codes); restitution (only in the Criminal Code of RSFSR); the social reprimand; confiscation of property; deprivation of military and other ranks. Punishment imposed on servicemen in the short-term military service may consist of an assignment to a disciplinary battalion for a period ranging from three months to two years. People found guilty of loitering or begging, or leading some other parasitic way of life, may also be subject to punishment in the form of assignment to an educational-labor dispensary for a period from one to two years.

Pending its abolition, application of the death penalty—by shooting—is allowed as an exceptional measure of punishment for crimes against the State (treason, espionage, terrorism, and subversion), for murder under aggravating circumstances, and also in other instances specifically provided for in the Soviet legislation, for example, in the case of an assault under aggravating circumstances on the life of a militiaman or a member of a volunteer public order squad; rape under aggravating circumstances (of a minor, group rape, or resulting in the death of the victim); aircraft hijacking under aggravating circumstances; embezzlement of state or social property on an especially large scale. Persons under eighteen years of age at the time of the commission of a crime and women who were pregnant at the time of the commission of a crime or at the time of sentencing or at the time of execution, are not subject to the death penalty.

The death penalty may be imposed by the court only in a case when its application is necessary in view of special circumstances aggravating the responsibility and the exceptional danger of the person who has committed the crime. The grounds for the application of the death penalty must be given in the judicial decision.

Imposition of Punishment

The court must impose punishment in strict accordance with the law and within the limits established by relevant articles of criminal codes. In imposing punishment, the court, guided by socialist legal consciousness, takes into consideration the nature and degree of social danger of the committed crime, the degree in which criminal intention was put into effect (if the crime was not completed), the degree and nature of the participation of each of the perpetrators if a crime was committed in complicity, the personality of the offender, and the mitigating or aggravating circumstances.

Taking into account the nature and degree of social danger of the committed crime, the personality of the offender, and other circumstances of the case, the court may, when it finds that it is possible to rehabilitate and re-educate the offender without isolating him or her from society while exercising due supervision over the offender, impose a suspended sentence of deprivation of liberty coupled with compulsory involvement in work throughout the period of punishment. This form of sentencing may be applied with respect to the offender who is able to work and who has not been previously sentenced to the deprivation of liberty. In addition, the penalty provided for by the law may not exceed 3 years of deprivation of liberty if the crime involved is intentional and 5 years if it is based on recklessness.

In imposing punishment on a person sentenced for the first time to deprivation of liberty for a term of up to three years, the court may suspend the execution of the sentence for a term from one to two years. In this case, the court may impose certain obligations: to undertake work or schooling, to refrain from visiting specified localities, to undergo a specific medical treatment (for example, an anti-alcohol therapy), etc.

When in imposing punishment in the form of deprivation of liberty or corrective labor, the court comes to the conclusion, taking into account the circumstances of the case and the personality of the offender, that it would be inappropriate for the offender to serve the punishment assigned, it may order the conditional non-execution of the punishment and establish a probationary period from one to five years.

Taking into consideration the exceptional circumstances of the case and the personality of the offender, the court may deem it necessary to impose an extraordinarily mitigated punishment, that is, below the minimum limit provided for by the law for the given crime.

Some studies indicate that fewer than fifty percent of offenders are sentenced to deprivation of liberty, twenty percent to corrective labor and seven percent are fined. Forty percent of those sentenced to deprivation of liberty for a period from one to three years receive conditional sentences including the duty to work. Stay of execution of the sentence has been applied to every fifth convicted minor and to every second juvenile, when such procedure was allowed by the law.

Most extraordinarily mitigated punishments were imposed for rape under aggravating circumstances (35.5 percent); the least frequently were such punishments imposed for infliction of grievous bodily injuries (1.7 percent); punishments near the lowest penalty limit most frequently imposed for malicious hooliganism (72.3 percent) and least frequently for premeditated murder under aggravating circumstances (38 per cent); middle-range penalties were most frequently imposed for theft of personal, state, or social property (15 percent), and rarely for resistance to a militiaman (3.1 percent); most of the punishments which were near maximum limit were imposed for premeditated murder under aggravating circumstances (58.6 percent), while the least of such sentences involved rape (11.8 percent). In a study which surveyed 19 categories of crime, in 16 of them most sentences were below the medium sanction provided for by the law; the punishment imposed by the court was "shifted" toward the highest limit of punishment only in two of these categories: premeditated murder and hooliganism, both in the absence of aggravating circumstances.

Relief from Punishment

A person who has committed a formally prohibited act may be relieved of criminal responsibility when it is deemed that, by the time of investigation or court proceedings, the act has lost its socially dangerous nature or the person has ceased to be socially dangerous because of a change in the circumstances.

A person who has committed a crime may be relieved from punishment by the court decision where it is deemed that, by virtue of his or her subsequent impeccable behavior and honest attitude to work, such person by the time of the court hearing, is not socially dangerous.

A person who has committed a formally prohibited act which does not present a major social danger may be relieved from criminal responsibility where it is deemed that the rehabilitation and re-education of this person is feasible without the application of criminal punishment. In this event one of the following decisions provided for by the law may be made:

(1) to bring the person to administrative responsibility;
(2) to transfer the case to a comrades' court for its consideration;
(3) to transfer the case to a commission for minors;
(4) to assign the person to the supervision of a social organization or work collective (Art. 43 of the Fundamentals).

Compulsory Medical and
Educational Measures

A person who was *non compos mentis* at the time of the commission of a socially dangerous act, or a person of sound mind who has committed a crime but who before the judgment was rendered by the court, or during the execution of his sentence has become *non compos mentis*, may be subject to compulsory medical measures in the form of commitment to a psychiatric hospital. The decision in this matter belongs exclusively to the court. The treatment may be discontinued by the judicial ruling based upon certification by the medical facility that such person has recovered from the illness or that the latter has taken a course which makes the application of medical measures no longer necessary. Where the court does not deem it necessary to apply the said measures to the mentally deranged person, and, likewise, in the case of their discontinuance, the court may transfer such person to the care of relatives or guardians with compulsory medical supervision (Articles 58-61 of the Russian Penal Code).

To an alcoholic or drug addict who has committed a crime the court may apply, following medical certification of the perpetrator, both compulsory treatment and punishment for the crime committed. Such persons, sentenced to deprivation of liberty, are subject to compulsory treatment during the period of their confinement and, if necessary, following their release. A person sentenced to punishment not involving the deprivation of liberty and a person released from places of confinement are subject to compulsory treatment of alcoholism and drug addiction in medical facilities. The treatment may include a drug therapy and work regime. The court discontinues the compulsory treatment upon the recommendation of the medical facility (Art. 62 of the Penal Code of the Russian Republic).

When the court finds that the rehabilitation of the person under 18 who has committed a crime which presents no significant social danger is feasible without the application of criminal punishment, the court may apply compulsory educational measures which do not constitute punishment. These measures include: apology to the victim; reprimand, strict reprimand or a warning; transferring the minor to the custody of his or her parents or persons acting in their place; or assigning the juvenile to a work collective of social organization—with their consent—or to individual citizens, upon their request, for strict supervision; assigning a social education worker to the offender and placing the minor in a special facility for education, reform, or treatment (Art. 63 of the Penal Code of the Russian Republic).

III. Criminal Procedure

Principles of Criminal Procedure

The main sources of criminal procedure are: the Fundamentals of Criminal Procedure of the USSR and the Union Republics adopted on December 25, 1958, and the Republican Codes of Criminal Procedure, promulgated on the basis of the Fundamentals.

As provided for by Art. 151 of the USSR Constitution, justice in the USSR is administered only by the courts. No other authority may establish that a person is guilty of committing a crime: this belongs exclusively to the competence of the courts.

There are no special courts in the USSR. All citizens and officials are subject to the jurisdiction of general courts. "Justice is administered in the USSR on the principle of equality of citizens before the law and the court" (Art. 156 of the Constitution of the USSR).

As has already been mentioned, all Soviet judges are elected. This is one of the guarantees making judges and people's assessors (lay judges) independent and subject only to the law (Art. 155 of the USSR Constitution).

Any pressure or influence on judges aimed at making them render certain decisions is condemned by the law. True, most judges are Communists, but membership in the Communist Party does not restrict their actual independence. On the contrary, the Party Central Committees has strictly forbidden the local Party organs to interfere with the administration of justice. If such a prohibition is not observed by the local party leader, the latter is strictly punished, maybe even dismissed from his post, and the event is published in newspapers and magazines.

Criminal cases are almost never decided by a single judge sitting alone. In courts of first instance, cases are heard by one judge and two people's assessors; in the higher courts (courts of appeal and supervision) by three professional judges. Only in some rare cases of minor semi-administrative violations (e.g., petty hooliganism, petty speculation, etc.) a people's judge hears the case alone. Maximum penalty in such cases in 15 days' detention.

People's assessors hear all cases in the first instances, including cases in the Supreme Court of the USSR. People's assessors have the same rights as professional judges in decision-making on all matters of fact and law; all decisions are taken by a majority vote.

Article 157 of the USSR Constitution proclaims that proceedings in all courts shall be open to the public. Hearings *in camera* (behind the closed doors) are allowed only in cases provided for by the law (sex offenses, juvenile delinquency, cases connected with state secrets). Even in hearings behind the closed doors all rules of procedure must be observed.

The Soviet Union is a multinational state. In consequence, Court proceedings are conducted in the language of the union or autonomous Republic, of the autonomous province, or in the language the majority of the population of the area. The accused, the victim, and other persons participating in court proceedings who do not know the language in which they are being conducted, are ensured the right to become fully acquainted with the materials of the case. The services of an interpreter during the proceedings and the right to address the court in their own language are provided for by Art. 159 of the Constitution of the USSR.

The principle of presumption of innocence governs the whole Soviet criminal procedure. The main content, the core of the principle is provided for in Art. 160 of the 1977 Constitution of the USSR: "No one may be adjudged guilty of a crime and subjected to punishment as a criminal except by the judgment of a court and in conformity with the law." The Guiding Explanation issued by the Plenum of the Supreme Court of the USSR on June 16, 1978, reads: "The accused shall be deemed not guilty until his guilt has been proven in accordance with the procedure provided for by the law and established by a final court decision."

Presumption of innocence is provided for by other legal rules as well. For example, the court, the procurator, the investigator, and the person conducting the inquiry have the legal duty to undertake all measures allowed by the law for a comprehensive, thorough, and objective scrutiny of the circumstances of the case and expose with an equal force the circumstances which may lead to the conviction or the acquittal of the accused and also those which may mitigate or aggravate his responsibility. The court, the procurator, the investigator, and the person conducting preliminary inquiry may not shift the duty of proof to the accused. They are prohibited from seeking to obtain testimony from the accused through the use of force, threats, or any other illegal means (Art. 141 of the Fundamentals). Thus, testimony which was not given voluntarily is simply not admissible. In general, admission by the accused of his guilt is always approached with utmost caution. As expressed by Art. 77 of the Russian Code of Criminal Procedure, "An acknowledgment of guilt by the accused may be used as the basis for accusation only if corroborated by the totality of evidence available in the case."

Another important rule has been codified in the Fundamentals: "A judgement of conviction may not be based on assumptions and shall be rendered only where, in the course of the court hearing, the defendant's guilt in committing the crime has been proved" (Art. 430 of the Fundamentals). In other words, it is not assumption (even if reasonable) or probability (the highest as the case may be) but only accurate knowledge, which represents absolute truth as regards the relevant facts, that can serve as the basis for conviction. In consequence, the Guiding Explanation of the Supreme Court of the USSR of June 16, 1978, summarizes nicely the basic elements of the presumption of innocence: "The law stipulates that the burden of proof lies on the prosecutor. Hence, it is not admissible to put on the accused the burden of proving his innocence. The finding of guilt may not be based on assumptions. All doubts must be resolved in favor of the accused unless the doubts can be eliminated".

Another important principle is that of participation in criminal proceedings of members of the public. This principle is a reflection of one of the main trends in the development of the Soviet political system, that of broadening of socialist democracy. The 1977 Constitution and the new text of the Communist Party's Program (1986) envisage an ever greater involvement of citizens in running state and public affairs, the enhancement of the role of social organizations, and the need for constantly taking into account the public opinion. Soviet political doctrine holds that the USSR is, at present, a state of the whole people, without any class conflicts. In building developed socialism, the USSR relies on the conscientiousness of the masses and individual citizens, on their initiative and active work.

**Participants in
Criminal Proceedings**

The court is the main and principal participant in the trial. During criminal proceedings the other participants may address the court with different motions, present evidence, etc., but they are not able to make any decisions. This is a unique right of the court. The primary duty of the court is to establish the truth.

The Soviet theory of criminal procedure as well as judicial practice does not recognize formal (judicial) truth as a ground for conviction. The court decision should reflect objective (material) truth. This means that the conclusions reached by the court should fully correspond to what has taken place.

Preliminary (pre-trial) investigation of criminal cases is conducted by the investigators from the Procurator's Office, the Ministry of the Interior, or the State Security Committee. Their responsibilities are defined by law. Only some simple cases are examined by other agencies of inquiry, e.g., militia, fire brigade, etc. They function according to the same procedures, with minor exceptions, as the investigator does.

Investigators from the Procuracy have the right to investigate any case. In practice the majority of cases are investigated by the investigators from the Ministry of Interior. But the cases of murder and some instances of malfeasance in office, including crimes committed by the procurators and investigators from the procuracy, may be handled only by the procuracy.

Investigators of the State Security Committee investigate serious crimes against the State (treason, espionage, terrorism, subversion, etc.) a complete list of which is provided by the law (Art. 126 of the Russian Code of Criminal Procedure). Investigators of the State Security Committee are bound by the same rules which are established by the republican codes for investigators of the Procurator's Office and Ministry of the Interior. The Procurator's Office supervises investigations conducted by the Committee. The Committee's investigator must obtain the procurator's consent for a search, to detain a suspect, and to commit a case to trial.

The procurator supervises observance of the law. He is in charge of preliminary investigation. He exercises procedural direction and supervision over the work of all investigators, including those of the Ministry of the Interior and the State Security Committee. The prosecutor has broad and authoritative power; he may vacate unlawful decisions taken by the investigator, discharge an investigator, give the investigator binding directives, terminate cases, etc.

During the trial, the procurator acts on behalf of the State action, but must withdraw the accusation if the judicial investigation does not confirm the substance of the accusation. The procurator is obliged to submit a protest to a higher court concerning each unlawful or unsubstantiated judgment. However, the procurator has no authoritative or directive power *vis-à-vis* the court. He himself must obey the court's rulings.

The procurator's powers are provided for by an All-Union Law on the Procurator's Office of the USSR (1979), and are therefore identical in all the Union Republics.

Upon completing a preliminary investigation, the investigator or the procurator must advise orally or in writing the organization, enterprise, collective farm, etc., that their employee has committed a crime and that his case is being transferred to the court. Such information is usually made public at a general meeting of the workers or employees of the given enterprise or at a trade union meeting. People discuss the event and may decide to authorize one of their members to represent them in court. The appointed person is instructed to either support the prosecution or defend the colleague on behalf of the collective. The representative is guided by his conscience and facts exposed at the court's hearings. Depending on the course of the judicial investigation, he may change his position even if it differs from the one taken by the collective which appointed him. At present, a social prosecutor or a social defender participates in about every eighth judicial proceeding.

The accused, thanks to the presumption of innocence, enjoys ample rights which allow him to exercise the right to defense. The accused has the right to know what he is accused of; to present evidence; to enter petitions; to file complaints over the actions and decisions of the investigator, the procurator, the court; to make challenges; to acquaint himself, upon completion of the preliminary investigation, with all the material of the case; and to have defense counsel.

The accused person may be detained only by a court decision or on the warrant of a procurator (Art. 54 of the Constitution of the USSR). In the event of an unjustified detention, the accused person may file a complaint with a procurator at a higher level. The law does not make provision for the hearing of such complaints in a court.

As a general rule, pre-trial detention is allowed only for a period of up to two-months. In exceptional cases, the length of detention may be extended by the procurator of a Region, and then by the procurator of the Union Republic. Detention for the maximum term, that is, nine months, must be approved by the Procurator-General of the USSR. In practice, in the vast majority of cases, the length of pre-trial detention does not exceed two to three months.

In exceptional cases a suspect may be detained without the warrant of a procurator. This may take place when the suspect has been caught *in flagranti* (red handed), if stolen objects have been found in his possession, etc. This form of short detention may not continue for over

72 hours after which the detainee must be released or the procurator's warrant for arrest issued.

Advocates (professional defense attorneys), representatives of trade unions and of other social organizations may act as defense counsels. The defense counsel is requested to participate by the accused or by his relatives. On the accused's request, the investigator, the procurator, or the court must assign a defense counsel for him, and may relieve the accused, fully or in part, from payment for the advocate's services. In this case, the fee will be paid by the State.

The defense counsel participates in the criminal case from the moment when the preliminary investigation is completed and the accused person has been handed a record of the proceedings. However, if the accused person is a minor, deaf or blind, etc., the defense counsel may participate from the moment the indictment has been presented, i.e., when the accused has been handed the document where the investigator sets forth the essence of the accusation and specifies the charge. From the moment the indictment has been presented, the defense counsel may also participate in any other case but only with the prosecutor's consent. In practice, the consent is given rather frequently.

From the moment the defense counsel begins to participate in the case, he has the right—and needs no special permission—to meet the accused privately without any limits on the number and length of meetings; to acquaint himself with all the material of the case and to take notes; to take part, with the permission of the investigator, in certain investigatory actions; to file complaints against the actions and decisions of the investigator, the procurator, and the court.

The advocate has no right to abandon the defense of the accused once he has accepted the case. The accused, however, may dismiss the defense counsel at his own initiative at any stage of the investigatory or judicial proceedings.

The participants in criminal proceedings may also include: a victim, that is, a person who suffered moral, physical or property damage caused by the crime; a civil plaintiff, that is, the person or organization whose property is damaged by the crime; and a civil respondent, that is, the person who bears responsibility for the property damage caused by the crime (often it is the accused himself; it may also be his parents, legal representatives, etc.). In principle, the rights of these participants are equal to those of other participants. They may present evidence, make motions and challenges, acquaint themselves with the materials of the case, and file complaints over the actions and decisions of the investigator, the procurator, and the court.

Stages of Criminal Proceedings

Initiation of case. Case initiation is the initial stage of criminal proceedings. At this stage, the agency conducting the inquiry, the investigator, the procurator, or the judge, having been notified that a crime has been committed, prepares a special procedural act called the decree on the initiation of a criminal case. It is only after this action that acts aimed at the detection of evidence (searches, interrogations, etc.) are allowed.

Preliminary investigation. This is the second stage of the proceedings. The investigator has the duty to establish all the circumstances of the crime and the perpetrator. Having this aim in mind, the investigator conducts interrogations, searches, examinations, and other investigatory actions. When enough evidence has been obtained, he presents a decree in which he names the accused. Then, he makes a decision concerning the preventive measures which are to be taken with regard to the accused (bail, pre-trial detention, etc.) and continues to collect evidence. An investigation must be terminated if the period of limitation has expired, if it has been established that the accused person did not commit the offense, when an amnesty act has been promulgated, etc. However, if none of the above circumstances applies, and if the evidence collected points to the guilt of the accused, the investigator prepares an indictment and submits the case to the procurator. The latter has the duty to verify the materials of the case and to examine whether the rights of all the participants in the proceedings have been observed. Following this, he approves the indictment and refers it for substantive examination to the trial court.

Committal for trial. This stage is like a filter which screens off, as it were, cases which for various reasons do not merit going to trial. In this way, the persons against whom criminal proceedings have been instituted without sufficient grounds have an additional guarantee that they will not be tried. It must be emphasized that this stage the question of guilt is not yet being decided. The court does not verify the evidence but, makes only a prima facie determination whether any evidence exists in the case, determines whether the indictment is based on facts and whether formal requirements have been observed. In consequence, the decision to commit a person for trial does not mean he or she is guilty.

Committal for trial is, as a rule, accomplished by a judge acting alone. In some cases, however (where the judge disagrees with the conclusions reflected in the indictment, in cases of minors, etc.), the question has to be decided collectively, that is by the judge and two people's assessors. A procurator's opinion must be attached. As a result, the case may be terminated, sent back for additional investigation, or committed for trial.

The filtering function of this stage is reflected primarily in the fact that a significant percentage of cases are returned by the court to the procurator for an additional investigation. This happens when the court finds violations of procedural rules (e.g., the accused person has not been fully acquainted with the material of the case), instances of incorrect legal description of the act, or instances of incomplete examination of the circumstances of the case (e.g., if the accused person's alibi has not been verified, or the age of a minor has not been accurately established). Also, at this stage matters connected with the trial—such as the participation of the procurator, defense counsel, expert, etc., are resolved.

Court hearing. The court trial is the main, central stage in the criminal proceedings. Evidence is examined orally, directly, and without interruption. The adversary principle is fully applied here: the parties (the prosecutor, accused, defense counsel, victim, civil plaintiff, and civil respondent) enjoy equal rights in presenting evidence, participating in the scrutiny of the evidence, and in filing petitions (Art. 38 of the Fundamentals of Criminal Procedure).

The law states that in the following instances the participation of a defense counsel in the court proceedings is mandatory: (1) where a state prosecutor or a social prosecutor participates in the trial; (2) where the accused is a minor; (3) where the accused is incapable of exercising his right to defense on his own due to his physical or mental handicap; (4) where the accused does not speak the language in which the proceedings are conducted; (5) where a person is accused of committing a crime for which the death penalty may be imposed; (6) when more than one offender is tried jointly and the interests of one are in conflict or where at least one of them has a defense counsel (Art. 49 of the Russian Code of Criminal Procedure).

A court hearing is divided into several stages: a preparatory stage where the appearance of all summoned is checked, possible challenges are raised, etc.; a judicial investigation where the court and the parties interrogate the accused and the witnesses, assess the evidence, read protocols and other documents; a court debate where the parties evaluate the evidence and discuss the possible verdict; and the final statement by the accused.

The court hearing is completed and the decision in the case is rendered. The court may base its judgment only on the evidence which has been examined during the judicial hearing. The decision is prepared on the basis of the discussion held in a separate consultation chamber and no persons other than the judge and the two people's assessors examining the case may be present. All questions are settled by a simple majority vote. A judge or people's assessor in the minority may write a dissenting opinion.

Appeal proceedings. Any participant in the trial has the right to appeal the decision, within seven days, to a higher court. The punishment shall not be increased if the appeal has been lodged only by the convicted offender. The appeal court is not bound by the specifics of the appeal and examines the case in its entirety and with respect to all the persons convicted.

The procurator, the defense counsel, the convicted person and the victim may participate in the appeal hearing. Witnesses are not interrogated; only case files are examined. As a result of the examination of the case by way of appeal, the court may leave the judgment unchanged, vacate the judgment and refer the case for a new trial or a new investigation, vacate the judgment and terminate the case, or change the sentence to a milder one.

Execution of the judgment. This is the final stage of criminal proceedings. At this stage, the judgment has become final. It may not be appealed or vacated by the appeal court and it must be implemented. Obviously, the actual implementation of the punishment is not part of criminal proceeding. However, at this very last stage some procedural questions may arise such as suspension of the execution of punishment, relief from punishment due to illness, or conditional release from punishment before the expiration of the term, etc.

Finally, one may also distinguish the stage of *judicial supervision* and that of *re-opening of cases* because of newly discovered circumstances. These stages are aimed at an examination of the judgments which have already become final. Those measures are extraordinary in nature and we will not dwell upon them.

Summary proceedings are not widespread in the USSR. Since 1958, cases of willful non-support, minor acts of hooliganism, petty theft of state property, illegal tree-cutting, unlawful hunting, and some other minor offenses may be tried under a simplified procedure, with only a summary record being compiled. However, court hearings in these cases are conducted according to regular criminal procedure.

Proceedings involving cases of juvenile delinquency, committed by persons under 18 years of age, do not differ, in the most essential elements, from those of adults. However, there are additional procedural requirements to be noted: the conditions of life and education of the minor, the participation of any adult instigators must be ascertained; pre-trial detention is allowed only in exceptional cases, usually the minor is placed in care and custody of his parents or guardians; the interrogation of a minor is conducted with the participation of an educator; the participation of the defense counsel is mandatory; committal for trial is always made collectively; parents, or persons acting on their behalf, are summoned to court hearings and have the right to present evidence, to participate in the examination of evidence, to file petitions and to make challenges; minors more often than adults are sentenced to various educational measures, such as making apologies to the victim, or restitution, instead of criminal punishment.

IV. Execution of Penal Measures (Corrections)

The basic source of Soviet law of corrections is the Fundamentals of Corrective Labor Legislation of the USSR and the Union Republics, adopted on July 11, 1969.

Only a sentence which has been passed by a court of law and which has become final constitutes grounds for the execution of punishment.

Deprivation of liberty, exile, restricted residence, and corrective labor are deemed corrective-labor measures. Deprivation of the right to hold specified offices or to engage in specified activity, fines, public reprimand, confiscation of property, deprivation of military rank, and other forms of punishment provided for by the legislation of the Union Republics are not corrective-labor measures.

The basic means for the rehabilitation of persons on whom punishment in the form of corrective-labor measures was imposed are: the regime of serving the sentence; socially useful labor; political-educational work; and general and vocational-technical instruction.

Types of Corrective-Labor Institutions

The corrective-labor institutions executing sentences of deprivation of liberty include prisons, corrective-labor colonies, and educational labor colonies.

Men serving punishment are assigned as follows: those sentenced for the first time for crimes based on recklessness serve punishment in settlement colonies designed for this type of offender; those sentenced for the first time to deprivation of liberty for a term not exceeding five years for intentional crimes which are not grave and not listed in the law, are assigned to settlement colonies for persons who have committed intent-based crimes; those convicted for the first time of crimes which are not grave and are not listed as such in the law serve punishment in the colonies with a general regime; those sentenced to deprivation of liberty for the first time for grave crimes are assigned to colonies with a reinforced regime; those who are either convicted for especially dangerous crimes against the State or who have already served punishment in the form of deprivation of liberty are sent to colonies with a strict regime; those who are deemed especially dangerous recidivists, and convicts whose death sentences have been commuted by way of pardon or amnesty are directed to colonies with a special regime.

Women sentenced for the first time to deprivation of liberty for crimes based on recklessness serve punishment in settlement colonies designed for this category of offenders; those convicted for the first time of intentional crimes which are not grave and not enumerated by the law are sent to settlement colonies for persons who have committed intentional crimes; all other women sentenced to deprivation of liberty are assigned to colonies with a general regime but women convicted for especially dangerous crimes against the State, those deemed especially dangerous recidivists and those whose death sentence has been commuted to deprivation of liberty by way of pardon or amnesty, are assigned to colonies with a strict regime (Art. 14 of the Fundamentals).

Male minors sentenced to deprivation of liberty for the first time serve punishment in educational-labor colonies with a general regime; those who have previously served punishment in the form of deprivation of liberty are sent to educative-labor colonies with a reinforced regime. Female minors serve punishment in educative-labor colonies with a general regime (Art. 16 of the Fundamentals).

The conditions of serving sentences, that is, the number of visits, parcels, and freedom of movement within the territory of the colony vary from one category of colony to another. In corrective-labor settlement colonies of all types the convicts are kept under surveillance without guard; in the hours from the waking signal to the retirement signal, they can move freely within the bounds of the colony; with the permission of the colony's administration they may travel for work or study without surveillance outside the colony but within the bounds of the respective Region, Territory, Autonomous or Union Republic; they may wear civilian clothes, carry money and valuables, and use money without restriction; with the permission of the colony's administration and if housing conditions permit, they may live in the colony with their families, buy a dwelling house in accordance with the law in force, and set up a personal household in the colony's territory. Persons who have convincingly demonstrated progress in their rehabilitation may be transferred to such settlement colonies from colonies with general, reinforced, or strict regimes to encourage their rehabilitation (Art. 20 of the Fundamentals).

Prison sentences are served by especially dangerous recidivists sentenced to imprisonment; by persons who upon the attainment of 18 years of age have committed especially dangerous crimes against the State or other grave crimes for which they have been sentenced to deprivation of liberty for a term exceeding five years; and by convicts transferred, by a court ruling, from corrective-labor colonies for malicious violations of the regime. Prisons have two regimes: general and strict. A strict regime is applied to convicts which have previously served a term of imprisonment; persons sentenced to imprisonment for crimes committed in places of confinement; persons transferred from colonies to serve punishment in a prison; and persons transferred to a strict regime as a penalty for malicious violations of the institutional rules. A strict regime may be imposed for a period from two to six months (Art. 15 of the Fundamentals).

Employment of Persons
Serving Deprivation of Liberty

The administration of corrective-labor institutions has the duty to ensure the enlistment of the convicts in socially useful work with due consideration for their work ability and, if possible, their qualifications. An eight-hour working day is established for persons serving punishment in corrective-labor colonies and prisons; they are given one day off per week. The duration of the work day of the convicts serving punishment in corrective-labor colonies and the provision of days off every week is established in conformity with the general labor law rules. The work safety rules and labor protection regulations established by the general labor legislation apply in full.

The work of persons sentenced to deprivation of liberty is remunerated in accordance with its quantity and quality and on the basis of the norms and rates in effect in the national economy. The convicts' earnings are credited to them, with deductions representing partial reimbursement by them of the cost of maintenance of corrective-labor facilities. In educational-labor colonies, regardless of all deductions, not less than 45 percent of the total earnings of the convicts who do not violate the institutional rules must be credited to their personal accounts. Fifty percent or more of the total earnings of the convicts serving punishment in corrective-labor settlement colonies of all types is credited to their personal accounts (Articles 27-29 of the Fundamentals).

Conditional Release from Punishment Before the Expiration of Full Term; Substitution of Lighter Punishment

Adult, able-bodied persons serving punishment in places of confinement, with the exception of convicts serving sentences in settlement colonies, provided such persons can be further rehabilitated and re-educated without isolation from society, may be conditionally released by the court after they have actually served part of the term provided for by the law. The release is coupled with obligatory supervised labor in places determined by the agencies in charge of the execution of the sentence (Art. 53² of the Russian Penal Code).

Conditional pre-term release from punishment or substitution of a lighter punishment for the unserved part of the punishment may be applied by the court with respect to persons sentenced to deprivation of liberty, those conditionally sentenced to deprivation of liberty with obligatory labor, and those sentenced to exile, restricted residence, corrective labor or assignment to a disciplinary battalion or to an educational-labor dispensary, when such convicts have demonstrated their rehabilitation by exemplary conduct and honest attitude to work and have already served part of the term required by the law (Art. 53 of the Russian Penal Code).

Measures to Combat Recidivism

Some researchers have found that the proportion of recidivists is 3 percent among persons relieved of criminal responsibility with the transfer of the case to a comrades' court; five percent among persons relieved from criminal responsibility and transferred on parole; nine percent of those sentenced to corrective labor; and fifteen to eighteen

percent among persons conditionally released from places of confinement before the expiration of the term. Recidivism among persons who
have served a custodial penalty varies depending of the length of the
sentence, the type of colony, previous conviction record, and type of
crime, but is estimated at approximately forty percent. Eighty percent of
crimes committed by persons who have served punishment are perpetrated within three years following their release. The rate of recidivism is
highest within six months following the convicts' release.

The Soviet law makes provision for a range of special measures aimed
at the prevention of recidivism. Persons released from places of
confinement are provided with free travel to the place of their residence
or employment, and also with food or money for the duration of their
travel. They may also be given a lump-sum subsidy from a special fund.

Persons released from places of confinement shall be provided with
work (taking into account, if possible, their profession), within 15 days
after applying for help in obtaining employment. Instructions of the
executive committees of local Soviets of People's Deputies (local
government bodies) concerning the provision of employment to such
persons are binding on the heads of enterprises, institutions, and
organizations. The disabled and the aged shall be placed, at their
request, in homes for the disabled and the aged. Minor orphans shall be
sent to boarding schools or placed under guardianship under statutory
procedure (Art. 47 of the Fundamentals). Work collectives are obliged
to provide assistance to corrective-labor institutions in the effort to
obtain the rehabilitation and re-education of the convicts and, following
the latter's release from punishment, render assistance to them in job
placement and organize their everyday life.

Especially dangerous recidivists released from places of confinement
are placed under administrative supervision. Such supervision is also
established over some other categories of persons released from places
of confinement if either of the following conditions is present: (1) the
behavior of such persons in the places of confinement evidenced their
obstinate unwillingness to undertake an honest job and to follow the
path of rehabilitation, (2) after they have served their term of
punishment, or after they have been conditionally released from
punishment before the expiration of their term, they systematically
violated public order and the rules of socialist community life and
ignored warnings of agencies of the interior to discontinue anti-social
behavior.

**Supervision Over the
Execution of Punishment**

The 1979 Law on the Procurator's Office of the USSR (Articles 42-45) mandates that procurators exercise supervision over the observance of laws in places of confinement, preliminary detention, deprivation of liberty (prison and colonies), and during the execution of punishments which do not involve deprivation of liberty as well as in the application of other compulsory measures assigned by the court. The procurator may visit the institutions listed above at any time and does so systematically. He reads the documents on the basis of which the persons there were detained or put in preliminary detention, or sentenced to deprivation of liberty or to compulsory treatment or education. The procurator verifies the lawfulness of the orders, directives, and rulings issued by the administrative bodies of these institutions. He also interviews the persons in custody and those with regard to whom compulsory measures have been applied.

The procurator has the duty to suspend the execution of the orders, directives, and rulings issued by the administration of such institutions, and to file protests against them if they are contrary to the law. The procurator's rulings are binding for the administration of such institutions.

The procurator has the duty to immediately release from custody persons who are kept in places of confinement unlawfully or who have been detained or put in preliminary detention, or subjected to compulsory medical treatment or education in violation of the law.

All issues arising in connection with the execution of sentences (for instance, connected with the granting of a stay in the execution of a sentence, release due to illness, conditional pre-term release from punishment, replacement of the unserved part of the sentence by a milder punishment, etc.) shall be settled by the court with mandatory participation of the procurator.

8

Poland

STANISLAW J. FRANKOWSKI

Poland is over 1,000 years old. Once one of the greatest powers in Europe (sixteenth and seventeenth centuries), it was divided in the nineteenth century by its three neighbors (Prussia, Austria, and Russia), and is now a middle size country. It has a population of 37 million and covers a territory about the size of New Mexico.

In the past, Poland was often a battleground because of its location (Germany to the west, Russia to the east). During World War II, Poland lost one-sixth of its population and in 1945, with victory over the Nazis, was literally in ruins. Its capital, Warsaw, a flourishing city of 2.6 million before the war, was almost completely destroyed.

The Soviet Army entered the territory of prewar Poland in July of 1944 while fighting the Germans, and since then the country has been in the Soviet sphere of influence. The Communist Party (the Polish United Workers' Party) is a constitutionally recognized leading political force and it purports to exercise control over all important aspects of social and political life. The Party is a sovereign body of power (as is the communist party in every country following the Soviet model of communism). In Western terms, the Party combines the powers of the Parliament, the Cabinet, the Ministries, and all local authorities. The Political Bureau is its highest body combining, in fact, the roles of the supreme legislature, policymaker, and executive body. The Secretariat of the Central Committee (the executive cabinet) runs all the day-to-day affairs of the country. The membership of the Secretariat overlaps, to some extent, with that of the Politbureau. The head of the Secretariat (the First Secretary of the Party's Central Committee, currently, General Wojciech Jaruzelski) is, *ex officio*, also the chairman of the Political Bureau and, thus, the real leader of the country. Under the Secretariat exists the huge apparatus of the Party's Central Committee with its numerous departments that encompass, almost without exception, all aspects of the country's political, social, economic, and cultural life. This central body of real authority directly extends its power to all provinces, down to the finest administrative district, via the local committees of the party. All other institutions, such as the Parliament, the Council of Ministers, the local administrative bodies, the Army, the trade unions, the youth organizations, and even professional and civic associations, function under the constant and rigorous supervision of the party bodies. Most important, the formalized system of political appointments ("nomenklatura") enables the Party to fill all important positions outside the party's apparatus.

It must be stressed that the picture presented above is simplified. In fact, postwar Communist Poland has never been a fully totalitarian country and in many respects is unique among all other communist nations. First, almost 80% of the land is privately owned and cultivated. This is a clear deviation from classical Marxist thought according to which private ownership of major means of production (including land) must be abolished in a communism-building society. Polish farmers are not big landowners but they are economically independent and their lives cannot be as regimented as that of workers of a state-owned factory.

Second, the Catholic Church is flourishing. Poland is said to be a country of paradoxes and this is certainly one of them: a country run by a communist government with a predominantly Catholic population (over 90% of Poles consider themselves Roman-Catholics). When Karol Wojtyla was elected Pope John Paul II in 1979, the Church's spiritual power over the Polish nation became even greater. Although the Party owns or controls all the media (TV, radio, newspapers, and so on), it does not control the sermons delivered every Sunday by thousands of clergymen. With the imposition of martial law in December of 1981 and the downfall of Solidarity, the Church has become the most respected public institution.

Last but not least, Poland was the first communist country in which the working class revolted against the ruling party elite and created an independent political structure of its own. August of 1980, when Solidarity was born, was certainly a breathtaking event not just for the

Poles. In December of 1981, when the Martial Law was imposed, the movement was crushed. Nevertheless, General Jaruzelski was correct when he once said that Poland will probably never be the same: There shall be no return to either the Solidarity period (at least in the foreseeable future) nor to the pre-Solidarity one. Indeed, too much has changed, primarily in the sphere of social consciousness between August 1980 and December 1981. To put it bluntly, the Communist Party will not relinquish its power, but Poland must and will be governed differently given the many distinctive features of its sociopolitical life. It seems that the communist regime, out of necessity, has accepted this reality, however unpleasant: The relative openness in political life, fairly substantial religious and academic liberties, the existence of semiofficial political opposition (including the underground Solidarity), all these phenomena are virtually unknown in other communist countries (except, perhaps, Yugoslavia) and make everyday life tolerable, although not acceptable to most Poles.

Nevertheless, the current leadership has not been able to gain popular support and the deep sociopolitical and economic crisis will certainly continue for the years to come. The Polish nation remains divided, the opposition movement unabated (although weakened) and the Catholic Church gains more and more strength and respectability. At the same time, the highly centralized Polish economy is not able to meet the most basic needs of the population. The standard of living in 1985 was lower than in 1979 and the debt to the West is growing steadily (estimated at 32 billion U.S. dollars in 1986).

General Description of
the Legal System

Polish law belongs to the socialist family of laws, but historically it is a part of the Romano-Germanic family with emphasis placed on the codified law—the law built in a systematic manner and phrased in general, abstract language. Formally, judicial decisions are not the source of law. For all practical purposes, however, Supreme Court decisions, especially the so-called "Practice Directives" must be viewed as universally binding, legal rules. Particularly until 1970, when the old, prewar legislation was still in force, the role of Supreme Court decisions was immense. In several instances, the Court's directives were in clear conflict with statutory rules. In the 1970s, the role of Supreme Court directives was of special importance in the field of sentencing. Almost invariably the Court favored tough penal policy by urging lower courts to apply harsh penalties either with respect to certain categories of offenders (e.g., recidivists) or certain categories of offenses (e.g., rape or offenses against social property).

In 1969, the new codes were passed: the Penal Code, the Code of Penal Procedure, and the Code on the Execution of Penalties. They all became effective on January 1, 1970. In 1971, the Code of Violations, acts of minor importance, formally not criminal offenses, was passed. In this way the Polish criminal law almost in its entirety has become codified. Very few changes were introduced in the 1970s.

After the creation of Solidarity in August 1980, the system of criminal justice became a subject of immense criticism. In October of 1980, over 100 Polish academics signed a memorandum urging the government to modernize the system along the lines of humanism and respect for human rights. In particular, the scholars were critical of the following basic deficiencies existing since 1945: an instrumental approach to criminal law, an overcriminalization of social and political life, an extremely harsh system of punishments, unsatisfactory protection of offender's procedural rights, and difficult prison conditions. In 1981, several progressive drafts were prepared, including some sponsored by the Solidarity. The December 1981 Decree on the State of War (known in the West as the Martial Law Decree) closed a very promising chapter in the postwar history of Poland.

The legislative changes introduced by the Decree, as well as by the subsequent legislation, may be divided into two categories. Some are emergency-type regulations, dictated clearly by narrow political considerations, which made the above mentioned shortcomings of the system only more pronounced. A good example of this retrograde trend are the two Laws of May 10, 1985, one amending the Penal Code and the Code of Criminal Procedure, the other one, On Special Criminal Responsibility (in force until June 30, 1988) containing a set of rules increasing the harshness of criminal law and simplifying the criminal procedure. The laws were strenuously opposed by the overwhelming majority of Polish scholars and by the Church. On the other hand, some other post-1981 legislative reforms are more in tune with the body of law reflected in the Codes of 1969. In particular, one may mention the new Law on the Prevention of Alcoholism, the Law on Juvenile Delinquency and Demoralization (both of October 26, 1982), and the Law on Prevention of Drug Addiction of January 31, 1985.

As far as the functioning of the system in practice is concerned, it is easily noticeable that the communist power elite has often used the system of criminal justice as a means of achieving current political goals defined exclusively by this very elite. In general, but especially in periods of political tensions, the law is perceived and used primarily as the instrument of political power. Its role is not to limit the state power, but to strengthen it. Short-term political expediency easily prevails over the letter of the law. Only in the period of relative political stability is the law given some autonomy, remaining, however, always at the mercy of political leaders.

Amount, Structure, and Dynamics of Criminality

In every country a gap exists between "official" and "actual" criminality. It is quite probable, though, that in communist Poland this gap has been more considerable, due primarily to the instrumental approach to the criminal justice system as a whole. For a long time it was claimed for propaganda reasons that the crime rate in communist Poland was much lower than in prewar, capitalist Poland. The alleged decrease in criminality was usually attributed to the new sociopolitical conditions that promote behavior patterns based on mutual respect and cooperation as opposed to capitalist individualism and competitiveness. No doubt, in certain categories of crimes the decline was real (e.g., in 1937, 1,306 persons were convicted of murder while in 1966 only 306). But it is difficult to tell with scientific certainty whether the overall level of criminality is lower than before the war because of the changing extent of criminalization, the "dark" number, the inaccuracies or even falsifications in reporting, and other problems too numerous to mention. But recently, according to official statistics, a significant increase in crime took place beginning in 1980 and continuing through 1984. This increase in crime (alleged or real), was given as a reason for introducing a series of laws providing for drastic penal measures and the simplification of criminal proceedings. This trend culminated in May 1985 with the promulgation of the already mentioned legislation. Already in April of 1986, it was announced that in 1985 the number of criminal investigations dropped for the first time in several years (by 3% compared to 1984) and the decline was attributed, of course, to the functioning of the Laws of May of 1985. Nevertheless, according to the same official sources, the level of criminality was still 50% higher than in the 1970s. Some Polish criminologists indicate that the statistical increase in criminality may not properly reflect reality and imply that the crime figures may have been artificially inflated.

According to official statistics, every fourth traditional crime may be causally related to the use of alcohol. In 1985, 77% of those suspected of murder, 82% suspected of rape, and 87% suspected of robbery were found drunk during the alleged commission of the crime. In passing, it may be noted that alcoholism has been, no doubt, one of the major social problems in postwar Poland. The number of persons drinking frequently is currently estimated at over 4 million and 500,000 are considered problem drinkers requiring medical treatment. In recent years, drug-related criminality has also become a source of considerable concern.

Political criminality, although statistically insignificant, has been the source of embarrassment for Jaruzelski's government. The use of the "stick and carrot" policy has become the rule. Each wave of arrests and convictions of underground Solidarity activists and other opposition figures has been invariably followed by an amnesty law and the political detainees were freed (e.g., 700 in 1984 and 300 in 1986).

Scope of Criminal Law

From one point of view, Polish criminal law may be described as modern: It does not attempt to regulate public morals. Adultery, prostitution, and homosexual practices among consenting adults in private were decriminalized already before the War. Social parasitism is not, strictly speaking, considered a crime, unlike most communist countries, although the Law of 1983 provides for the application of penal measures with respect to persons systematically evading socially useful work.

On the other hand, since the state is directly involved in running the economy, criminalization in this area is more extensive than in capitalist countries. For example, one may be held criminally liable for mismanagement while running a state firm if serious losses result. Another area of broad criminalization is politically oriented activities. A series of regulations promulgated after December 1981 were clearly aimed at suppressing various forms of social unrest and protest.

In the last two decades, the extent of criminalization has changed due to the process of differentiation between criminal offenses and semi-administrative violations. The latter are, as a rule, minor breaches of regulatory-type rules and are tried by administrative tribunals. Fines are the most frequently used sanctions; when the sentence is deprivation of liberty (the maximum time limit is three months), the decision is subject to judicial review. In practice, though, in some instances judicial supervision is purely illusory due to deficient procedural mechanisms. Two other features are noteworthy: (a) some violations were formerly classified as crimes (e.g., petty thefts or drunk driving); (b) in the last decade or so, the law of violations has been increasingly used to deal with antigovernment protesters. Charges of participating in unlawful demonstrations or gatherings, possession of printing appliances, and so on, have been brought against many political opponents of the regime. Short-term deprivation of liberty has often been imposed.

Structure and Functioning
of Law Enforcement Agencies

The police in Poland are centralized, as in most countries. They are subordinate to the Ministry of Internal Affairs. The functions of the police (called the People's Militia) are manifold: to protect public order, to prevent crime, and, finally, to detect and investigate crime. Regarding the latter function, it must be stressed that police are not expected to act on their own but always under the supervision and guidance of the procurator.

The procurator's office is hierarchically organized on a countrywide basis with the Procurator General at the top. The principal function of procurators, as defined by law, is to ensure the strict observance of law by all state organs as well as by citizens. It may be said that the procurator is the key element in the Polish legal system, as in other socialist countries. The Procurator General is usually very highly ranked in the party hierarchy. In the field of criminal justice, the procurator is the one who either conducts preliminary investigations or supervises investigations carried on by other agencies. It is up to the procurator to indict suspects and act as a public accuser at trial. In public perception this is the main function of the procuracy.

In 1983, the Committee for the observance of Law, Public Order and Social Discipline, headed by the Minister of Interior, was created. This interdepartmental body, unknown in other communist countries, is charged with a duty of streamlining and coordinating the activities of all law enforcement agencies.

Courts are divided into three levels: local, district, and the Supreme Court. Most criminal cases are heard by local courts. District courts are primarily appellate in their function; they are also first instance courts in cases of serious offenses. The Supreme Court has appellate jurisdiction only. But it must be emphasized that its role is also to ensure the uniformity of judicial practice. In reality, the Supreme Court is used as the medium through which the party's general policies are transmitted to lower courts and, indirectly, to other state agencies.

The independence of judges has been constitutionally proclaimed. Especially since December 1981, though, they have been subject to close political scrutiny and supervision. In fact, as a result of an elaborate system of promotions, transfers, rewards, disciplinary penalties (including dismissal), judges in communist Poland have always been kept in subservient positions. It is worth noting that Supreme Justices are appointed for a five year period while all other judges until the age of retirement.

Finally, a few words about attorneys. In order to become a practicing attorney one must be admitted to the bar. The bar is a self-governing body composed of many collectives of attorneys. The collective is organized on a cooperative scheme. Profits are evenly divided among its members, but only up to a certain limit; the remainder goes to those who contributed most. Expenses are shared equally. An attorney may take any case; however, in practice, especially in large cities, most attorneys specialize either in civil or criminal matters. The social prestige of attorneys is quite high and they usually make more money than either judges or procurators. The Minister of Justice is authorized by law to perform certain supervisory functions over the bar. In the last decade, some prominent attorneys who have defended political activists have been subjected to disciplinary proceedings, suspension, and other forms of harassment.

Judges, procurators, and attorneys must receive legal training at the university level. As a matter of interest it may be noted that many Polish judges and procurators, especially at the lower levels, are women.

Substantive Criminal Law

The Principle of Legality

One of the fundamental principles of Polish law is the rule, expressed clearly in the Penal Code, that there can be no crime and therefore no punishment without being provided for by law. This means that no one can be subjected to criminal liability without having committed an act prohibited by the law in force, and no punishment other than that provided by the law may be applied (Article 1). It means the analogy rule, according to which criminal responsibility may also be based on the commission of an act that is only similar but not identical to the one prescribed explicitly by the law in force, is alien to the Polish criminal justice system. But it must be noted that there is less need for the rule of analogy under the Polish system in view of the broad language used fairly often by the legislature to define offenses.

The rule of strict construction has not been formally accepted but, for example, the Supreme Court quashed the conviction of an offender charged with an escape from a penal institution when it turned out that the offender was, in fact, a youth kept in a special correctional center. According to the 1977 ruling, the escape from a facility of that kind is not covered by the statute that refers only to penal institutions. It shows that, in general, courts tend to accept the interpretation favoring the accused. On the other hand, in many instances, especially when the case has political overtones, judges do not hesitate to interpret the law expansively. For example, in 1982, a person who painted on the wall the words "December 1981 will not be forgotten" was found guilty of the offense described as dissemination of "false information which may cause damage to the interest of the Polish People's Republic." Later on, though, the conviction was overturned by the Supreme Court.

The Code further requires that human conduct not only be formally prohibited by law but also socially dangerous to constitute an offense. This requirement is characteristic of socialist criminal law. This law is not satisfied with the legal prohibition: If the social danger of a formally prohibited act is not existent or is deemed insignificant, the act shall not constitute an offense. In such situations, the case must be dropped and may be transferred to a social court, to a disciplinary commission, or to another similar organ. The criterion of social danger, thus, reduces the scope of criminal responsibility. To avoid any misunderstanding, it must be emphasized that the social danger of an act cannot, by itself, make the act criminal. It is absolutely necessary that the act be formally prohibited by law. On the other hand, the concept of social danger makes the law more flexible, but always in favor of the accused: Some cases may be dismissed as noncriminal if their social danger is deemed to be insignificant. But it must not be ignored that this power gives a great deal of discretion to the law enforcement agencies.

Concerning retroactivity of laws, criminal responsibility may be incurred only when an act is prohibited by the law in force at the time of the commission of the act. This means that criminal laws in Poland are not retroactive. The principle of nonretroactivity was violated at least twice in Poland. A Decree passed in 1945 provided for criminal responsibility for "the traitors of the Polish Nation." This law was applied to those Polish nationals who, during the war, voluntarily changed their nationality by becoming German subjects. This form of conduct was not deemed criminal when it took place. Another Decree dealt with those responsible for the September 1939 defeat against Hitlerite Germany, again, not a crime at the time of its commission. The two Decrees were soon repealed; the second Decree was hardly ever used. Finally, it must be mentioned that serious objections have been raised with respect to the Martial Law Decree. The text of the Decree was promulgated only on December 14 but the Decree provided explicitly that it became effective on December 13.

The rule of nonretroactivity, however, is not deemed applicable to judicial decisions. As a result, a more extensive judicial interpretation is immediately adopted in the case under review even if the act, at the time of its commission, was not considered criminal in light of previous judicial decisions based on the same statute. The most striking example is the Supreme Court decision of the mid-1950s pertaining to willful nonsupport of a family member. In accordance with the law in force at that time (the relevant article of the 1932 Penal Code), the offense was not committed unless the nonsupport resulted in the poverty of a person entitled to support. Nevertheless, the Supreme Court decided that it was enough if the person deprived of support lived "under very difficult conditions"—clearly something less than the "poverty" required by the law. Formally, the law was not changed, but the scope of criminality was de facto extended. The new interpretation of the law (later quickly abandoned) was applied instantly to the offender whose case was reviewed by the Supreme Court. It must be noted that this evidently unjust outcome is fairly typical of the Romano-Germanic family of law, based on the fictitious (from a practical point of view) idea that judicial decisions do not constitute the source of law. Namely, it is assumed that the function of the court is to declare only what the law is and not to create it.

Finally, a few words on the concept of "void for vagueness." In short, the concept (in the American sense) has no place in the Polish legal system. First, there is no constitutional rule requiring that criminal laws be specific. Nevertheless, all Polish scholars emphasize that it is absolutely necessary to have criminal laws written in a precise and clear manner. Many offenses, though, following the European tradition, are described rather broadly. This is particularly true in the field of political offenses. But until recently the idea of supremacy of Parliament was understood in such a way that all properly passed laws were unconditionally valid and were not subject to any external control from the point of view of their compatibility with the Constitutional principles. In 1982, the Constitutional Tribunal was created. It is a body appointed by the Parliament to declare whether the laws conform to constitutional standards. It is far from clear, though, whether in the absence of a specific constitutional requirement of clarity and precision of criminal laws, a broadly phrased criminal statute could be declared as being not in compliance with the Constitution.

Age of Criminal Responsibility

As a general rule, persons over 17 at the time of the commission of an offense incur criminal responsibility. A person between 13 and 17 is a juvenile and is handled differently. A juvenile over 16 may be treated as an adult in exceptional cases, namely, if he or she commits one of several very serious offenses listed by the Code and if it seems highly probable that correctional or educational measures designed for juveniles would be ineffective. In these cases, however, the death penalty may not be the sentence. An offender over 17 but under 18 who has committed a less serious offense may be treated by the court as a juvenile and correctional or educational measures may be applied in place of penal measures.

The last category of offenders distinguished on the basis of age is a "youth," that is, a person under 21 at the time the court verdict is passed. The law says that while imposing a penalty on a youth, the court aims first to rehabilitate the youth by, for example, educating or teaching him or her a trade. In practice, though, the emphasis on rehabilitation often means increased social control and, in extreme cases, even a prolonged period of incarceration.

Responsibility of Corporations

Criminal responsibility of corporations is unknown in Poland as it is in all other socialist countries (except Yugoslavia). It is claimed that the personal responsibility of corporation officers is far more effective. Further, the soundness of corporate criminal responsibility in a communist country is put in doubt since all large corporations are social (state) property. Would it be advisable for the state to criminally punish its own enterprises? Some scholars say, however, that especially in such areas as the protection of the environment, where it is usually difficult to identify the individual offender and where in most cases only those on the lowest echelons are brought to responsibility, corporate criminal responsibility would be far more effective and just.

Mental Element (*Mens Rea*)

Another basic rule of Polish criminal law is that no crime can be committed without a guilty mind (*mens rea*). Consequently, strict liability, that is, liability irrespective of offender's fault, is rejected. The Code makes the following distinctions regarding the forms of *mens rea*: intent (direct or oblique), recklessness, and inadvertent negligence. The dividing line is drawn between intent and recklessness: All offenses based on intent are considered intentional; all other offenses, nonintentional. This distinction is of vital importance because nonintentional offenses are punishable only in cases provided for explicitly by law. In fact, there are relatively few nonintentional offenses known to the Code; basically, only intentional commission of an act constitutes an offense. It is imperative to have this limitation in mind while analyzing the scope of criminalization.

Ignorance of the criminal law does not preclude responsibility; the penalty, however, may be mitigated. Only exceptionally, when the ignorance is excusable, will the responsibility be excluded. For example, if a foreign tourist is misinformed by a Polish customs officer and, as a result, violates currency regulations, the tourist must be absolved if his or her ignorance is considered unavoidable. Until recently it seemed that the problem of ignorance of criminality was mostly of academic interest. However, some lawyers tried to rely on this defense while defending their clients charged under the Martial Law Decree. They claimed that the defendants had no opportunity to acquaint themselves with the provisions of the brand new Decree that criminalized—for the first time in the history of Poland—certain acts, such as participating in strikes. In most instances, this line of defense was not successful; the courts assumed that it was enough that knowledge of criminality of the acts charged was obtained from the mass media proclamation of the Decree; neither actual availability nor knowledge of the official text of the law were deemed relevant.

Preparation, Attempt, Complicity, Conspiracy

Mere preparation is not punishable unless the law provides otherwise. Instances of this kind are very rare (for example, espionage, treason, and similar serious political offenses). Curiously enough, mere preparation to commit a murder is not punishable. Attempt, as a rule, is punishable within the limits provided for the completed offense. Thus, theoretically, one could be sentenced to death for attempted murder. Obviously, in practice, attempts are treated more leniently.

When dealing with complicity, the Code distinguishes among the perpetrator, co-perpetrator, aider, and instigator. The perpetrator is not only the person who has committed an offense by himself or herself, but also the person who has directed the commission of a prohibited act by another. This unusual form of perpetration was introduced by the new Code to deal with organized crime, mainly of an economic nature. As a consequence, the leader ("brain") of a group organized to appropriate social property is to be regarded as the perpetrator even if he or she personally has not participated in the acts of appropriation.

Aiding and instigating are considered separate and independent forms of the commission of an offense. Theoretically, the instigator and aider are responsible for their own crime (e.g., murder committed in the form of instigation) even if the person instigated or to whom the aid was given has made no attempt to commit an offense or has been acquitted for whatever reason. In practice, such cases are seldom prosecuted.

The concept of conspiracy in the American sense is not known. Entering into an agreement with another person for the purpose of committing an offense constitutes one of the forms of preparation and is punishable only in those rare cases when the law explicitly so provides. But participation in an association (some organizational ties among the members must exist) having as its purpose the commission of a crime does constitute a separate offense.

Defenses

The Code lists the following circumstances that preclude penal responsibility: necessary defense, higher necessity, insanity, justified risk, and insignificant social danger.

The limits of particular defenses have been delineated rather broadly. For example, while describing the state of necessity, the Code states that the defense is allowed (from the point of view of criminal law) to sacrifice the good of even a slightly greater value in comparison with the good protected, if the danger is imminent and cannot be averted otherwise. Even if the limits of the state of necessity are exceeded, the court may apply extraordinary mitigation of the penalty or waive its imposition. The latter also applies to necessary defense.

The definition of insanity is composed of two parts. First, the Code specifies that offenders, to be adjudged insane, must have been incapable at the time of commission of a prohibited act of recognizing its significance or controlling their conduct. Second, the Code specifies the grounds of the above mentioned psychological dysfunctions: mental deficiency, mental illness, or any other disturbance of the mental function. Insane offenders are not subject to criminal liability because they are not deemed blameworthy. As a consequence, they cannot be punished. However, special preventive measures may be applied. In practice, the defense of insanity is raised only when the offense charged is a capital one. Finally, insanity does not exclude criminal responsibility if the perpetrators have culpably put themselves into the state of insanity, for example, by excessive drinking of alcohol. Due to widespread consumption of alcohol in Poland, the legislature decided to ignore the rule "no crime without a guilty mind" in order to protect society from aggressive offenders acting in the state of acute insobriety. To afford them the defense of insanity would be contrary to public interest.

Special attention should be given to justified risk. This concept may be applied in many areas of social life, for example, in medicine or sports. But in Poland, as in any communist country where most enterprises are social property, the concept of justified risk is of particular importance in economic life. The managers of state-owned enterprises who, while acting reasonably, undertake risky decisions resulting in economic losses, will not bear criminal responsibility, if they intended to bring an advantage to the socialized economy or to conduct technical or economic experiments.

Other defenses such as consent or custom, not mentioned by the Code, have been elaborated by scholars and by judicial decisions.

Penal Measures

According to most scholars, Polish criminal law is based on the idea of just, "deserved" punishment: Punishment should be proportionate to the gravity of an offense. One could say that this is nothing but retribution in its modern shape, that is, free of any feeling of vengeance or hate toward the offender. It must be stressed, however, that the gravity of the offense is not the only factor to be taken into account by the judge in the process of sentencing. Attention should also be paid to the idea of special and general prevention. Incidentally, it is symptomatic that the Code does not utilize the term "general prevention," not to mention "general deterrence," but speaks instead of the "social impact of punishment." The former terms have certain connotations (intimidation of large masses of the population by excessively harsh penalties) that the legislature wanted to avoid.

The Code, while specifying the guidelines for judicial sentencing, attempts to reconcile the sometimes conflicting aims of punishment: to satisfy the social feelings of justice (the idea of "deserved" punishment), special prevention, rehabilitation of the offender, and, finally, general prevention (understood by the drafters as forming desirable attitudes in the society at large). There can be no doubt that especially after 1981 the shift toward general deterrence in the strict sense of intimidation is noticeable both on a legislative and judicial level.

Further, on many occasions, the Supreme Court urged lower courts to rely on the guideline that—in a concrete case—would enable the imposition of a harsher sentence. For example, the idea of proportionality was stressed with respect to property offenses (the value of stolen property being the primary consideration) and the incapacitation needs were emphasized when the Supreme Court elaborated on the sentencing of recidivists.

The penal policy of the Code has been usually described by the term "polarization." According to this idea, taken from the Soviet Union, first-time offenders, committing relatively minor offenses, shall be treated with considerable leniency, sometimes even outside the system of criminal justice, while recidivists and those committing especially grave crimes shall be dealt with extreme harshness. The policy of polarization, as actually implemented, coupled with other factors, has made the Polish criminal justice system one of the world's most punitive systems.

Kinds of Penal Measures and Their Distribution in Practice

Polish criminal law is characterized by a great variety of penal measures at the disposal of the judge. They may be divided into penalties and preventive measures.

The death penalty, described by the Code as "of an extraordinary character," must not be applied to persons who were under 18 at the time of commission of an offense, nor to a pregnant woman. In no case is the imposition of the death penalty mandatory. The judge is always empowered to impose a penalty of deprivation of liberty for 25 years, even if the penalty of death is the only penalty provided by the statute under which the offender is charged. The penalty is provided for in the Code (excluding the Military Part) for the following offenses: treason, espionage, seditious conspiracy, terrorist acts, sabotage, murder, armed robbery, and organizing or directing a major economic swindle. All in all, there are 24 capital crimes known to the current Polish legislation.

The exact number of death sentences imposed and actually implemented in postwar Poland is difficult to ascertain. It is interesting to note that the history of the death penalty may be related, only to a point, to the political transformations of the country. In the period immediately following World War II, thousands of war criminals were punished with death. In the Stalinist period (1949-1954) well over 1,000 death sentences were imposed; a substantial number were politically motivated. In the period between 1955 and 1969, 113 death sentences were imposed, an average of 8 per year; in almost every case for an especially heinous murder. A few persons received the death sentence for economic offenses but, in the end, only 1 was executed. It must be explained at this point that in the last 30 years, in approximately two-thirds of the cases, the death sentences have been commuted by the Council of State to long terms of imprisonment.

Despite a fairly significant number of death sentences handed down, the problem of the death penalty was not extensively debated. In the period 1955-1957, a few short articles against it were published in influential and widely read weekly magazines. Often the pronouncement of Karl Marx was recalled that a society that wants to be deemed civilized cannot tolerate the death penalty. Curiously enough, in some instances the words of the founder of the communist ideology had to be deleted following a censor's intervention.

Not surprisingly, the new Code retained the death penalty. Despite the declaration on the "extraordinary character" of the penalty, the number of death sentences meted out in the period 1970-1980 reached 120; an average of 11 sentences per year, compared to 7 per year in the 1960s. Again, the punishment was almost invariably imposed only in the worst cases of murder. However, no data concerning military courts are available.

In 1980, the problem of the death penalty emerged within the criminal law reform movement. The Solidarity-sponsored Commission suggested that the penalty be abolished (except wartime offenses), while the Commission appointed by the Minister of Justice was in favor of curtailing the application of the penalty by narrowing down the scope of offenses punishable by death to treason and murder. The Commission also proposed that a rule requiring the unanimous votes of the judges to impose the penalty be adopted. In general, though, the Commission was rather cautious and recommended that the whole subject be publicly discussed.

The imposition of martial law in December of 1981 brought this stage of the debate to an end. However, the reform movement of the Solidarity era has had a lasting effect also in this field. The number of death sentences meted out in the 1980s has been slightly lower than during the previous decade. Some scholars indicate that the current trend may herald the forthcoming abolition of the death penalty in practice before it is abolished *de jure* (by law). This seems to be wishful thinking.

Deprivation of liberty, formerly called imprisonment, may be adjudged for a period of 3 months to 15 years or, exceptionally, for 25 years. If the penalty imposed does not exceed 2 years (or 3 years, in the case of a nonintentional offense), the execution of penalty may be conditionally suspended. This is often called a "suspended sentence." The offender remains under supervision during the test period and several restrictions may be imposed. The suspended sentence used to be a favorite noncustodial alternative of Polish judges. The 1985 Law on Special Criminal Responsibility significantly restricted the scope of availability of this measure, in particular, by prohibiting the judge from suspending the sentence with respect to offenders convicted of crimes against persons if they were drunk at the time when the offense was committed.

Immediate imprisonment is also widely used by Polish courts, despite the findings of many empirical studies that it neither deters nor rehabilitates. In addition, the average length of sentence has increased considerably in the last 15 years. A prison sentence in the range of 3 to 6 months has become a rarity. This change is, one can assume, the intended consequence of the penal policy geared toward general deterrence. Another interesting feature is the significant decrease in the number of those sentenced to deprivation of liberty under the 1969 Code. In other words, fewer people are now sent to prison than before 1970, but those sent remain there much longer.

All in all, the frequent use of relatively long prison terms manifests the highly repressive nature of the Polish system of justice. Under the 1969 Code, the absolute number and the rate of prison sentences have remained fairly stable. The total number of convictions averaged 150,000 per year. Approximately one-third were immediate prison sentences; the number of suspended prison sentences was even higher. Roughly speaking, out of 100 persons convicted by Polish courts in the last 15 years, 30 went directly to prison and 40 had their prison sentences suspended. When the conditions attached were not met, the prison sentence was activated; the failure rate has been around 10%. In the absence of comprehensive official data for the period under discussion, it may only be estimated that well over 50,000 prisoners are received into prisons in any given year. Since, at the same time, the average length of the sentence has dramatically increased, the prison population has become very high. In the last 15 years it has probably fluctuated between 75,000 and 130,000 (no official data have been available for each year), that is, between 200 and 350 per 100,000 population. It was officially reported on December 31, 1985, that the prison population reached 110,000. These figures (which include pretrial detainees but exclude those serving short-term deprivation of liberty imposed as a consequence of the violation conviction as well as those detained as a result of military court judgments) are extremely high by any standards. Both in absolute terms and on a per capita basis Poland's prison population is larger than in all other European communist countries (except the Soviet Union where no data on prison population are published), not to mention Western Europe.

It is worth noting that 11 amnesty laws have been passed in communist Poland. For example, in 1984, 35,000 prisoners were released. After each amnesty law, though, the prison population has returned fairly quickly to the preamnesty level.

Limitation of liberty is a new kind of penal measure (modeled to some extent on the Soviet penalty of correctional work) introduced by the Code to limit the use of short-term imprisonment that in the 1960s was the subject of scholarly criticism. Its essence is mandatory unremunerated work for social purposes performed at liberty under supervision. In addition, several restrictions are imposed, such as a prohibition on freely changing place of residence and the duty to report regularly to administrative authorities, to make restitution for damages caused, or to apologize publicly to the injured person. In theory, emphasis has been shifted from compulsory work as the key element of the penalty to the conditions under which the work is to be performed and to the restrictions to which the convicted person is subjected. In practice, though, punitive elements have often been present.

The newly introduced measure was, especially right after the Code went into force, considered by judges as a substitute for the fine, not—as intended—for the deprivation of liberty. This demonstrates that, in practice, a measure of an intermediate gravity tends to replace more lenient measures, not more severe ones, if no specific sentencing guidelines to the contrary are given by the legislature. Second, the limitation of liberty was used rather rarely. But by the mid-1970s the number of limitation of freedom sentences was quite impressive. Those sentenced were required to perform simple, manual works, such as cleaning the streets, gardening, and road building. In the 1980s, the penalty has been used less often, mainly due to the practical difficulties involved in the process of its implementation. Some have objected to the idea from the very beginning on the ground that the penalty constitutes involuntary servitude, prohibited by several international documents to which Poland is a party.

A fine may be levied as a separate penalty or it may be adjudged in conjunction with deprivation of liberty. In the second situation, the purpose of the fine is clearly to intensify criminal repression by hurting an offender financially. This form of fine is to be imposed when the offense was directed against social property.

In the early 1950s, fines were viewed in Poland with great suspicion as supposedly incompatible with some basic ideological premises of socialism. It was claimed that a fine was a penal measure typical of capitalist systems in which almost everything, even the criminal justice system, is profit oriented. It was also maintained that fines are, by their very nature, clearly discriminatory because they cannot seriously affect the rich while they are unbearable for the poor. Nowadays, the approach to fines is totally different. The 1969 Code's emphasis on economic sanctions was criticized in the Solidarity period as excessive. Some claimed that the whole criminal justice system was perceived by the ruling party elite as almost the only profitable branch of the state economy.

The reliance on economic sanctions has increased since December of 1981. In particular, the 1985 Law On Special Criminal Responsibility significantly raised the limits of fines and provides, for example, that in the case of corruption of public officials the amount of the fine adjudged must be ten times higher than the amount of the bribe offered.

It must be pointed out that under the legislation currently in force, in some instances the court must impose a long-term imprisonment, coupled with a heavy fine and confiscation of the offender's property, either in whole or in part. It is difficult to comprehend how a convicted person could be reasonably expected to pay the fine. One must also add that court costs to be paid by the offender have been considerably increased. As a result, many offenders, unable to bear a great financial burden, have to serve additional prison terms (up to 2 years) for their default.

Conditional quashing of criminal proceedings is another measure introduced by the Code. It occupies an intermediate position between the unconditional withdrawal of charges and all other penal measures. It may be applied toward offenders without prior conviction if the social danger of the act is not substantial, if the circumstances of its commission are not in doubt, and if the applicable penalty would otherwise be a fine, limitation of liberty, or deprivation of liberty not exceeding 3 years. The Code of Criminal Procedure empowers not only the court but also the procurator to conditionally quash the proceedings. This solution evoked much controversy since many scholars and practitioners were opposed to conferring on the procurator the power that should belong exclusively to the judiciary, namely, establishing that the offender has indeed committed the crime. The conditional quashing has been used often in practice, mostly by procurators.

To sum up, the Polish sentencing system is characterized by the following features: (a) the penalty of death is currently used less frequently; (b) middle- and long-term immediate prison sentences are imposed often, making the system extremely harsh; (c) the growing reliance on economic sanctions results in the impoverishment of fairly large masses of population; and, (d) a fairly substantial number of less serious offenses are handled through a nonjudicial channel.

Special Treatment of Juveniles;
Recidivist, Insane, Drug
and Alcohol Offenders

The Law of October 26, 1982, has created a separate, nonpenal, comprehensive system of treatment of juvenile delinquents. As explained by the drafters, the emphasis is on measures of educational and rehabilitative measures rather than dispositions punitive in nature. The best interest of the child should be the guiding criterion. The jurisdiction in juvenile matters is vested in family courts, unfortunately severely understaffed (in the end of 1985 there were 950 family court judges while the needs were estimated at 1,200). The new law allows the family court judge to intervene early in the lives of juveniles, that is, without waiting for the commission of an act that would constitute a crime if committed by an adult. In other words, such acts as drinking of alcoholic beverages, the use of drugs, truancy, prostitution, or other forms of antisocial but noncriminal behavior, symptomatic of the juvenile's demoralization, may result in the imposition of certain, allegedly treatment-oriented, sanctions. In 1985, every fifth juvenile case involved noncriminal delinquency. Other categories of cases (termination of parental rights or cases involving acts criminal in nature) have remained rather stable in the last years, although a slight increase of criminal cases, attributed to the demographic changes, was registered in the period 1984-1985.

The 1982 Law provides for a wide variety of measures. They include placement under custody of youth organization, work collective, a private individual or a probation officer; placement in correctional center or in a protective correctional center; finally, placement in a training center. The court may also place a youth in a medical establishment or in a foster family. At the end of 1985, over 200,000 offenders were within the juvenile justice system. Most of them remained at liberty, but were under various forms of supervision. As far as custodial measures are concerned, almost 5,000 juveniles were detained in correctional or training centers. The length of stay is indeterminate and should be determined by the rehabilitation effects.

The Law of January 31, 1985, on the Prevention of Drug Addiction provides that the family court may order an involuntary commitment of a youth to a special medical facility and extend the stay after the age of majority if a longer treatment period is needed. At the end of 1985, only 26 young drug addicts were involuntarily treated in special facilities. Such a small number is surprising in view of the widespread use of drugs among Polish youths.

Recidivists, in particular the multiple ones, are handled in a harsh manner. The imposition of deprivation of liberty is, practically speaking, mandatory. In addition, the Code introduced two other special measures. The first, protective supervision, runs for a period of three to five years from the time of release from a penal institution. The recidivist under supervision is subjected to many restrictions, including a prohibition on freely changing his or her place of residence. The second measure is placement in a social readaptation center. The center is designed for those multiple recidivists who have served deprivation of liberty, but are deemed not fully adapted to regular life in society. The minimum length of stay is 2 years; the maximum, 5 years.

The very idea of the center as well as its implementation in practice came under heavy attack in 1981. As it turned out, it was virtually impossible to perform any kind of rehabilitative activities in an establishment containing only the most hardened criminals. Further, prolonged stay in the center was perceived by the residents as continuation of their serving a regular prison sentence. In fact, a regular prison and a readaptation center were in most instances indistinguishable.

Offenders declared insane are committed to a psychiatric hospital or to another appropriate medical institution if their remaining at liberty presents a serious danger to the legal order. It must be emphasized that the commission of an act prohibited by the law is a necessary prerequisite for the use of this preventive measure. The length of stay is not fixed in advance and depends on treatment progress. The same rules apply to those whose responsibility at the time of the commission of an offense was partially diminished. In practice these measures are used infrequently.

With regard to alcoholics, the Code allows placement in detoxification treatment centers prior to serving the penalty adjudged. The minimum length of stay is 6 months, the maximum 2 years. The court decides on the release, taking into account results of the treatment. There are a few other Code provisions dealing with alcohol offenders. For example, when conditionally suspending the execution of deprivation of liberty, the court may impose a duty to refrain from abusing alcohol and/or to submit to medical treatment. The same duty may be imposed on the multiple recidivist remaining under protective supervision.

Parole

Every person serving a deprivation of liberty term may be conditionally released early if several specific requirements are met. First, there must exist a positive prognosis that the perpetrators, after their release, will respect the legal order. In particular, that they will not commit a new offense. The decision regarding conditional release should be based, above all, on the evaluation of the offenders' behavior in the penal institution. Conditional release may take place after at least two-thirds of the penalty has been served. When a youth is involved, at least one-half of the sentence must be served; for a multiple recidivist, at least three-fourths. The portion of the penalty remaining to be served constitutes a test period. The May 1985 Law on Special Criminal Responsibility provides that certain categories of recidivists shall not be subject to parole. This innovation was met with particularly strong scholarly criticism because the early release is especially appropriate as a motivational tool while dealing with recidivists.

Criminal Procedure

Liberal or Conservative?

Criminal procedure, perhaps as no other branch of law, may serve as a highly responsive barometer detecting and reflecting the political climate of a country. This is understandable because criminal procedure directly affects civil rights and liberties.

Two conflicting trends may be distinguished in the development of the law of criminal procedure in communist Poland: the liberal one that culminated in promulgation of the 1969 Code of Criminal Procedure (with all its numerous shortcomings) and the retrogressive one that is best exemplified by the 1985 Law on Special Criminal Responsibility. As a result, the current law of criminal procedure is a peculiar mixture and it is difficult to tell which of its components are permanent and normal and which only temporary and deviant. The analysis that follows will rely primarily on the model reflected in the Code as a point of departure. But it must be kept in mind that the model actually in force is much different due to the recent legislative changes, not to mention the ever existing gap between the law on the books and the law as applied.

Adversary or Inquisitorial?

Criminal trials in Poland are not as spectacular as in some other countries. In most cases there are no surprises: The main body of evidence is known in advance to the court and to the parties. It has been gathered during the pretrial investigation conducted either directly by the procurator or by the (People's Militia) under the procurator's guidance and supervision.

The emphasis on pretrial investigation is one of the principal features of Polish criminal procedure. The second characteristic feature is active participation of the court during the trial. In practice, a trial is aimed at verifying the accuracy of evidence collected during the investigation. The leading role in this process is played by the judge. The judge is supposed to be familiar with all the relevant findings of the investigation as they appear in the files submitted with the indictment, a document in which the charges and the evidence in the case are specified in detail. It is up to the judge to hear the accused, to interrogate the witnesses and experts, and to undertake all actions he or she deems necessary to reach a just verdict. Theoretically, the duty of the Polish judges is not to decide who is the winner in a duel played in front of them between the defense attorney and the accusing party, but to establish the guilt or innocence of the accused by all legally accepted means. With some exaggeration, it might be said that the defense attorney, the accusing party, and other parties play only supporting roles. For example, their lack of initiative would not relieve the court of the duty of clarifying a given matter if this seems indispensable from the point of view of justice. If the defense attorney fails to summon an important witness who might help establish the accused's alibi, the witness should be summoned by the judge. In practice, though, most judges are conviction prone as is reflected by a high conviction rate.

It may already have become clear that Polish criminal procedure is a blend of the so-called inquisitorial and adversary system, with "inquisitional" elements prevailing, especially during the pretrial investigation. According to the majority of Polish legal scholars, the advantages of an adversary system are indisputable, but only when there exists a true equality of parties involved. For example, if only a small fraction of defendants can afford a good defense attorney of their choice, the adversary system in its pure form may lead to inequality based on economic differences. But it is also clear that the inequality of the parties may result from other than economic factors. It has been a fact of life in Poland that the two state agents involved, the professional judge and the procurator, easily dominate all other actors taking part in the court drama: defense attorneys, defendants, private accusers, civil plaintiffs, and so on. Polish scholars have for years accentuated the need for a real, not just formal, equality of all the parties.

Fundamental Principles of
Polish Criminal Procedure:
Theory and Reality

The first fundamental principle is called the "principle of objective truth." All decisions in criminal cases should be based only on well-established facts, not on legal fictions. It is, therefore, the duty of all official bodies, including the procurator, to do everything in their power to establish relevant facts, regardless of whether those facts speak in favor of the accused. This truth-finding function is, in a way, restricted by another basic principle: All facts may be established only in a manner allowed by the law. The search for truth is certainly understandable and commendable. The principle of "objective truth," imported from the Soviet theory, may be thus seen as a natural rejection of "formal theory of proof," feudal in origin. However, all modern systems have rejected the old scheme that had accepted a wide gap between the objective reality and the "judicial" one, that is, the one established as a result of interplay of highly formal rules of evidence of extremely doubtful validity. This kind of triumph of form over substance is certainly not acceptable to any modern legislator. But the emphasis on objective truth in Poland and other communist countries goes much further: Since the primary goal of criminal proceedings is to establish the "truth," the substance clearly comes to the forefront while the form is often neglected. The rule of "free evaluation of evidence" becomes sometimes a substitute for an elaborate set of evidentiary prohibitions that play such an important role in the West, particularly under the common law, in protecting the accused's procedural rights. In contrast, the rules of evidence have been hardly developed in Poland; the defendant's procedural rights are, generally, not properly guaranteed by the law in force and often sacrificed in practice for the sake of establishing the "truth." An acquittal based on the constable's blunder (to use Justice Cardozo's famous remark) is almost unthinkable.

The third principle is "objectivity of official organs": All state organs involved in criminal proceedings must be impartial while performing their duties. This rule, closely related to the principle of objective truth, is binding not only upon the court but theoretically also upon the procurator and other agencies involved in criminal proceedings. In practice, though, the procurator and the defendant are clearly on opposite sides. The former's main function is to prepare the case for trial and represent the state during judicial proceedings. The instances in which the prosecutor would deliberately act in favor of the accused are exceedingly rare.

The issue of judicial independence has already been briefly mentioned. Let us now add a few comments. Is it possible to immunize judges from political pressures in a situation where the law is seen primarily as an instrument of current policy and, moreover, where the power structure of the country has been ossified, that is, the hegemonic role of the Communist Party has been accepted by all other officially recognized political entities and reflected in the Constitution? Theoretically, judges in Poland are bound only by the law and no one is authorized to instruct them how to decide a particular case. But in practice judges function in a tightly controlled environment and are subject to various, usually indirect, pressures. It may be pertinent to note that all administrative positions are occupied by members of the Party who enjoy a great amount of discretionary power as far as promotions, transfer, rewards, and the like are concerned. Several attempts were made during the Solidarity period to revive the self-government of judges. In particular, it was urged that the system of politically oriented appointments to administrative positions be replaced by a democratic process of elections.

Finally, the principle of "presumption of innocence" is, no doubt, considered one of the most fundamental premises of criminal proceedings. The Code provides explicitly that the accused is deemed innocent until his or her guilt has been proved in the manner provided by the law. This statement has been interpreted by most Polish scholars to mean that all official bodies are required to consider and treat the accused as innocent until the accused is declared guilty by the court. It is not entirely clear, though, how to apply this rule to the procurators, especially in a situation when they decide to place the suspect in pretrial detention.

In every country, the presumption of innocence is binding only upon criminal justice agencies and "trials by the media" often take place. In a mature, Western-type democracy, based on the idea of political pluralism, the magnitude of the problem is incomparably smaller. But in Poland, as in any communist country, a defendant found "guilty" by the government-controlled media has little chance (and virtually no chance if the case is political in nature) of being acquitted by a judiciary controlled by the same power center (unless the acquittal is seen expedient from a political point of view).

In at least one point, the current Polish law is in conflict with the presumption of innocence. The Law on Special Criminal Responsibility of 1985 prohibits conditional suspension of imprisonment with respect to certain categories of offenders. There are some exceptions, though. If the defendant has compensated fully the damage caused by his offense (and if some other conditions are met), the court may conditionally suspend the execution of imprisonment. Since the trial in Poland is not divided into a "guilt" and "sentencing" stage (the guilty verdict is immediately followed by the announcement of the penalty imposed), the defendants maintaining their innocence during trial are faced with an extremely difficult choice: If they decide to compensate for the damage, it will surely be considered as their de facto admission of guilt; if they do not compensate the damage, they may lose the chance of getting a suspended sentence. Especially when the defendant is awaiting trial in custody (a frequent occurrence in Poland), the pressure to plead guilty and compensate for the damage allegedly caused is enormous.

The presumption of innocence is accompanied by one subsidiary rule, namely, the one on the burden of proof. For ages it has been a golden principle of Polish criminal procedure that the burden of proof is on the accusing party in the sense that if this party does not succeed, the accused must be declared innocent and unconditionally acquitted. This rule has been expressed rather clumsily by the Code: "Unresolvable doubts shall not be interpreted in disfavor of the accused" (Article 3, par. 3). In judicial practice, though, certain presumptions disfavoring the accused do function.

In passing, it is interesting to note that the Code does not clearly specify the standard of proof required in criminal cases. The Code's formula ("Judges shall make decisions on the basis on their own conviction which shall be based upon evidence presented and its evaluation, with due consideration to the principles of science and personal experience"—Article 4, par. 1) is clearly unsatisfactory.

Rights of a Defendant
at Various Stages of
Criminal Proceedings

Three phases of criminal proceedings may be distinguished: preparatory proceedings, the court proceedings, and appellate proceedings. In each phase a defendant enjoys somewhat different rights. In general, it is a point of public concern that the balance between the powers of state agencies and the rights of the citizens involved has not been properly struck.

In many instances, the first step leading to the initiation of a criminal case is a short detention that precedes a formal opening of the case. Detention is an action undertaken either by a private individual (the apprehended suspect, caught "red handed," must be then immediately turned over to the police) or—in most instances—by the police themselves. According to the Code, detention may take place if there is reason to believe that the person apprehended has committed the offense and it is feared that such person may go into hiding or may tamper with the evidence. The Code further specifies that "the person detained should be released as soon as the reasons for his detention cease to exist" (Article 206). If, however, within 48 hours no copy of the order for his or her pretrial detention has been presented, the person detained shall be immediately released. Even on its very face, the regulations are deficient: The police are not required to state in writing the reasons for the detention, the decision to detain is not subject to any control or review; no mention is made regarding how serious an offense has to be to warrant detention. If literally applied, Article 206 would allow for detention even in cases of the most trivial offense, for which the penalty applicable is only a fine. Not surprisingly, in the last ten years police detention has been used fairly often as a purely preventive or repressive measure, especially while dealing with the political opposition. In some cases, purely fictitious reasons were given by the police (e.g., the theft of a typewriter reported by the neighbor). Sometimes, the police did not even pretend that they had any legitimate reason for detention. For example, they would round up a group of dissidents on the eve of a planned antigovernment demonstration and release them within 48 hours. Sometimes, the same persons were detained many times in a row and the intervals between the detentions were as short as twenty minutes. This way of dealing with political opponents was indirectly condoned by the Procurator General (the guardian of socialist legality) in a circular letter to regional procurators, made public by the Solidarity at the end of 1980. Several improvements in the detention system were then suggested: (a) the police should be required to state the reasons for detention in writing; (b) the duration of detention should be limited to twenty-four hours; (c) some form of external supervision should be introduced; (d) the detained should be entitled to legal representation; and (e) detention should be allowed only if the offense allegedly involved is punishable by imprisonment of a certain length, unless it is impossible to establish the identity of the suspect.

None of these suggestions aimed at curbing the abuses of law has been implemented. Quite to the contrary, the Law on the Ministry of Interior of July 14, 1983, has significantly broadened the detention powers of police and security forces. The Law empowers those bodies to apply preventive measures with respect to the persons who "violate or endanger the public order" (Article 7, par. 5) when this is advisable to prevent the commission of a crime or a violation against the public safety and order, in particular, when the danger to life or health or considerable damage to property is imminent. The maximum length of detention (48 hours) has not been changed.

The first formal stage in a criminal case is preparatory proceedings. According to the Code, investigations in criminal matters shall be conducted by the procurator who, in turn, may delegate to the police either the performance of specific investigating actions, for example, search and seizure, or the conduct of the investigation in full. In practice, most criminal investigations are carried out by the police and the procurator's supervision is perfunctory. Complaints about mistreatment by the police or about physical abuse of suspects to extract confessions are frequently heard. A few years ago, the idea of reintroducing the concept of an examining judge (known before the War) who would conduct the investigation in more serious cases or supervise criminal investigations conducted by other agencies in less serious cases became popular and was explicitly endorsed by the Solidarity.

When suspects have been identified, the first step is to inform them immediately of the charges against them. From this moment on, the suspects may retain a defense attorney. In some instances, a defense attorney must be appointed *ex officio*. The suspects are then to be interrogated, but have the privilege of refusing to answer any question asked. They may demand that the reasons justifying the charge be put in writing and delivered to them. Later, the suspects or their defense attorneys may submit motions to have certain actions performed during preparatory proceedings. They may also request to participate in the actions undertaken by an investigating agency. In some cases, the suspects' presence is mandatory, for example, if certain actions cannot be repeated, such as a highly complicated reconstruction of events that allegedly had taken place. Upon completion of preparatory proceedings, suspects have an unrestricted right to acquaint themselves with all collected evidence that has been selected by the investigating agency to be used in their case. Also, a defense attorney must be given access to the files. Then each of them may file a motion that certain actions be performed to supplement the evidence. If it is decided to perform the acts indicated by the suspects or their defense attorney, the latter's request to be present during these actions cannot be denied. On average, preparatory proceedings do not take more than three months.

It must be emphasized that preparatory proceedings are the crucial part of criminal proceedings in Poland, since at this stage the most vital decision is rendered: whether to prosecute or to quash the proceedings (unconditionally or conditionally). It has been a well-established practice for many years that doubtful cases are not sent to court. In consequence, the decision to prosecute is practically tantamount to conviction.

The next step is the preparation of the indictment. A written form is required. The public prosecutor (who is, in most cases, the procurator) must immediately notify the suspect (who from this moment on is called the accused) about this action.

Now starts the next phase—the court proceedings. The court, having examined whether the indictment conforms to the formal requirements, sends a copy of it to the accused. Later, the date of the main trial is set and the accused must be notified about it at least seven days in advance. Since there is no problem of court congestion, the case is usually scheduled to be heard within a month.

The trial takes place in a courtroom, some architectural elements of which are worthy of our attention. As almost everywhere in continental Europe, at the very end of the room there is a rostrum, approximately two-feet high, on which stands a large, rectangular table. Judges sit in front of the table. On their right, by the same table, sits a public prosecutor and on the left, a court clerk recording the proceedings. The accused sits on a bench at ground level on the extreme right. Just in front of the accused is a bench for his or her attorney so that they can communicate freely. On the opposite side there are two benches: one for a private prosecutor or for a civil plaintiff and one for their attorneys. A witness box is in front of the main table. It is intriguing that the public prosecutor sits on the same level as the judges, while the defense attorney is on lower ground with the client. The explanation usually given is that both the public prosecutor and the judge represent the state, so there should be no distinction made in regard to location.

The trial begins with a brief judicial interrogation of the accused as to his or her name, address, occupation, family situation, criminal record, and so on. Then the prosecuting party reads the indictment. Afterward, the judge addresses the accused by asking whether the accused understood the charge, whether he or she pleads guilty or not guilty, and whether he or she intends to offer any explanations. Also at this stage the accused has the unrestricted right to remain silent or not to answer specific questions if it is deemed advisable. As recalled in 1977 by the Supreme Court, this way of defense must not be interpreted in disfavor of the accused. In practice, the accused usually pleads not guilty and decides to present his or her version of the events, considering it to be advantageous to do so at the beginning of the trial. The accused's explanations should not be interrupted by the judge. After the accused has finished, the judge will ask questions. Already at this point the main purpose of the judicial activity is to establish the truth. Therefore, some of the questions will be absolving, some accusatory; some throwing a favorable light on the accused, some clearly demonstrating blame. When the judge completes the interrogation, the floor is given to a public prosecutor, then to a defense attorney, assuming that, as in a typical case, there are no other parties involved. It must be emphasized that the accused does not testify under oath, but merely voluntarily offers explanations that will be evaluated as any other evidence. A 1972 Supreme Court decision is worth mentioning here. A defendant, while defending himself in court, stated that a policeman used unlawful force during the interrogation. The defendant was later charged with a crime of false accusation, and the conviction was affirmed by the Supreme Court. Most Polish scholars are critical of this decision, pointing out that although the law is silent on the subject of the defendant's freedom of speech, it does grant immunity to the defendant's lawyer. By analogy, the same right should be given to the defendant.

Later, witnesses and experts are called and other evidence is presented. As before, the leading role is played by the judge, who is the one who starts asking questions and asks most of them, while other parties sit mute, taking notes. Obviously, the public prosecutor, as well as the accused and his or her attorney, also have a right to question people summoned by the court and they exercise this right in almost every instance. The judge may waive or modify any question, since the judge is in charge of conducting the trial in the manner required by law.

The trial ends with concluding speeches. The prosecutor speaks first, followed by other parties such as the civil plaintiff. The final word belongs to the defense attorney and to the accused. If the prosecutor decides to reply, the defense attorney and the accused must be given the floor once again. This is a rule without exception—the defending side is always allowed to speak last. In a typical case, the court hearing takes no more than one and a half hours. Concluding speeches are usually condensed, free of rhetoric.

After the speeches, the court recesses to prepare the verdict. The debate is secret and only the judges and the court clerk may be present. No records are made. First, the question of guilt or innocence must be decided. As in all other circumstances, a majority vote is binding. The professional judge casts his or her vote last not to influence the two lay assessors but, as has already been mentioned, in practice he or she is the one who decides the case. If the outcome is against the accused (as is usually the case), the debate centers on the kind and amount of punishment. When this issue is resolved, the verdict is immediately announced in public. The reasons justifying the verdict must be orally presented. In most instances the presentation is schematic, composed usually of well-worn phrases ("taking into account the totality of the evidence . . ." and so on).

At the very end, the presiding judge asks whether the accused understood the meaning of the verdict passed. If the accused answers in the affirmative, the judge informs the accused of the legal requirements regarding his or her right to appeal and gives some details on this subject. In sum, a typical criminal case in Poland involving one accused defended by one attorney, a procurator, and two or three witnesses would take about two hours of courtroom time.

Appellate proceedings may be instituted by the defendant as well as the prosecutor. Both have equal rights in this respect: Both may appeal against the conviction or acquittal, both may appeal against the sentence claiming the penalty is manifestly disproportionate. Their appeal may be based on either legal or factual grounds. Most appeals instituted by the procurator are in disfavor of the defendant. If the appeal had been instituted only by the convicted defendant, the appellate courts may not worsen the defendant's situation.

Unless the case is set for a retrial, the verdict passed by the appellate court becomes final. At this time there is very little room for maneuver. In exceptional cases only, the so-called extraordinary appeal may be launched to the Supreme Court either by the Procurator General or by the Minister of Justice or, finally, by the Chief Justice of the Supreme Court. Also, in some narrowly defined situations, there exists a possibility of reopening the case. This may happen, for example, when the conviction was based on perjury. In practice, these two legal remedies are used rather frequently and they perform a vital political role, in particular, by forcing the judges to increase the severity of sentencing. For example, in 1985, the Procurator General launched an extraordinary appeal in 487 cases. In 481 instances the penalty imposed on the defendant was viewed as being too lenient. The Supreme Court agreed with the Procurator General in 94% of the cases.

Pretrial Detention

Awaiting trial in custody is a common occurrence in Poland (approximately one-fifth of prisoners are usually pretrial detainees) and the law in this area is glaringly deficient.

The Code of Criminal Procedure explicitly provides that the aim of pretrial detention is to prevent the suspect from evading justice. In practice, though, pretrial detention is applied as a coercive measure (to induce the suspect to admit the guilt) or as a purely repressive one (as an "advance" punishment).

The initial decision to detain belongs to the procurator; the person detained may either file a complaint to the court or a motion to the procurator at a higher level. The success rate is exceedingly low (less than 10% of complaints meet with the court's approval). This may be, in part, explained by the fact that procurators rely exclusively on a clause of the Code that refers to whether the act allegedly committed by the suspect was of a "substantial social danger" (Article 217). This extremely elusive formula facilitates the abuse of procurator's powers. In practice, no substantive reasons are usually given why in a particular case the alleged crime meets the statutory criterion.

No time limit is fixed by the 1969 Code regarding the duration of pretrial detention. In a few known cases, the suspects awaiting trial spent several years in prison despite the fact that the decision to detain a suspect for a period exceeding six months is reviewable by the Supreme Court upon motion of the suspect (Article 222). A sample study of 100 pretrial decisions, conducted in the early 1980s, brought astonishing results. The study concerned only detainees charged with less serious crimes (misdemeanors) and in each case the decision to detain was overturned by the court before the verdict has been rendered. Nevertheless, only in 12 cases were the defendants detained for less than one month. In 44 cases, they were detained for a period between one and three months, in 35 between three and six months, and nine detainees were held for over six months. In general, the judicial control over pretrial detention is considered purely illusory.

According to the Code, people awaiting trial in custody may communicate freely with their defense counsel in private. However, the Code states also that in special situations a procurator or a person appointed by a procurator may be present during such a meeting. In exceptional cases, the procurator may even prohibit any personal contact between suspects and their attorneys. In practice, the exception has become the rule. Procurators often make it extremely difficult for defense attorneys to communicate freely with their clients. This means that the person detained is cut off from the outside world and remains at the mercy of the agencies conducting the investigation. Some attorneys, well-aware of the reality, do not even attempt to get access to their clients.

As a rule, those under pretrial detention are later convicted by the courts and almost always they are sentenced to immediate imprisonment the length of which is not shorter than the period already spent in detention (incidentally, by law, the time spent in custody must be fully credited to the penalty adjudged). To make the point clear: The chances of being convicted are much higher for those awaiting trial in custody; also, the sentences meted out are usually harsher.

Finally, it must be mentioned that instead of pretrial detention, bail or police supervision may be applied. It is also possible for a third party to guarantee the suspect's further participation in the case. In practice, these measures are used infrequently (pretrial detention has been used in the last 15 years 2.5 times more often than all other noncustodial measures combined).

In the Solidarity-period discussions of 1980-1981, the following improvements were postulated: (1) The decision to detain a suspect should belong exclusively to the judge; (2) The clause referring to the "social danger" of the act should be eliminated; (3) Pretrial detention must not be used either for repressive or coercive purposes; (4) A defense attorney must have free access to his client; and (5) The maximum length of a pretrial detention should be fixed by the Code (at 2 years). Needless to say, all this is just a history today.

The Law On Special Criminal Responsibility of May 1985, indicative of the new, more repressive approach, introduced some innovations in the field of pretrial detention as well. It provides that if the offense charged is a felony or if the alleged offender is a recidivist (as defined by Article 60 of the Penal Code or by the 1971 Tax Penal Law), pretrial detention is mandatory unless it would create grave danger to the suspect's life or health or would cause especially grave damage to the accused or his or her family. This regulation means, for all practical purposes, that if the procurator decides to charge the suspect with a felony, the suspect will be immediately deprived of liberty and, ultimately, the prison sentence will be imposed.

Expedited Proceedings

The Code of Criminal Procedure, as originally passed in 1969, provides that expedited proceedings are to be used with respect to offenders who committed petty offenses of a hooligan character (defined rather loosely by Article 59 of the Penal Code). The proceedings are initiated by the police information; no formal indictment is necessary. The offenders must be brought to court within 48 hours and their cases must be heard immediately. The sentence (the maximum length was fixed at one year) is subject to appeal within seven days (instead of the regular fourteen days). The appellate court must review the case within one month.

The Law on Special Criminal Liability has substantially broadened the scope of expedited proceedings by extending it to offenses other than of hooligan character and by increasing up to three years of imprisonment the penalty that may be imposed. The Law also provides that all cases tried under expedited proceedings shall be heard by a professional judge acting alone and that if the penalty imposed is immediate imprisonment, the defendant must be immediately detained. The defendant's appeal, which must be lodged within seven days, shall be reviewed within 21 days. Finally, the sentence may be rendered in the defendant's and his or her attorney's absence if the defendant was properly served. The May 1985 Law as a whole has been severely criticized by a majority of Polish scholars, but the section on expedited proceedings was a subject of particular indignation. The scholars pointed out that the defendant's right to defense has been reduced, practically speaking, to zero, in violation of Poland's international law obligations. In fact, the May 1985 Law has extended expedited proceedings to the point that they have become an alternative system of handling numerous kinds of criminal cases. Under the Law, efficiency clearly prevails over due process: A sentence of three years of imprisonment may be rendered by a single judge in absentia, the defendant then is immediately detained, and the time limits to lodge an appeal are exceedingly demanding.

Lay Participation
in Criminal Proceedings

In Poland, as in all other communist countries, the participation of the public in criminal proceedings has been presented as one of the distinguishing features of the communist model of criminal justice. In reality, though, civic participation is minimal. In the 1970s, a great majority of criminal cases were heard by a panel made up of one professional judge and two people's assessors. Theoretically, each member of the panel had equal rights. In practice, as has been mentioned, the professional judge easily dominated over the two lay judges and the instances when the case was decided by two-vote majority of lay judges were infrequent. As may be recalled, the May 1985 Law on Special Criminal Responsibility has drastically curtailed lay participation in criminal proceedings: All cases tried under expedited proceedings are heard by a professional judge sitting alone.

It must be emphasized at this point that lay assessors do not participate in appeal proceedings when the law requires a panel of three professional judges. This means that every decision rendered by a first instance court with participation of lay judges may be corrected by a tribunal composed only of professional judges. And, needless to say, the Supreme Court decisions are made only by a panel of professional judges.

The significance of other forms of lay participation in criminal proceedings in Poland is also negligible. The Code provides for a social representative. The representative is not a party to the trial, but a person who, acting on behalf of the collective that had appointed him or her, may make motions and may be given the floor, but is not expected to act in favor of or against the accused. This person's only role is to represent the public interest violated by the alleged offender. Several social organizations are empowered to appoint a social representative who would act on their behalf. It is up to the court to decide whether to admit a social representative appointed by the organization. In practice, the instances in which a social representative participates in criminal trial are infrequent.

Finally, on several occasions the Penal Code provides for the participation of the public if certain measures are to be applied. For example, while conditionally quashing the proceedings the court may require that a pledge be given by a social organization to which the perpetrator belongs or by a collective where he or she works. The same condition may be attached when the decision to conditionally suspend the execution of imprisonment is at stake.

Execution of Penal Measures
(Corrections)

Aims and Basic Principles

The Code on the Execution Penalties states clearly that penalties "shall be executed in a humanitarian manner and with respect for the human dignity." Then the Code provides that the only aim of the implementation of prison sentences is to rehabilitate offenders, to accustom them to socially useful work, and thereby prevent their relapse into crime. No reference to the idea of general deterrence has been made in this context.

The Code declares that all inmates shall be classified, directed to the appropriate penal institution, and assigned an appropriate regimen (depending on the regimen, inmates have different duties and privileges). The purpose of classification is to prevent mutual demoralization and to create favorable conditions for the application of individualized treatment measures. The classification group to which an inmate belongs is determined by a penitentiary commission, the collective organ existing within each penal institution. The type of penal institution and the conditions of incarceration are prescribed either by the court imposing the sentence or by the penitentiary court. The latter is also empowered to order modifications in the process of the execution of penalty; only exceptionally may the decision be made by the penitentiary commission. Depending on progress in rehabilitation, the inmates may be transferred from one type of penal institution to another, and the regimen under which they serve the penalty may also be changed (for the better, which should be the rule, but also for the worse). In theory, the Polish correctional system is thus based on the principle of progression.

The classification group, the type of penal institution, and the conditions of incarceration are supposed to be determined on the basis of such factors as age, previous criminal record, length of sentence, susceptibility to resocialization, and character of the offense. In practice, it is the gravity of the offense that decisively influences the decision. This is especially true in the first stage of the execution of penalty.

The correctional system is highly complex and diversified. There are six types of institutions. In addition, inmates placed in whatever types of penal institution may be subjected to one of four different regimes: mitigated, basic, intense, and severe. Briefly, the six types of penal institutions may be described as follows. Labor-centers are semi-open institutions in which two types of regimes (basic, mitigated) may be applied. They are for convicts who begin serving a penalty not exceeding five years. In practice, the majority of convicts are placed in labor-centers. Ordinary penal institutions are for those serving long-term sentences and for those convicted of offenses of a hooligan character. Transitional penal institutions are open-type institutions for those who have served at least two years in another type of institution and who are in the last stage of serving the penalty. Youth institutions are for those who are under 21 and who were under 21 at the commencement of their term and have a relatively short time to serve. The emphasis in these institutions should be on vocational training and sports activities. Special penal institutions are reserved for multiple recidivists. In those institutions the mitigated regimen is not applied.

Penal institutions for those requiring special medical-educational measures house alcoholics, drug abusers, and all convicts with mental disturbances. Those who require these special measures constitute at least 10% of all inmates.

The sentenced person is obligated to perform assigned work or to pursue training, to observe the order and discipline of the institution, to maintain proper relations with other inmates, and to have a conscientious attitude toward work. It is clear, however, from the foregoing summary of pertinent regulations that emphasis has been placed on productive work as the inmates' basic duty. In practice, this duty is strictly enforced. The employment of the sentenced person is also considered to be one of his or her basic rights. Remuneration for the work performed and working hours correspond with generally accepted standards. However, substantial deductions to cover maintenance costs of inmates and for other purposes are made.

The kinds and scale of rewards are specified in the Prison Rules. The Code mentions only that rewards are granted by the director of the penal institutions to those who distinguish themselves by their exemplary attitude and particularly by diligence in work or training. The Code also declares that the highest reward is a pass to leave the penal institution for a period up to five days.

The Code is more detailed when describing the most severe disciplinary penalties, such as reduction in the remuneration for work performed, deprivation or limitation of visits, a hard bed in a solitary cell up to 14 days, and placement in an isolated section from one to six months. Penalties are imposed by the director of the institution, who may request an opinion from the penitentiary commission. Placement in an isolated section requires the prior consent of the penitentiary judge. It is important to observe that the judge is obligated to annul or modify any decision concerning the disciplinary punishment if that decision is contrary to law or to the principles of penitentiary policy.

Implementation of Imprisonment
Sentences in Practice

In the years 1944-1955, the administration of penal institutions was under the authority of the Ministry of Internal Affairs (then called the

Ministry of Public Security). At the same time, it was the responsibility of the Procuracy to supervise implementation of the penalties in accordance with the law. Because the Ministry was formally and factually independent from the Procuracy, a procurator charged with the supervision of penal institutions was in practice concerned mostly with purely legal aspects of imprisonment (the length of stay, legal validity of a warrant, and so on) and did not interfere in the internal life of penal institutions. In 1956, the administration of penal institutions was transferred to the Ministry of Justice (a special department charged with the administration of penal institutions was then created). This move was considered a major step toward the elimination of serious abuses of law that were fairly prevalent in the early 1950s. The supervision performed by the procurator, however, was retained. The above model was accepted by the 1961 Code. It declares, first of all, that all penal institutions are subordinate to the Minister of Justice (the special department in charge of penal institutions is now called the Main Bureau of Penal Institutions). Second, the Code introduced two new institutions: the penitentiary court and the penitentiary judge. The Code specifies that supervision exercised by a penitentiary judge shall consist primarily of ensuring the propriety of the execution of the penalty and particularly the methods and measures of penitentiary treatment employed. The supervision exercised by the procurator primarily includes ensuring the legality of the execution of the penalty and observance of the rights and duties of inmates. It must be noted that the penitentiary judge and the prosecutor have an unlimited right to enter the premises of any institution. They also have the right to examine documents and demand explanations from administrators, to converse in private with inmates, and to investigate inmates' grievances and petitions.

As was exposed in the period of heated discussions between August 1980 and December 1981, the model of corrections heralded by the drafters as humanitarian and based on modern principles of individualized rehabilitation was plagued by many problems. All in all, prison conditions were extremely difficult. Considerable overcrowding, scarce food, poor hygiene, the lack of proper recreational and educational activities, and, above all, the emphasis on hard, manual labor made prisoners' lives miserable. The treatment of prisoners was in many instances brutal. In 1974, the Provisional Prison Rules were passed by the Minister of Justice. In many respects they enhanced the rigidity of the Code that itself was far from liberal. It became clear that, under the circumstances, the only realistic goal of the correctional activities could be the protection of prisoners from moral as well as physical degradation. But even this limited goal could not always be attained. After a long period of confinement the released were not able to function normally upon returning to society. A high recidivism rate was one of the indicators of this phenomenon. In the Spring of 1981, the Rules were modified to provide for more humane treatment. At the same time, two civic organizations were spontaneously created to assist prisoners and monitor the functioning of correctional institutions. Several prison riots took place later that year. Usually they were met with very strong measures; some resisters were killed. The Martial Law Decree only aggravated the situation. The prison population swelled. Under the Decree, many thousands of political activists, some of them popular and enjoying great public respect, were interned. This was the period when for the first time in many years a sizable part of the Polish prison population was not composed of conventional prisoners such as thieves, robbers, or traffic offenders. Despite tremendous social pressure, the Government refused to acknowledge the existence of political criminals as a legally separate category enjoying certain privileges mandated by various international documents. On the whole, however, the treatment of internees was probably better than the one accorded regular convicts. The internees were released in December of 1982 when the Martial Law was suspended. Some of them, though, were put on trial, convicted, and imprisoned.

Concluding Remarks

Some see Swiss cheese as consisting almost exclusively of large holes but others decide to ignore the holes and enjoy the cheese. It seems that some readers of this chapter may feel that I was overly preoccupied with the "holes" of the Polish criminal justice system and missed the enjoyment of the substance. Would such criticism be well-taken? How do the "consumers" themselves evaluate the system? The results of an April 1986 public opinion poll demonstrate unequivocally that a substantial number of Poles do not give their system of criminal justice even a passing grade. Roughly speaking, only every fifth respondent believed that the police performed their duties "well" and every third gave this rating to judges and procurators ("well" was the highest grade that could be given). Even more revealing is the fact that only every sixth respondent was of the view that no one in Poland is above the law. Interestingly enough, among those who think that some are more equal than others, Communist Party members constituted almost two-thirds. Those findings are, no doubt, indicative of a high degree of dissatisfaction and distrust among the population at large toward the Polish law enforcement agencies.

Bibliography

Compiled by James Milles,
Bibliographer and Instructor in
Legal Research at Saint Louis
University School of Law (USA)

This bibliography is composed of the major books and articles in English describing the criminal justice systems of the foreign countries included in this book.

England

Criminality

Advisory Committee on Drug Dependence, Home Office, *Rehabilitation of Drug Addicts* (1968).

Advisory Council on the Misuse of Drugs, Department of Health and Social Security, *Treatment and Rehabilitation: Report* (1982).

Alternative Strategies for Coping with Crime (N. Tutt ed. 1978).

Anderton, C. J., *Crime in Perspective* (1979).

Baldwin, J. & A. E. Bottoms, *The Urban Criminal: A Study in Sheffield* (1976).

Bancroft, J. H., *Deviant Sexual Behaviour: Modification and Assessment* (1974).

Bean, P., *Rehabilitation and Deviance* (1976).

Borkowski, M., *Domestic Violence* (1983).

Borland, M., *Violence in the Family* (1976).

Borrell, C. & B. Cashinella, *Crime in Britain Today* (1975).

Burns, A., *To Deprave and Corrupt: Pornography, Its Causes, Its Forms, Its Effects* (1972).

Cabinet Office, *Vandalism* (1979).

Committee on Prostitution, British Social Biology Council, *Women of the Streets: Sociological Study* (1955).

AUTHOR'S NOTE: The compiler wishes to acknowledge the guidance and advice of Professor Stanislaw Frankowski.

262

Cook, T., *Vagrant Alcoholics* (1975).
Creighton, S., *Trends in Child Abuse* (1984).
Croft, J., *Concerning Crime* (Home Office Research Studies No. 75, 1982).
Department of Health & Social Security, *Child Abuse Reports: A Study of Inquiry* (1982).
Eekelaar, J., *Family Violence* (1978).
Farrier, D., *Drugs and Intoxication* (1980).
Foakes, J., *Family Violence* (1984).
Freeman, M., *Violence in the Home* (1978).
Glatt, M. M., *Drugs, Society and Man: A Guide to Addiction and Its Treatment* (1974).
Gunn, J. & D. P. Farrington, *Abnormal Offenders, Delinquency and the Criminal Justice System* (1982).
Home Office, *Tackling Vandalism* (1979).
Hough, M. & P. Mayhew, *The British Crime Survey* (Home Office Research Studies No. 76, 1982).
McClintock, F. H. & N. H. Avison, *Crime in England and Wales* (1968).
Miller, N., *Battered Spouses* (1975).
Sandford, J., *Prostitutes: Portraits of People in the Sexploitation Business* (1975).
Thorman, G., *Family Violence* (1980).
Weissman, J. C. & R. L. Dupont, *Criminal Justice and Drugs: The Unresolved Connection* (1982).
West, D. J., *Murder Followed by Suicide* (1965).
West, D. J., *Understanding Sexual Attacks* (1978).
West, D. J., *Delinquency: Its Roots, Careers and Prospects* (1982).

Law Enforcement Agencies

Abrahams, G., *Police Questioning and Judges' Rules* (1964).
Browne, D., *The Rise of Scotland Yard* (1956).
Bunyard, R. S., *Police: Organization and Command* (1979).
Cain, M. E., *Society and the Policeman's Role* (1973).
Calvert, F., *The Constable's Guide to Powers of Arrest & Charges* (7th ed. 1982).
Critchley, T. A., *History of the Police in England and Wales* (Rev. ed. 1978).
Ditchfield, J. A., *Police Cautioning in England and Wales* (1976).
Home Office, *Report of the Committee Appointed to Consider the Authorized Procedures for the Interrogation of Prisoners Suspected of Terrorism* (Cmd. 4901, 1972).
Home Office, *Handling of Complaints Against the Police: Report of the Working Group for England and Wales* (Cmd. 5582, 1974).
Home Office, *Crime Prevention and the Police* (1979).
Home Office, *Police Interrogation: An Observational Study in Four Police Stations* (1980).
Home Office, *The Establishment of an Independent Element in the Investigation of Complaints against the Police: Report of a Working Party* (Cmd. 8193, 1981).
Home Office, *Police Complaints and Discipline Procedures* (Cmd. 9072, 1983).
Leigh, L. H., *Police Powers in England and Wales* (2nd ed. 1984).
Mark, R., *Policing a Perplexed Society* (1976).

Moody, S. R. & J. Tombs, *Prosecution in the Public Interest* (1982).

Moriarty, C.C.H., *Police Law* (24th ed. 1981).

Morris, P. & K. Heal, *Crime Control and the Police: A Review of Research* (Home Office Research Studies No. 67, 1981).

Wegg-Prosser, C., *The Police and the Law* (2nd ed. 1979).

Whittaker, B., *The Police* (1964).

Criminal Law

Advisory Council on the Penal System, *Powers of the Courts Dependent on Imprisonment: Report* (1977).

Advisory Council on the Penal System, *The Length of Prison Sentences: Interim Report* (1977).

Advisory Council on the Penal System, *Sentences of Imprisonment: A Review of Maximum Penalties* (1978).

Borrie, G. J. & N. V. Lowe, *The Law of Contempt* (2nd ed. 1983).

Bradshaw, S., *Drug Misuse and the Law* (1972).

Brody, S. R., *The Effectiveness of Sentencing: A Review of the Literature* (Home Office Research Study No. 35, 1976).

Brownlie, I., *Law of Public Order and National Security* (2nd ed. 1981).

Caird, R., *A Good and Useful Life: Imprisonment in Britain Today* (1974).

Clarkson, C. & H. Keating, *Criminal Law: Text and Materials* (1984).

Cook, R. J. & P. Senanayake, *Human Problem of Abortion: Medical and Legal Dimensions* (1979).

Coote, A. & T. Gill, *Battered Women and the New Law* (2nd ed. 1979).

Cross, R. & P. A. Jones, *Cases and Statutes on Criminal Law* (1977).

Curzon, L. B., *Criminal Law* (2nd ed. 1978).

Edwards, J.L.J., *Mens Rea in Statutory Offences* (1955).

Elliot, D. W. & J. C. Wood, *A Casebook on Criminal Law* (4th ed. 1982).

Fitzgerald, M. & J. Muncie, *System of Justice: Introduction to the Criminal Justice System in England and Wales* (1983).

Gibson, E., *Homicide in England and Wales, 1967-1971* (1975).

Gillies, P., *The Law of Criminal Conspiracy* (1981).

Halnan, P., *Drinking/Driving and the New Law* (1984).

Hollis, C., *The Homicide Act* (1964).

Home Office, *The Brixton Disorders, April 10-12, 1981: Report of an Inquiry* (Cmd. 8427, 1981).

Home Office, *Review of Criminal Justice Policy, 1976* (1977).

Howard, C., *Strict Responsibility* (1963).

Kenny, C. S., *Outlines of Criminal Law* (19th ed. 1966).

Koestler, A., *Reflections on Hanging* (1956).

Kohl, M., *The Morality of Killing: Sanctity of Life, Abortion and Euthansia* (1974).

Law Commission, *No. 83, Criminal Law: Report on Defenses of General Application* (1977).

Law Commission, *No. 89, Criminal Law: Report on the Mental Element in Crime* (1978).

Law Commission, *Working Paper No. 102, Criminal Law: Attempt and Impossibility in Relation to Attempt, Conspiracy and Excitement* (1980).

Levy, L., *Treason Against God: A History of the Offences of Blasphemy* (1980).
National Council for Civil Liberties, *Vagrancy, an Archaic Law: Memorandum of Evidence to the Home Office Working Party on Vagrancy and Street Offenses* (1975).
Progress in Penal Reform (L. Blom-Cooper ed. 1974).
Radzinowicz, L., *Ideology and Crime: A Study of Crime and and Its Social and Historical Context* (1966).
Reshaping the Criminal Law (P. R. Glazebrook ed. 1978).
Royal Commission on Capital Punishment, *Report* (Cmd. 8932, 1953).
Shapland, J., J. Willmore, & P. Duff, *Victims in the Criminal Justice System* (1985).
Simpson, A.W.B., *Pornography and Politics: Look Back to the Williams Committee* (1983).
Smith, J. C. & R. Hogan, *Criminal Law* (5th ed. 1983).
Stephenson, G., *Criminal Law and Consumer Protection* (1983).
Stirrat, G. M., *Legalized Abortion: The Continuing Dilemma* (1979).
Thomas, D. A., *Principles of Sentencing: The Sentencing Policy of the Court of Criminal Appeal* (2d ed. 1979).
Walker, N., *Crime and Punishment in Britain* (2d ed. 1968).
Walker, N., *Sentencing Theory, Law and Practice,* (1985).
Walther, N., *Blasphemy in Britain: The Practice and Punishment of Blasphemy, and the Trial of "Gay News"* (1977).
Williams, G., *The Sanctity of Life and the Criminal Law* (1958).
Williams, G. L., *Criminal Law: The General Part* (2nd ed. 1961).
Williams, G. L., *Textbook of Criminal Law* (2nd ed. 1983).
Williams, G. L., *The Mental Element in Crime* (1965).
Wootton, B., *Crime and Penal Policy* (1978).
Wootton, B., *Crime and Criminal Law: Reflections of a Magistrate and Social Scientist* (Hamlyn Lecture No. 15, 2nd ed. 1981).

Criminal Procedure

Anderson, R., *Representation in the Juvenile Court* (1978).
Archbold, J. F., *Pleading, Evidence and Practice in Criminal Cases* (41st ed. 1982).
Baldwin, J. & M. McConville, *Negotiated Justice: Pressures on Defendants to Plead Guilty* (1977).
Baldwin, J. & M. McConville, *Jury Trials* (1979).
Barnard, D., *Criminal Court in Action* (2nd ed. 1980).
Cavenagh, W. E., *Guide to Procedure in the Juvenile Court* (1982).
Chamblis, W. & R. Seidman, *Law, Order and Power* (2nd ed. 1982).
Clegg, J. & E. Cowsill, *Evidence: Law and Practice* (1984).
Cross, R., *Outline of the Law of Evidence* (1980).
Devlin, *The Criminal Prosecution in England* (1960).
Emmins, C. J., *Practical Approach to Criminal Procedure* (2nd ed. 1983).
King, M., *Bail or Custody* (2nd ed. 1973).
Knight, M., *Criminal Appeals: A Study of the Powers of the Court of Appeal, Criminal Division* (1970 & Supp. 1975).
May, R., *Modern Law of Criminal Evidence* (1984).
May, R., *Criminal Evidence* (1986).
Pain, K. W., *Practice and Procedure in Juvenile Courts* (1982).
Stone, R., *Entry, Search and Seizure* (1985).

Corrections

Bochel, D., *Probation and After-Care: Its Development in England and Wales* (1976).
Briggs, D., *In Place of Prison* (1975).
Cavandino, P., *Parole: The Case for Change* (1973).
Cooks, R.A.F., *Home Office Approved Probations Hostels* (1956).
Davies, M., *Prisoners of Society: Attitudes and After-Care* (1974).
Fielding, N., *Probation Practice* (1984).
Fitzgerald, M., *Prisoners in Revolt* (1977).
Fitzgerald, M. & J. Sim, *British Prisons* (2nd ed. 1982).
Fox, L. W., *The English Prison and Borstal Systems* (1952).
Harding, J., *Employment and Probation and After Care Service Handbook* (1979).
McConville, S., *Uses of Imprisonment: Essays on the Changing State of English Penal Policy* (1975).
Prisoners Past and Future (J. Freeman ed. 1978).
Short, R., *Care of Long Term Prisoners* (1979).
Wright, M., *Making Good: Prisons, Punishment and Beyond* (1982).

Nigeria

Criminality

Alemika & Kayode, *Some Predictors of Recidivism: A Study of the Inmates of a Nigerian Prison*, 5 Int'l J. Comp. & Applied Crim. Just. 187 (1981).
Bienen, *Criminal Homicide in Western Nigeria, 1966-1972*, 18 J. Afr. L. 57 (1974).
Kayode, *Some Notes on a Research into Crime and Punishment in Nigeria*, 11 Aust. & N.Z. J. Criminology 241 (1978).
Milner, *Sanctions of Customary Criminal Law: A Study in Social Control*, 1 Nig. L.J. 173 (1965).
Oloruntimehin & Olofunmilayo, *A Study of Juvenile Delinquency in a Nigerian City*, 13 Brit. J. Criminology 157 (1973).
Oloyede, *Juvenile Delinquency in Nigerian Law*, 4 Nig. L.J. 50 (1973).
Recent Developments in the Field of the Prevention of Crime and the Treatment of Offenders, Int'l Rev. Crim. Pol'y 20, (1962, at 77).

Law Enforcement Agencies

Carter & Marenin, *Police in the Community, Perceptions of a Government Agency in Action in Nigeria*, African Legal Stud. 9 (1977).
Jearey, *The Structure, Composition and Jurisdiction of Courts and Authorities Enforcing the Criminal Law in British African Territories*, 9 Int'l & Comp. L.Q. 396 (1960).
Nwogugu, *Abolition of Customary Courts—The Nigerian Experiment*, 20 J. Afr. L. 1 (1976).
Ohonbamu, *Dilemma of Police Organization Under a Federal System: The Nigerian Example*, 6 Nig. L.J. 73 (1972).

Criminal Law

Adaramaja, *Character as Basis of Criminal Liability in Nigerian Law*, 3 Nig. L.J. 116 (1969).

Adeyemi, *Death Sentence and the Young Offender*, 8 Nig. L.J. 26 (1967).

Adeyemi, *Homicide by Reckless or Dangerous Driving (Summary Trial and Punishment) Edict, 1968—An Unfortunate Legislative Exercise*, 3 Nig. L.J. 172 (1969).

Aguda, *Definition of Crime in Nigerian Law*, 4 Nig. B.J. (April 1963, at 26).

Aguda, *Consent and Homicide*, 5 Nig. B.J. 48 (1964).

Aguda, T. A., *Principles of Criminal Liability in Nigerian Law* (1966).

Aremu, *Parties to Conspiracy as Combinations of Principal Offenders in Nigeria*, 9 Anglo-Am. L. Rev. 105 (1980).

Aremu, *Criminal Responsibility for Homicide in Nigeria and Supernatural Beliefs*, 29 Int'l & Comp. L.Q. 112 (1980).

Bassey, *Obtaining Credit by Fraud in Nigeria*, 4 Nig. B.J. (July-August, 1963, at 21).

Bienen, *The Determination of Criminal Insanity in Western Nigeria*, 14 J. Mod. Afr. Stud. 219 (1976).

Brett, L. & I. McLean, *The Criminal Law and Procedure of Lagos, Eastern Nigeria and Western Nigeria* (1963).

Brett & McLean's The Criminal Law and Procedure of the Six Southern States of Nigeria (C. 0. Madarikan & T. A. Aguda, 2nd ed. 1974).

Browne, *An Operational Study of the New Penal Code of Northern Nigeria*, 39 U. Det. L.J. 465 (1962).

Carew, *Our Penal Policy and the Prison System*, 4 Nig. L.J. 60 (1969).

Coker, *Focus on Nigerian Criminal Law (II)*, 1 Nig. B.J. 2 (1958, at 10).

Cottrell, *Recent Nigerian Cases on State Privilege*, 6 Nig. L.J. 60 (1972).

Criminal law Reform in Northern Nigeria, 24 Mod. L. Rev. 604 (1961).

Emiko, *A Reflection on the Nigerian Corrupt Practices Decree*, 19 J. Indian L. Inst. 17 (1977).

Essien, *The Northern Nigeria Penal Code*, 5 N.Y.L. Sch. J. Int'l & Comp. L. 87 (1983).

Gledhill, A., *The Penal Codes of Northern Nigeria and the Sudan* (1963).

Hedges, *Liability Under the Nigeria Criminal Code: A Historical and Comparative Study*, in *The Changing Law in Developing Countrys 184* (J.N.D. Anderson ed. 1963).

Hedges, R. Y., *Introduction to the Criminal Law of Nigeria (excluding the Northern Region)* (1962).

Ibeziako, E. A., *An Outline of the Defense of Bona Fide Claim of Right* (Ibez Library Series No. 1, 1973).

Ijalaye, *Contempt of Court in Nigeria: A Re-evaluation*, 11 Nig. B.J. 98 (1973).

Iyizoba, *Aiding a Crime after Its Completion*, 11 Nig. L.J. 65 (1977-1980).

Karibi-Whyte, *Res Furtiva in Nigerian Criminal Law*, 4 Nig. B.J. (July- August 1963, at 26).

Karibi-Whyte, *Some Recent Amendments to the Criminal Code*, 3 Nig. L.J. 156 (1969).

Karibi-Whyte, *Unlawful Possession in the Criminal Code*, 8 Nig. L.J. 11 (1967).

Kasunmu & Omabegho, *Provocation as a Defense Under the Nigerian Criminal Code*, 14 Int'l & Comp. L.Q. 1399 (1965).

Kahlil, *Criminal Law Reform in Nigeria*, 5 J. Islamic & Comp. L. 51 (1974).

Milner, A., *The Future of Sentencing in Nigeria* (1970).

Milner, A., *The Nigerian Penal System* (Law in Africa No. 23, 1972).

Morris, *How Nigeria Got Its Criminal Code*, 14 J. Afr. L. 137 (1970).

Naish, *A Redefinition of Provocation Under the Criminal Code*, 1 Nig. L.J. 10 (1964).
Northern Region of Nigeria, *Notes on the Penal Code Law* (2nd ed. 1963).
Okonkwo, *Accidental Manslaughter*, 1 Nig. L.J. 253 (1965).
Okonkwo, *Note on Reform of the Nigerian Criminal Code*, 1 Nig. L.J. 293 (1965).
Okonkwo, *Assaulting a Police Officer in the Execution of His Duty*, 7 Nig. L.J. 1 (1973).
Okonkwo, *The Defence of Bona Fide Claim of Right in Nigeria*, 17 J. Afr. L. 271 (1973).
Okonkwo, *Unlawful Act Doctrine and the Defence of Accident*, 11 Nig. B.J. 93 (1973).
Okonkwo, C. & M. Naish, *Criminal Law in Nigeria* (1964).
Okonkwo, C. & M. Naish, *Okonkwo and Naish on Criminal Law in Nigeria* (2nd ed. 1980).
Olorunmodimu, J. A., *Nigerian Decided Criminal Cases in Nutshell* (1973).
Owoade, *Some Aspects of Criminal Law Reform in Nigeria*, 16 Nig. B.J. 25 (1980).
Owoade, *Some Aspects of the Law of Homicide*, 7 Indian Socio-Legal J. 37 (1981).
Rewane, *Contempt of Court in Nigerian Criminal Law*, 1 J. Afr. L. 172 (1957).
Smith, *Admissions Received Through Interpreters: An African Hearsay Problem*, 1 Nig. L.J. (November 1964, at 26).
Uvieghara, *Strike Actions and the Criminal Law*, 6 Nig. L.J. 88 (1972).
Vukor-Quarshie, *Corporate Criminal Liability: An Additional Chapter to the Criminal and Penal Codes of Nigeria*, 2 Jahrbuch für Afrikanisches Recht 141 (1981).

Criminal Procedure

Adesanya, *The Constitutional Privilege of an Accused to Refuse to Give Evidence: Republic v. El Mann Examined*, 6 E. Afr. L.J. 264 (1970).
Adesanya, *The Exclusion of the Application of the Nigerian Codified Form of Common Law of Evidence from the Customary Courts and the Machinery for Filling the Gaps*, 20 N. Ir. L.Q. 349 (1969).
Adesanya, *Voluntary Confession and the Privilege Against Self-Incrimination in Nigeria*, 4 Nig. L.J. 64 (1970).
Aguda, T. A., *The Law of Evidence in Nigeria* (2nd ed. 1974).
Aguda, T. A., *Law and Practice Relating to Evidence in Nigeria* (1980).
Aihe, *Preventive Detention in Nigeria*, Rev. Int'l Comm'n Jurists (December 1972, at 68).
Akanki, *Proof of Customary Law in Nigerian Courts*, 4 Nig. L.J. 20 (1970).
Akinkgube, *Corroboration in the Nigerian Law of Evidence*, 7 Nig. L.J. 61 (1973).
Akpambgo, *Magistrates' Courts Law (Amendment) East Central State of Nigeria Edict No. 23 of 1971*, 6 Nig. L. Q. 133 (1972).
Aremu, *Voluntariness of Confessions in Nigerian Law*, 11 Nig. L.J. 33 (1977-1980).
Asian-African Legal Consultive Committee, *The Recognition and Enforcement of Foreign Judgments, Service of Process and Recording of Evidence in Civil and Criminal Cases*, in *Report of the Seventh Session Baghdad 1965* (1965).
Bairamian, V. R., *Criminal Procedure and Evidence in Nigeria: Synopsis of Reported Judgments of the Supreme Court, 1963 to 1966* (1971).
Cottrell, *Aspects of the Problem of the Representation of Defendents* in *Criminal Proceedings*, 2 Nig. L.J. 32 (1967).
Delano, *Bail*, 4 Nig. L.J. 35 (1969).

Elias, *The Office and Duties of the Federal Attorney-General in Nigeria,* 6 Nig. L.J. 149 (1972).

Elias, *Some Considerations on the Administration of Criminal Justice in Nigeria,* 20 Int'l Rev. Crim. Pol'y 3 (1962).

Emiko, *"No Case Submission" Under the Nigerian Law,* 18 J. Indian L. Inst. 493 (1976).

Fagbemi, *Res Gestae and the Nigerian Evidence Act,* 7 Lawyer (Lagos) 22 (1978).

Ibironke, *Prima Facie Case in Criminal Proceedings,* 2 Nig. L.J. 24 (1967).

Ijalaye, *The Nigerian Extradition Decree 1966,* 4 Nig. L.J. 37 (1970).

Jones, J. R., *Some Cases on Criminal Procedure and Evidence in the Northern States of Nigeria* (1969).

Jones, J. R., *Criminal Procedure in the Northern States of Nigeria* (1975).

Ksunmu, *Admissibility of Illegally Obtained Evidence in Nigeria—Based on Sada and Another v. The State,* 3 Nig. L.J. 83 (1969).

Kasunmu, *"Improper" Admission of Inadmissible Evidence: The Effect of Failure to Object,* 6 Nig. L.J. 31 (1972).

Kodilinye, *Proof of Guilt Under the Indian Hemp Decree 1966,* 12 Nig. B.J. 69 (1974).

Nwabuez, B.O., *The Machinery of Justice in Nigeria* (Butterworth's African Law Series No. 8, 1963).

Nwogugu, *Abolition of Customary Courts—The Nigerian Experiment,* 20 J. Afr. L. 1 (1976).

Ojo, *Execution of Warrants Outside Region (State) of Issue,* 6 Nig. L.J. 139 (1972).

Okonkwo, *The Submission "No Case to Answer" in* Criminal Proceedings, 6 Nig. L.J.1 (1972).

Olubunmi, *Res Gestae and the Nigerian Evidence Act,* 11 Lawyer (Nigeria) 22 (1978).

Omo-Agege, *The Rule Against Hearsay—A Case for Its Abolition,* 7 Lawyer (Nigeria) 13 (1978).

Oretuyi, *Bill of Rights in Nigeria 1969-1975: What Has It Accomplished in the Administration of Criminal Justice?,* 9 E. Afr. L. Rev. 1 (1976).

Oretuyi, *Presumption of Innocence Under the Nigerian Law,* 7 Indian Socio-Legal J. 169 (1981).

Richardson, S. S. & T. H. Williams, *The Criminal Procedure Code of Northern Nigeria* (Law in Africa No. 7, 1963).

Rudd, G. R., *The Nigerian Law of Evidence* (1964).

Scott, *Criminal Procedure: A Comparative Note on Joint Trials,* 19 Int'l & Comp. L.Q. 585 (1970).

Skelton, *Standards of Procedural Due Process Under International Law vs. Preventive Detention in Selected African States,* 2 Hous. J. Int'l L. 307 (1980).

Tobi, *Right to Counsel in Nigeria,* 5 Int'l Legal Prac. 75 (1980).

Williams, *The Criminal Procedure Code of Northern Nigeria: The First Five Years,* 29 Mod. L. Rev. 258 (1966).

Zalman, M. & G. Zalman, *Cases and Materials on the Law of Criminal Procedure in the Northern States of Nigeria* (1969).

Corrections

Asuni, T., *Corrections in Nigeria,* in International Corrections 163 (1982).

Elias, T. O., *The Prison System in Nigeria* (1968).

Milner, *Sanctions of Customary Criminal Law: A Study in Social Control*, 1 Nig. L.J. 173 (1965).

Mittlebeeler, *Collective Punishment*, 8 J. Islamic & Comp. L. 27 (1978).

Richardson, *Training for Penal Reform in Northern Nigeria*, 13 J. Afr. Admin. 38 (1961).

Varia

Mittlebeeler, *Race and Jury in Nigeria*, 18 How. L.J. 88 (1973).

Ofori-Amankwa, *Penal Code and the Criminal Code: Their Origin and Differences*, 8 J. Islamic & Comp. L. 49 (1978).

West Germany

Criminality

Ingraham, B., *Political Crime in Europe: A Comparative Study of France, Germany and England* (1979).

Kaiser, *Child Abuse in West Germany*, 2 Victimology 294 (1977).

Kappel & Leuteritz, *Wife Battering in the Federal Republic of Germany*, 5 Victimology 225 (1980).

Mergen, *Sexuality and Criminal Law in Terms of Anthropological and Social Conflicts*, in *Criminology Between the Rule of Law and the Outlaws* 139 (1976).

Oehler, *Criminal Violence and Its Control in the German Federal Federal Republic*, in *Studies in Comparative Law* 109 (E. Wise & G. Mueller ed. 1975).

Rasch, *Psychological Dimension of Political Terrorism in the Federal Republic of Germany*, 2 Int'l J. L. & Psychiatry 79 (1979).

Law Enforcement Agencies

Adlam, G., *Juvenile Courts in the Federal Republic of Germany*, Crim. L. Rev. 401 (1956).

Boehm, *Modern Juvenile Courts: Germany*, 17 Int' I. J. Offender Therapy & Comp. Criminology 184 (1973).

Herrmann, *The Independence of the Judge in the Federal Republic of Germany*, in *Contemporary Problems in Criminal Justice* (Tokyo 1983).

Criminal Law

Albrecht & Johnson, *Fines and Justice Administration: The Experience of the Federal Republic of Germany*, 4 Int'l J. Comp. & Applied Crim. Just. 3 (1980).

Arzt, G., *Responses to the Growth of Crime in the United States and West Germany: A Comparison of Changes in Criminal Law and Societal Attitudes*, 12 Cornell Int. L. J. 43 (1979).

Association Internationale de Droit Penal, *The Criminal Justice System of the Federal Republic of Germany, Proceedings of the Conference* sponsored by the American

National Section AIDP, The Goethe Institute of Chicago, de Paul University, College of Law. Held in Chicago, April 12, 1980 (Toulouse 1981).

Daly, *Intoxication and Crime: A Comparative Approach*, 27 Int'l & Comp. L. Q. 378 (1978).

Jescheck, *The Doctrine of Mens Rea in German Criminal Law—Its Historical Background and Present State*, 8 Comp. & Int'l L. J. S. Afr. 112 (1975).

Jescheck, *Modern Criminal Policy in the Federal Republic of Germany and the Germany Democratic Republic*, in *Crime, Criminology and Public Policy: Essays in Honor of Sir Leon Radzinowicz* 509 (R. Hood ed. 1974).

Kaiser, *The Development of Methods and Measures of the Penal Law*, 45 Revue Internationale de Droit Penal 33 (1974).

Naucke, *An Insider's Perspective on the Significance of the German Theory's General System for Analyzing Criminal Acts*, 1984 B.Y.U.L. Rev. 305.

Positivist Roots of Criminal Law and the West German Criminal Law Reform, 10 Rut. Cam. L. J. 613 (1979).

Scheerer, *New Dutch and German Drug Laws: Social and Political Conditions for Criminalization and Decriminalization*, 12 Law & Soc'y Rev. 585 (1978).

Snyman, *The Normative Concept of Mens Rea: A New Development in Germany*, 28 Int'l & Comp. L. &. 211 (1979).

Criminal Procedure

Damaska, *Evidentiary Barriers to Conviction and Two Models of Criminal Procedure*, 50 U. Chi. 2 Rev. 281 (1973).

Damaska, *Reality of Prosecutorial Discretion: Comments on a German Monograph*, 29 Am. J. Comp. L. 119 (1981).

Eser, *Reform of German Abortion Law: First Experiences*, 34 Am. J. Comp. L. 369 (1986).

Goldstein & Marcus, *The Myth of Judicial Supervision in Three "Inquisitorial" Systems: France, Italy and Germany*, 87 Yale L. J. 240 (1977).

Herrmann, *Development and Reform of Criminal Procedure in the Federal Republic of Germany*, 11 Comp. & Int'l L. J. S. Afr. 183 (1978).

Krauss, *Reform of Criminal Procedure Law in the Federal Republic of Germany*, Jurid. Rev. 202 (1979).

Langbein, *Controlling Prosecutorial Discretion in Germany*, 41 U. Chi. L. Rev. 439 (1974).

Langbein & Weinreb, *Continental Criminal Procedure*, 87 Yale L. J. 1549 (1978).

Symposium: Comparative Criminal Justice Issues in the United States, West Germany, England, and France, 42 Md. L. Rev. 1 (1983).

Weigend, *Continental Cures for American Ailments*, 2 Crime and Justice (N. Morris ed. 381, 1981).

Corrections

Dunkel & Johnson, *Introduction of Therapy into Tegel Prison*, 4 Int'l J. Comp. & Applied Crim. Just. 233 (1980).

Ehrhardt, *The Concept of Correction of Delinquents in the West German Criminal Code of 1969/75*, 4 Austl. J. Forensic Sci. (December 1971, at 58).

Engel, *The Successful Treatment of a Habitual Criminal*, 22 Int'l J. Offender Therapy & Comp. Criminology 221 (1978).

Engelhardt, *Criminal Therapy Inside and Outside Prison*, 22 Int'l J. Offender Therapy & Comp. Criminology 201 (1978).

Horton, *Life Imprisonment and Pardons in the German Federal Republic*, 29 Int'l & Comp. L.Q. 530 (1980).

Huber, *Safeguarding of Prisoners' Rights Under the New West German Prison Act*, 2 S. Afr. J. Crim. L. & Crim. L. & Criminology 229 (1978).

Schneider & Scheerer, *Corrections in the Federal Republic of Germany*, in *International Corrections*, 39 (R. Wicks & H. Cooper ed. 1979).

Schueler-Sprigorum, *A Critical Comparison of the British Detention Centers and the German Jugendarrest Systems*, 3 Int's J. Criminology & Penology 201 (1975).

Legislation (including drafts)

Alternative Draft of a Penal Code for the Federal Republic of Germany, American Series of Foreign Penal Codes 21 (1977).

The German Code of Criminal Procedure, American Series of Foreign Penal Codes 10 (1965).

The German Draft Penal Code E 1962, American Series of Foreign Penal Codes 11 (1966).

The German Penal Code of 1871, American Series of Foreign Penal Codes 4 (1961).

(For further sources please refer to footnotes following Professor Herrmann's chapter.)

Sweden

Criminality

Alström, *A Study of Incest with Special Regard to the Swedish Penal Code*, 56 Acta Psychiatrica Scandinavica 357 (1977).

Carlsson, *Crime and Behavioral Epidemiology*, in *Biosocial Bases of Criminal Behavior* 25 (S. Mednick & K. Christiansen ed. 1977).

Carlsson, G. & G. Nordberg, *Crime: Trends and Recent Developments* (Report No. 3, 1976).

Crime and Crime Control in Scandinavia 1976-80 (N. Bishop ed. 1980).

Geis & Geis, *Rape in Stockholm: Is Permissiveness Relevant?*, 17 Criminology 311 (1979).

Hofer, Lenke, & Thorsson, *Criminality Among 13 Swedish Birth Cohorts*, 23 Brit. J. Criminology 263 (1983).

Kuhlhorn, E., *Crime Trends and Measures Against Crime in Sweden* (1980).

Lansing, *Historical Development of the American Judicial and Swedish Administrative Approaches to Juvenile Justice*, 14 Comp. & Int'l L. J. S. Afr. (March 1981, at 56).

Löfmarck, *White-Collar Economic Crime in Sweden: The Doctor as Criminal*, 25 Scandinavian Stud. in L. 109 (1981).

Medhus, *Criminality Among Female Alcoholics*, 3 Scandinavian J. Soc. Med. 45 (1975).

National Council for Crime Prevention, *Swedish Studies on Juvenile Delinquency* (1976).

National Swedish Council for Crime Prevention, *Young Offenders: Research Results and Policy Application of the 1956 Study of Young Offenders* (1975).

Peltoniemi, *Current Research on Family Violence in Finland and Sweden,* 7 Victimology 252 (1982).

Persson, *The Level of Crime in Society and Individual Criminality: Two Data Problems in a New Type of Criminological Studies,* 18 Statistisk Tidskrift 409 (1980).

Research and Development Division, National Swedish Council for Crime Prevention, *Crime: Trends and Recent Development* (Report No. 8, 1977).

Roslund & Larsun, *Crimes of Violence and Alcohol Abuse in Sweden,* 14 Int'l J. Addiction 1103 (1979).

Sarnecki, J., *Juvenile Delinquency in Sweden* (1980).

Schjolberg, *Computer-Assisted Crime in Scandinavia,* 2 Computer L. J. 457 (1980).

Votey, *Scandinavian Drinking-Driving Control: Myth or Intuition,* 11 J. Legal Stud. 93 (1982).

Law Enforcement Agencies

Akermo, K., *A Review of the Swedish Police System,* 42 RCMP Gazette 4 (1980, at 1).

Efraimsson, *Crime Prevention in the Newly-Organized Swedish Policy,* 26 Int'l Crim. Police Rev. 2 (1971).

Eriksson & Jorgensen, *The Application of Computerized Information Retrieval to Fingerprint Identifications,* 31 Int'l Crim. Police Rev. 194 (1976).

Eriksson, U. & E. Kuhlhorn, *The Police as Recreation Leaders—Two Attempts to Prevent Crime* (Report No. 3, 1977).

Lithner, *The Practical Training of Public Prosecutors in Sweden,* 5 Prosecutor 413 (1969).

Lithner, *The Prosecutor's Role,* 1967 Annales Internationales de Criminologie 427.

Police and the Social Order: Contemporary Research Perspectives (J. Knutsson et al. ed., National Swedish Council for Crime Prevention, Research and Development Division Report No. 6, 1979).

Criminal Law

Andenaes, *The Choice of Sanction, a Scandinavian Perspective,* in *Reform and Punishment* 3 (M. Tonry & F. Zimring, eds., 1983).

Aspelin, E., N. Bishop, H. Thornstedt, & P. Tornudd, *Some Developments in Nordic Criminal Policy and Criminology* (1975).

Bishop, *Developments in Criminal Law and Penal Systems, 1977: Sweden* Crim. L. Rev. 351 (1978).

Bogdan & Falk, *Reflections on Some International and Swedish Legal Rules Relating to Drug Offences,* Bull. on Narcotics (July-September 1977, at 1).

Edqvist & Wennberg, *Recent Legislation and Research on Victims in Sweden,* 8 Victimology 310 (1983).

Engstrom, *New Penal Provisions on Sexual Offenses Proposed in Sweden,* 21 Int'l J. Offender Therapy 264 (1977).

Jareborg, *Two Facts of Culpa,* 50 Revue Internationale de Droit Penal 307 (1979).

National Swedish Council for Crime Prevention, *A New Penal System: Ideals and Proposals* (Report No. 5, 1978).

Nelson, A., *Responses to Crime: An Introduction to Swedish Criminal Law and Administration* (New York University School of Law, Criminal Law Education and Research Center, Monograph Series No. 6, 1972).

Sellin, *Penal Reform in Sweden*, in *Modern Advances in Criminology* 35 (J. Edwards ed. 1974).

Sellin, T., *The Protective Code: A Swedish Proposal* (1957).

Sundberg, *Humanitarian Laws of Armed Conflict in Sweden, Ogling the Socialist Camp*, 16 Akron L. Rev. 605 (1983).

Sundeen, *Swedish Juvenile Justice and Welfare*, 4 J. Crim. Just. 109 (1976).

Thornstedt, *The Principle of Legality and Teleological Construction of Statutes in Criminal Law*, Scandinavian Stud. L. 213 (1960).

Thornstedt, *The Beginning and the End of Life From the Perspective of Swedish Criminal Law*, 14 Scandinavian Stud. in L. 25 (1970).

Thornstedt, *Euthanasia and Related Problems in Swedish Law*, 70 J. Legal Med. 32 (1972).

Thornstedt, *The Day-Fine System in Sweden*, Crim. L. Rev. 307 (1975).

Thornstedt, *Some Developments in Nordic Criminal Policy and Criminology: The Day-Fine System in Sweden*, 33 Int'l Crim. Police Rev. 265 (1978).

Zagaris, *Penal Reform in Sweden*, 9 Sw. U.L. Rev. 111 (1977).

Criminal Procedure

Berg & Cars, *Protection of Human Rights in Criminal Proceedings: National Report—Sweden*, 49 Revue Internationale de Droit Penal 340 (1978).

Ginsburg, *Comparative Study of Hearsay Evidence Abroad—Sweden*, 4 Int'l Law. 163 (1969).

Nordenson, *The Proposed Swedish Systems of Free Legal Assistance and of Compensation to Victims of Crime*, 70 J. Legal Med. 103 (1972).

Sellin, *Sweden's Substitute for the Juvenile Court*, Annals 137 (1949).

Stockdale, E., *The Technicians Move In*, in *The Court and the Offenders* 144 (1967).

Corrections

Conrad, J., *Crime and Its Correction: An International Survey of Attitudes and Practices* (1965 & reprint 1975).

Eriksson, *The Prison Administration's Work Schemes, The Future of Criminal Care in Sweden*, Nordisk Kriminalistik Arsbok 49 (1982).

Forssell, *The Training of Staff, The Future of Criminal Care in Sweden*, Nordisk Kriminalistik Arsbok 51 (1962).

Goransson, *Human Dignity in the Execution of Punishment*, in *Studies in Penology Dedicated to the Memory of Sir Lionel Fox* 108 (M. Lopez-Rey & C. Germain ed. 1964).

Kuhlhorn, E., *Non-Institutional Treatment: A Preliminary Evaluation of the Sundsvall Experiment* (1975).

Kuhlhorn, E., *Non-Institutional Treatment and Rehabilitation: An Evaluation of a Swedish Correctional Experiment, Shortened Version* (National Swedish Council for Crime Prevention No. 7, 1979).

Ludqvist, *The Organization of Prison Industries in Sweden*, Prison Service J. (January 1982 at 19).

Marnell, *Comparative Correctional Systems: United States and Sweden*, 8 Crim. L. Bull. 748 (1972).

Siegel, *Criminal Justice: Swedish Style: A Human Search for Answers*, 1 *Offender* Rehabilitation 291 (1977).

Ward, *Sweden, The Middle Way to Prison Reform?*, in *Prisons: Present and Possible 89* (M. Wolfgang ed. 1979).

Wickman, *Industrial Wages for Prisoners in Finland and Sweden*, in *Offenders and Corrections* 141 (D. Szabo & S. Katzenelson ed. 1978).

Legislation

The Child Welfare Act of Sweden (1965).

The Penal Code of Sweden as Amended Jan. 1, 1972 (T. Sellin, trans., The American Series of Foreign Penal Codes No. 17, 1972).

The Swedish Code of Judicial Procedure (American Series of Foreign Penal Codes No. 15, 1968; rev. ed., American Series of Foreign Penal Codes No. 24, 1979).

The Swedish Penal Code (The National Council for Crime Prevention, Sweden, 1986).

Varia

Becker, H. & E. Hjellemo, *Justice in Modern Sweden: A Description of the Components of the Swedish Criminal Justice System* (1976).

Nelson, A., *Crime and Responses to Crime* (1980).

Scandinavian Research Council for Criminology, *Scandinavian-Polish Workmeeting* (1981).

Japan

Criminality

Clifford, W. *Crime Control in Japan* (1976).

Evans, *Changing Labor Markets and Criminal Behavior in Japan*, 22 J. Asian Stud. 477 (1977).

Fornataro, *Further Comment on the Japanese White Paper on Crime*, 9 Crim. L.Q. 218 (1966).

Ingraham & Tokoro, *Political Crime in the United States and Japan: A Comparative Study*, 4 Issues Criminology 145 (1969).

The Juvenile Delinquent in Japan, 13 Brit. J. Criminology 170 (1973).

Koichi, *Victimological Studies of Sexual Crimes in Japan*, 1 Victimology 107 (1976).

Kumagai, *Filial Violence in Japan*, 8 Victimology 173 (1983).

Lunden, *Juvenile Delinquency in Japan Pre-War, War and Post-War Years*, 44 J. Crim. L. 428 (1953).

Lunden, *Violent Crimes in Japan in War and Peace, 1933-74*, 4 Int'l J. Criminology & Penology 349 (1976).

Martin & Conger, *A Comparison of Delinquency Trends*, 18 Criminology 53 (1980).

Miyazawa, *Victimological Studies in Japan*, 1 Keio L. Rev. 21 (1975).

Miyazawa, *Victimological Studies of Sexual Crimes in Japan*, 1 Victimology 107 (1976).
Wilson & Wilson, *Juvenile Delinquency in Japan*, Brit. J. Criminology 278 (1964).

Law Enforcement Agencies

Bayley, D., *Forces of Order: Police Behavior in Japan and the United States* (1976).
Hanajiri, *The Courts and Lawyers in Japan*, 162 N.Y.L.J. 1 (1967).
Hayakawa, *Age and the Judiciary in Japan*, 9 Kobe U. L. Rev. 1 (1973).
Nagashima, *Family Court in Japan*, 19 Juv. Court Judges J. 130 (1969).
Suzuki, *Problems of Disqualification of Judges in Japan*, 18 Am. J. Comp. L. 727.

Criminal Law

Abe, H., *Sentencing and Treatment: The Growing Emphasis on Therapeutic and Preventive Aspects of Criminal Justice in Japan* (1961).
Alston, *Japanese and American Attitudes toward the Abolition of Capital Punishment*, 14 Criminology 271 (1976).
Araki, *The Flow of Criminal Cases in the Japanese Criminal Justice System*, 31 Crime & Delinq. 601 (1985).
Armstrong, *A Perspective on Japanese Criminal Law and Procedure Law*, 5 Lawasia 179 (1974).
Bayley, *Learning About Crime—The Japanese Experience*, 43 Pub. Interest 55 (1976).
Dando, *Basic Problems in Criminal Theory and Japanese Criminal Law*, 35 Ind. L. J. 423 (1960).
Dando, *Criminal Law*, 4 Japan Sci. Rev. 27 (1953).
Dando, *Interrelation of Criminal Law and Procedure*, 2 Japan Ann. L. & Pol. 163 (1953).
Dando & Tamiya, *Conditional Release of an Accused in Japan*, in *Studies on Bail* 135 (C. Foote ed. 1966).
Fujiki, *Property and Criminal Law*, 2 L. Japan 120 (1968).
Hirano, *The Draft of the Revised Penal Code: A General Critique*, 6 Law in Japan 49 (1973).
Hirano, *Penal Protection of the Natural Environment in Japan*, 49 Revue Internationale de Droit Penal 185 (1978).
Hirano, *Some Striking Aspects of Japanese Criminal Law* (1961).
Jamazaki, *Illegal Practice of Medicine*, 3 Japan Ann. L. & Pol. 173 (1955).
Kikkawa, *Criminal Law*, 7 Japan Ann. L. & Pol. 175 (1959).
Kikkawa, *Criminal Law and Procedure*, 13 Japan Ann. L. & Pol. 65 (1965).
Kim, *Asian Criminal Law: A Comparison with Proposed Federal Criminal Code*, 14 S. Tx. L. J. 43 (1973).
Koshi, *The Japanese Legal Advisor, Crimes and Punishments* (1970).
Miyazawa, *Victimological Studies in Japan*, 1 Kyio L. Rv. 21 (1975).
Miyazawa, *Victimological Studies of Sexual Crimes in Japan*, 1 Victimology 107 (1976).
Ryu, *Is the Crime of Parricide Unconstitutional?*, 46 Rev. Jur. U.P.R. 555 (1977).
Saito, *The Provisional Draft of the Revised Criminal Code*, 2 Bull. Waseda U. Inst. Comp. L. 25 (1961).
Suzuki, *Politics of Criminal Law Reform: Japan*, 21 Am. J. Comp. L. 287 (1973).

Takikawa, *Mistake of Law*, 3 Japan Ann. L. & Pol. 159 (1955).
Uematsu, *Control of Sex Crimes by Penal Code of Japan*, 4 Hitotsubashi J. Arts and Sciences 15 (1964).
Uematsu, *Trends in the Revision of the Penal Code of Japan*, 3 Hitotsubashi J. L. and Politics 1 (1964).

Criminal Procedure

Abe, *Criminal Procedure in Japan*, 48 J. Crim. L. Criminology & Police Sci. 359 (1957).
Abe, *Police Detention and Arrest Privileges Under Foreign Law: Japan*, 51 J. Crim. L. Criminology & Police Sci. 429 (1960).
Abe, *Privilege Against Self-Incrimination: Japan*, 51 J. Crim. L. Criminology & Police Sci. 178 (1960).
Abe, *The Exclusionary Rule Under Foreign Law: Japan*, 52 J. Crim. L. Criminology & Police Sci. 284 (1961).
Abeyratne, *Aerial Piracy and Extended Jurisdiction in Japan*, 33 Int'l & Comp. L. Q. 596 (1984).
Beer, *Freedom of Information and the Evidentiary Use of Film in Japan: Law and Sociopolitics in an East Asian Democracy*, 65 Am. Pol. Sci. Rev. 119 (1971).
Benjamin, *Images of Conflict Resolution and Social Control: American and Japanese Attitudes Toward the Adversary System*, 29 J. of Conflict Resolution 13 (1975).
Dando, *Criminal Law*, 4 Japan Sci. Rev. 27 (1953).
Dando, *Interrelation of Criminal Law and Procedure*, 2 Japan Ann. L. & Pol. 163 (1953).
Dando, *Japanese Criminal Procedure Reform*, in *Essays in Criminal Science* (G. Mueller ed. 1961).
Dando, *System of Discretionary Prosecution in Japan* 18 Am. J. Comp. L. 518 (1970).
Dando, *Japanese Criminal Procedure* (B. George trans. 1965).
George, *The Impact of the Past Upon the Rights of the Accused in Japan*, 14 Am. J. Comp. Law 672 (1965).
George, *The "Right of Silence" in Japanese Law*, 43 Wash. L. Rev. 1147 (1968).
Ishada, *The Rights of the Suspect and of the Accused in Criminal Procedure in Japan* in Asian Judicial Conference, 4th, *Record* 300 (1970).
Meyers, *The Japanese Inquest of Prosecution*, 64 Harv. L. Rev. 279 (1950).
Niwayama, *Protection of Human Rights in Criminal Proceedings: National Report-Japan*, 49 Revue Internationale de Droit Penal 217 (1978).
Suzuki, *Discovery in Japanese Criminal Procedure*, 6 Kobe U. L. Rev. 13 (1968).
System of Discretional Prosecution in Japan, 18 Am. J. Comp. L. 518 (1970).
Tamiya, *On the Designation of Communication with Counsel*, 4 Law in Japan 87 (1970).
Woodsworth, *Some Impressions of Criminal Procedure in Japan*, 9 Law Soc'y Gaz. 185 (1975).

Corrections

Dando & Tamiya, *Conditional Release of an Accused in Japan*, 108 U. Pa. L. Rev. 323 (1960).
Hiramatsu, *History of Penal Institutions: Japan,* 6 Law in Japan 1 (1973).

Japanese Criminal Procedure (1965).

Koshi, G., *The Japanese Advisor: Crimes and Punishments* (1970).

Ochiai, *Offenders' Rehabilitation in Japan*, 1984 N.Z.L.J. 407.

Shikita, *Rehabilitative Programmes in the Adult Prisons of Japan*, 30 Int'l Rev. Crim. Pol. 11 (1972).

Shiono, *Use of Volunteers in the Non-Institutional Treatment of Offenders in Japan*, Int'l Rev. Crim. Pol'y, No. 27 (1969, at 25).

Suzuki, *Corrections in Japan in International Corrections* (R. Wicks & H. Cooper eds. 1979).

Tamita, *Conditional Release of Accused in Japan,* 105 Pennsylvania L. Rev. 323 (1960).

Yanagimoto, *Some Features of the Japanese Prison System*, 10 Brit. J. Criminology 207 (1970).

Legislation

The Code of Criminal Procedure (1949).

The Criminal Code of Japan: As Amended in 1947, and the Minor Offenses Law of Japan (1950).

Ministry of Justice, Japan, *The Constitution of Japan and the Criminal Statutes* (1957).

The Penal Code of Japan (As of 1954) (rev. ed. 1954).

Prostitution Prevention Act of 24 May 1956, 11 Int'l Rev. Crim. 130 (1957).

Varia

Bayley, *Learning About Crime: The Japanese Experience*, 44 Public Interest 55 (1976).

The Soviet Union

General

Basic Documents in the Soviet Legal System (W. Butler ed. 1983).

Berman, H. *Justice in the USSR* (1976).

Butler, W., *Russian and Soviet Law: An Annotated Catalogue of Reference Works, Legislation, Court Reports, Serials and Monographs on Russian and Soviet Law* (1976).

Butler, W., *Soviet Law* (Legal Systems of the World Vol. 1, 1983).

Feifer, G., *Justice in Moscow* (1964).

Hazard, J., *Communists and Their Law: A Search for the Common Core of the Legal Systems of the Marxism Socialist States* (1969).

Hazard, J., W. Butler, & P. Maggs, *The Soviet Legal System: The Law in the 1980s* (1984).

Maggs, P. & O. Ioffe, *Soviet Law in Theory and Practice* (1983).

Schwarzchild, *Variations on an Enigma: Law in Practice and Law on the Books*, 99 Harv. L. Rev. 685 (1986).

The Criminal Justice System of the U.S.S.R. (M. Bassiouni & V. Savitski eds. 1979).

Criminality

Chalidze, V., *Criminal Russia: A Study of Crime in the Soviet Union* (1977).

Connor, W., *Deviance in Soviet Society: Crime, Delinquency, and Alcoholism* (1972).

Hertsenzon, *Main Approaches to the Study of Criminality,* in *Recent Contributions to Soviet Criminology* 9 (1974).

Karpets, *Nature and Causes of Crime in the U.S.S.R.,* 5 Soviet L. & Gov't, No. 1 (1966, at 52).

Kudryatsev, *Relationship Between Theory and Practice in Organizing Action to Combat Criminality in the Union of Soviet Socialist Republics,* 29 Int'l Rev. Crim. Pol'y 3 (1971).

Kudryavtsev, *The Structure of Criminality and Social Change,* in *Recent Contributions to Soviet Criminology* 23 (1974).

Kuznetsova, *Comparative Criminological Study of Crime in Moscow (1923 and 1968-1969).* 11 Soviet L. & Gov't 177 (1972).

Minkovsky, *Effectiveness of Treatment Measures and Problems of the Typology of Juvenile Delinquents,* in *Recent Contributions to Soviet Criminology* 105 (1974).

Nature and Causes of Crime in the U.S.S.R., Trans. Soviet L. & Soc. Reg. No. 10 (1966, at 17).

Sakharov, *The Concepts of the Personality of the Offender,* in *Recent Contributions to Soviet Criminology* 63 (1974).

Sakharov, *On the Conception of the Causes of Crime in Socialist Society,* 15 Soviet L. & Gov't, No. 4 (1977, at 37).

Shelley, *Urbanization and Crime: The Soviet Case,* in *Readings in Comparative Criminology* (L. Shelley ed. 1981).

Shelley, L., *Soviet Criminology: Its Birth and Demise, 1917-1936* (1977).

Shtromas, *Crime, Law, and Penal Practice in the U.S.S.R.,* 3 Rev. Socialist L. 297 (1977).

Solomon, *Soviet Criminology—Its Demise and Rebirth, 1923-1963,* in *Crime, Criminology and Public Policy,* 571 (R. Hood ed. 1974).

Zeldes, *Juvenile Delinquency in the U.S.S.R.,* 4 Int'l J. Comp. & Applied Crim. Just. 29 (1978).

Zvirbul, *The Social and Historical Dimension in the Study of the Causes of Criminality,* in *Recent Contributions to Soviet Criminology* 41 (1974).

Law Enforcement Agencies

Adams, J., *Citizen Inspecters in the Soviet Union: The People's Control Committee* (1977).

Butler, W. *Comradely Justice Revisisted,* 3 Rev. Socialist L. 325 (1977).

Conquest, R., *The Soviet Police System* (1968).

Ginsburgs, *The Soviet Procuracy and Forty Years of Socialist Legality,* 18 Am. Slavic & E. European Rev. 34 (1959).

Kaminskaya, D., *Final Judgment: My Life as as Soviet Defense Attorney* (1982).

Karpets, *Principal Direction and Types of Activity of the Militia in the Soviet Union,* 33 Int'l Rev. Crim. Pol'y 34 (1977).

Levytsky, B., *The Uses of Terror: The Soviet Secret Police 1917-1970* (H. Piehler, trans., 1972).

Morgan, *People's Justice: The Anti-Parasite Laws, People's Volunteer Militia, and Comrade's Courts,* in *Miscellanea: Articles and Texts* 49 (Law in Eastern Europe No. 7, 1963).

Novikov, *Law on the Procuracy of the U.S.S.R.,* Soviet L. & Gov't, No. 2 (1981, at 34).

Smith, G., *The Soviet Procuracy and the Supervision of Administration* (1978).

Taylor, T., *Courts of Terror* (1976).

Terebilov, V., *The Soviet Court* (1973).

Timashelftt, *The Procurator's Office in the U.S.S.R.*, in *Law in Eastern Europe*, 8 (A. Szirmai ed. 1958).

Criminal Law

Adams, *Capital Punishment in Imperial and Soviet Criminal Law*, 18 Am. J. Comp. L. 575 (1970).

Beerman, *The Rule of Law and Legality in the Soviet Union*, 1 Rev. Socialist L. 97 (1975).

Berman, Cohen, & Russell, *A Comparison of the Chinese and Soviet Codes of Criminal Law and Procedure*, 73 J. Crim. L. & Criminology 238 (1982).

Bourtsley, *Capital Punishment in Russia*, 28 Law J. 251 (1983).

Dagel, *Criminal Law and Protection of the Environment in the U.S.S.R.*, 49 Revue Internationale de Droit Penal 297 (1978).

De Jong, *"An Intolerable Kind of Moral Degeneration": Homosexuality in the Soviet Union*, 8 Rev. Socialist L. 341 (1982).

Dobovik, *Efficacy of Criminal Law in Nature Conservation and in the Conditions of the Scientific and Technological Revolution*, in *The Development of Soviet Law and Jurisprudence*, 124 (Problems of the Contemporary World No. 68, 1978).

Effectiveness of Criminal Punishment, 4 Soviet L. & Gov't, No. 3 (1965-1966, at 30).

Feldbrugge, F., *Soviet Criminal Law* (Law in Eastern Europe No. 9, 1964).

Feldbrugge, *Criminal Law and Traditional Society: The Role of Soviet Law in the Integration of Non-Slavic People*, 3 Rev. Socialist L. (March 1977, at 3).

Feldbrugge, *What happened in Soviet Criminal Law?*, 11 Rev. Socialist L. 5 (1985).

Ginsburgs & Mason, *Soviet Criminal Law Reform: Centralized Uniformity Versus Local Diversification*, in *Essays in Criminal Science* 409 (G. Mueller ed. 1961).

Hazard, J., *Soviet Socialism and the Duty to Rescue*, in *20th Century Comparative and Conflicts Law* 160 (1961).

Lapenna, *Contemporary Crisis of Legality in the Soviet Union Substantive Criminal Law*, 1 Rev. Socialist Law 73 (1975).

Lapenna, I., *Soviet Penal Policy: A Background Book* (1968 & reprint 1980).

Makepeace, R., *Marxist Ideology in Soviet Criminal Law* (1980).

Mikiforov, *Fundamental Principles of Soviet Criminal Law*, 23 Mod. L. Rev. 31 (1960).

Osakwe, *Contemporary Soviet Criminal Law: An Analysis of the General Principles and Major Institutions of Post-1958 Soviet Criminal Law*, 6 Ga. Int'l & Comp. L. 437 (1976).

Pomorski, *Communists and Their Criminal Law: Reflections on Igor Andrejew's Outline of the Criminal Law of Socialist States*, 7 Rev. Socialist L. 7 (1981).

Pomorski, *Crimes Against the Central Planner: "Ochkovtiratel' stvo,"* in *Soviet Law After Stalin*, 291 (D. Barry, G. Ginsburgs, & P. Maggs, eds., Law in Eastern Europe No. 20, Pt. 2, 1978).

Pomorski, *Criminal Law Protection of Socialist Property in the U.S.S.R.*, in *Soviet Law After Stalin*, 223 (D. Barry, G. Ginsburgs, & P. Maggs eds., Law in Eastern Europe No. 20, Pt. 1, 1977).

Solomon, P., *Soviet Criminology: A Selective Bibliography* (1969).

Solomon, P., *Soviet Criminologists and Criminal Policy: Specialists in Policymaking* (1978).

Solomon, *Criminalization and Decriminalization in Soviet Criminal Policy, 1917-1941,* 16 Law & Soc'y Rev. (February 1982, at 9; reprinted in *Perspectives on Soviet Law for the 1980s* 123, F. Feldbrugge, & W. Simons, eds., Law in Eastern Europe 24, 1982).

Victorov, *Public Participation and Crime Prevention in the Union of Soviet Socialist Republics,* 27 Int'l Rev. Crim. Pol'y 38 (1969).

Criminal Procedure

Anashkin, *Basic Provisions of the Soviet Legislation on Criminal Procedure and Some Aspects of Its Application,* 29 Int'l Rev. Crim. Pol'y 18 (1971).

Anashkin, *Defense Counsel: Rights and Problems,* 9 Soviet L. & Gov't 300 (1971).

Fletcher, *The Ongoing Soviet Debate about the Presumption of Innocence,* 3 Crim. Just. Ethics 69 (1984).

Gorgone, J., *The Legislative Process in the U.S.S.R.: Soviet Jurists and the Reform of Criminal Procedure, 1956-1958,* (1974) (Ph.d. diss.).

Gorgone, *Soviet Criminal Procedure Legislation: A Dissenting Perspective,* 28 Am. J. Comp. L. 577 (1980).

Huskey, E., *The Politics of the Soviet Criminal Process: Expanding the Right to Counsel in Pre-trial Proceedings,* 34 Am. J. Comp. L. 93 (1986).

Libus, *Presumption of Innocence and Termination of Proceedings in Criminal Cases,* 21 Soviet L. & Gov't 50 (1982).

Luryi, *The Right to Counsel in Ordinary Criminal Cases in the U.S.S.R.,* in *Soviet Law After Stalin,* 105 (D. Barry, G. Ginsburgs, & P. Maggs, ed., Law in Eastern Europe No. 20, Pt. 1, 1977).

Luryi, *Special Courts in the U.S.S.R.: A Comment,* 8 Rev. Socialist L. 251 (1982).

Nikoforov, *Notes on Criminal Procedure in the U.S.S.R.,* in *The Accused: A Comparative Study* (J. Courts ed. 1966).

Osakwe, *Due Process of Law Under Contemporary Soviet Criminal Procedure,* 50 Tul. L. Rev. 266 (976).

Osakwe, *Modern Soviet Criminal Procedure: A Critical Analysis,* 57 Tul. L. Rev. 439 (1983).

Patterson & Doak, *Criminal Justice in Soviet Russia,* 4 Int'l J. Comp. & Applied Crim. Just. 113 (1980).

Petrukhin, *Presumption of Innocence: A Constitutional Principle of Soviet Criminal Justice,* 18 Soviet L. & Gov't, No. 2 (1979, at 3).

Savitskii, *Protection of Human Rights in Criminal Proceedings: National Report— U.S.S.R.,* 49 Revue Internationale de Droit Penal 389 (1978).

Shafir, *Right to Defence in Soviet Criminal Procedure and Possibilities for Expanding It,* 6 Soviet L. & Gov't, No. 1 (1967, at 29).

Smith, *Popular Participation in the Administration of Justice in the Soviet Union: Comrades' Courts and the Brezhnev Regime,* 49 Ind. L.J. 238 (1973).

Smith, *Procuratorial Campaigns Against Crime,* in *Soviet Law After Stalin,* 143 (D. Barry, G. Ginsburgs, & P. Maggs, ed., Law in Eastern Europe No. 20, Pt. 3, 1979).

Strogovich, *Adversary Proceedings and Trial Functions in Soviet Criminal Procedures,* 1 Soviet L. & Gov't, No. 3 (1962-1963 at 11).

Strogovich, *Defense Lawyer is Called Upon to Defend,* 9 Soviet L. & Gov't 320 (1971).

Strogovich, *On the Rights of the Individual in Soviet Criminal Procedure,* 15 Soviet L. & Gov't, No. 4 (1977, at 3).

Strogovich, *Presumption of Innocence and Termination of Criminal Cases for Reasons Other than Rehabilitation,* 22 Sov. L. & Gov't 50 (1983).

Strogovich, *Concerning Acquittal Because of Lack of Evidence of a Defendant's Participation in the Commission of a Crime,* 22 Sov. L. Gov't 21 (1983-1984).

Van den Berg, *Special Courts: Lessons from History,* 10 Rev. Socialist L. 63 (1984).

Corrections

Amnesty International, *Prisoners of Conscience in the U.S.S.R.: Their Treatment and Conditions* (2nd ed. 1980).

Bloch, S. & P. Reddaway, *Psychiatric Terror: How Soviet Psychiatry is Used to Suppress Dissent* (1977).

Bloch, S. & P. Reddaway, *Russia's Political Hospitals: The Abuse of Psychiatry in the Soviet Union* (1977).

Chalidze, *A Propos the Application of Corrective Labor Law in the U.S.S.R.,* in *Soviet Law After Stalin,* 71 (D. Barry, G. Ginsburgs, & P. Maggs, eds., Law in Eastern Europe No. 20, Pt. 1, 1977).

Effectiveness of Imprisonment for Rehabilitating Juvenile Criminals in the Latvian S.S.R., Trans. Soviet L. & Soc. Reg., No. 1 (1966, at 6).

Feldbrugge, *Soviet Corrective Labor Law,* in *Soviet Law After Stalin,* (D. Barry, G. Ginsburgs, P. Maggs, eds., Law in Eastern Europe No. 20, Pt. 1, 1977).

Feldbrugge, *Soviet Penitentiary Law,* 1 Rev. Socialist L. 123 (1975).

Feldbrugge, *The Soviet Penitentiary System,* 12 Rev. Socialist L. 5 (1986).

Georgadze, *Statute on the Labor Colonies for Minors of the U.S.S.R. Ministry for the Protection of Public Order,* 7 Soviet L. & Gov't 27 (1968).

Hinners, *Soviet Correctional Measures for Juvenile Delinquency,* 13 Brit. J. Criminology 218 (1973).

Solzhenitsyn, A., *The Gulag Archipelago 1918-1956* (1973-1978).

Struchkov, N., *Correction of the Convicted: Law, Theory, Practice* (1982).

Legislation

Code of Criminal Procedure of the R.S.F.S.R., in *The Soviet Codes of Law,* 157 (W. Simons ed., Law in Eastern Europe No. 23, 1980).

Corrective Labor Code of the R.S.F.S.R., in *The Soviet Codes of Law,* 321 (W. Somons ed., Law in Eastern Europe No. 23, 1980).

Criminal Code of the R.S.F.S.R., in *The Soviet Codes of Law,* 53 (W. Simons ed., Law in Eastern Europe No. 23, 1980).

Criminal Code of the R.S.F.S.R., in *The Soviet Codes of Law,* 53 (W. Simons ed., Law in Eastern Europe No. 23, 1980).

The Soviet Codes of Law (W. Simons ed., Law in Eastern Europe No. 23, 1980).

Soviet Criminal Law and Procedure: The R.S.F.S.R. Codes (H. Berman & J. Spindler, trans., Russian Research Center Studies 50, 2 ed. 1972).

Poland

Criminality

Bierzanek, *Planning of Human Resources for Crime Prevention in Poland,* 31 Int'l Rev. Crim. Pol'y 42 (1974).

Frankowski, *Causes of Criminality in Socialist Countries as Perceived by Socialist Criminology,* 22 Tijdschrift voor Criminologie (1980).

Godycka, *Alcoholism and its Treatment in Poland,* 18 Int'l. J. Offender Therapy & Comp. Criminology 106 (1974).

International Congress of Social Defense in Latin America, *Some Problems of Crime Prevention in Poland* (B. Hoyst ed. 1976).

Kojder & Kwasniewski, *Public Reaction in Poland to Deviant Behavior,* in International Centre for Comparative Criminology, *Second Regional Seminar* 21 (1975).

Mackowiak & Ziembinski, *Social Aspects of Sources of Criminality and of Its Prevention and Control,* Int'l Rev. Crim. Pol'y, No. 29 (1971, at 25).

Marek et al., *Alcohol as a Victimogenic Factor of Robberies,* 4 Forensic Sci. 119 (1974).

Marek, *Suicides Committed by Minors,* 7 Forensic Sci. 103 (1976).

Marek & Redo, *Drug Abuse in Poland,* 30 Bull. on Narcotics (January-March 1978, at 43).

Michalski, *Prevention of Criminality in Poland and Other Socialist States of Eastern Europe,* 35 Int'l Rev. Crim. Pol'y 44 (1979).

Morawski, *Attempts to Systematize Alcohology and Anti-Alcoholic Policies,* 18 Int'l J. Offender Therapy & Comp. Criminology 28 (1974).

Pelka-Slugocka & Slugocki, *Alcoholism and Female Crime in Poland,* 21 Int'l J. Offender Therapy & Comp. Criminology 174 (1977).

Plenska, *The Criminality of Women in Poland,* in *The Incidence of Female Criminality in the Contemporary World* 137 (F. Adler ed. 1981).

Walczak, *Planning Crime Prevention and Control in Poland,* Int'l Rev. Crim. Pol'y, No. 26 (1968, at 43).

Criminal Law

Cieslak, *The Problem of Depenalization in Contemporary Polish Criminal Law,* 25 Revue Internationale de Police Criminale 193 (1972).

Falandysz, *Scientific Session Dealing with New Codifications of Penal Law, Penal Procedure and Penal Executive Law,* 15 Droit Polonais Contemp. 51 (1971).

Frankowski, *Polish Criminal Justice System After World War Two—Selected Problems,* 44 U. Pitt. L. Rev. 139 (1982).

Frankowski, *Polish Supreme Court Directives as Sources of Criminal Law,* in *Anglo-Polish Legal Essays* 55 (W. Butler ed. 1982).

Frankowski & Zielinska, *Non-Custodial Penal Measures in European Socialist Countries,* 36 Int'l Rev. Crim. Pol'y 38 (1980).

Grajewski & Lammich, *Criminal Policy in Poland in Light of the Criminal Code of 1969,* 7 Rev. Socialist L. 407 (1981).

Greenberg, *Penal Sanctions in Poland: A Test of Alternative Models,* 29 Soc. Probs. (December 1980, at 194).

Kos-Rabcewicz-Zubkowski, *Provisions on Juvenile and Young Delinquents in the 1969-1971 Polish Penal Law Legislation,* 17 Osteuropa-Recht (October 1971, at 115).

Kos-Rabcewicz-Zubkowski, *Law and Order in Contemporary Poland*, 25 Can. Slavonic Papers 392 (1983).

Memorial by Polish Legal Scholars Submitted on 30 October 1980 to the Minister of Justice Prof. Dr. Jerzy Bafia on the Reform Of Prevailing Polish Criminal Law and Policy, Rev. Socialist L. 425 (1981).

Poklewski-Koziell, *Alternatives to Imprisonment in the New Polish Penal Code*, in *Studies in Comparative Criminal Law* 89 (E. Wise & G. Mueller eds. 1975).

Pomorski, *Lay Judges in the Polish Criminal Courts: A Legal and Empirical Description*, 7 Case W. Res. J. Int'l L. 198 (1975).

Pomorski & Defert, *Universally Accepted Norms and Their Implications in National Legal Systems: A Comparative Study of Polish and American Criminal Law and their Interaction with Modern International Human Rights Legislation*, 57 Denver L. J. 467 (1980).

Studnicki, *The Current Role of the Maxim "Ignorance of the Law is No Excuse,"* in International Congress of Comparative Law, Uppsala, 1966, *Rapports Polonais* 325 (1966).

Zielinska, *New Type of Sanction in Poland: The Non-Custodial Curtailment of Liberty*, 20 Int'l J. Offender Therapy & Comp. Criminology 65 (1976).

Criminal Procedure

Waltos, *The Phenomenon of Special Proceedings in Criminal Procedure*, 2 Comp. L. Y.B. 285 (1978).

Waltos, *Protection of Human Rights in Criminal Proceedings: National Report Poland*, 49 Revue Internationale de Droit Penal 245 (1978).

Waszczynski, *Criminal Process in the Polish People's Republic*, in *The Accused* 257 (British Institute Studies on International and Comparative Law 3, J. Coutts ed. 1966).

Corrections

Assist and Befriend or Direct and Control: A Report on Probation Services in Poland and England (J. Harper et al. ed. 1982).

Los & Anderson, *Subcultures in Correctional Institutions in Poland and the United States*, in *Readings in Comparative Criminology* (L. Shelley ed. 1981).

Moczydlowski, *Types of Penal Institution, Economic Organization, and Inmate Social Structure: Some Polish Examples*, 11 Int'l J. Soc. L. 305 (1983).

Pelka-Slugocka & Slugocki, *Advance Pay to Ex-Prisoners in Poland*, 20 Int'l J. Offender Therapy & Comp. Criminology 73 (1976).

Pelka-Slugocka & Slugocki, *The Impact of Imprisonment on the Family Life of Women Convicts*, 24 Int'l J. Offender Therapy & Comp. Criminology 249 (1980).

Rzeplinski, *Prison Staff in Poland in the Light of Legal Regulations and Actual Practice*, 27 Int'l J. Offender Therapy & Comp. Criminology 184 (1983).

Rzeplinski, *Prisoners' Rights in Poland*, 25 Int'l J. Offender Therapy & Comp. Criminology 178 (1981).

Wiewiorowski, *Abstract Laboratory Games as a Method of Assessing Cooperative and Exploitative Behavior in Prisoners*, in International Centre for Comparative Criminology, 2 *Troisieme Seminaire Regional* 135 (1977).

Varia

Borucka-Arctowa, *Citizen Participation in the Administration of Justice: Research and Policy in Poland,* in *Zur Soziologie des Gerichtverfahrens* 286 (L. Friedman & M. Rehbinder eds. 1976).
Kurowski, *General Principles of Polish Law,* (1984).
Scandinavian Research Council for Criminology, *Scandinavian-Polish Workmeeting* (1981).
Wagner, W., *Polish Law Throughout the Ages* (1970).

Legislation

Code of Criminal Procedure of the Polish People's Republic (S. Waltos ed. 1979).
Penal Code of the Polish People's Republic (W. Kenney & T. Sadowski, trans., in American Series of Foreign Penal Codes, No. 19, 1973).

About the Authors

George F. Cole is Professor of Political Science at the University of Connecticut. His published works include *Politics and the Administration Justice* (1973, Sage), *The American System of Criminal Justice* (Brooks/Cole, 1986, 4th edition), and *American Corrections* with Todd Clear (1986). He has studied the criminal courts in England and Yugoslavia under the auspices of the Fulbright-Hays Program.

Roseline A. Ekpenyong, born and raised in Nigeria, got her Ph.D. at Florida State University School of Criminology (Tallahassee). Currently, she is Assistant Professor of Criminal Justice at Michigan State University. Her research interests include comparative criminal justice systems, etiology, and prevention of juvenile delinquency, cross-cultural analysis of juvenile delinquency, and female criminality.

Stanislaw J. Frankowski taught almost twenty years at the University of Warsaw (Poland). Currently, he is Professor at Saint Louis University School of Law (USA). His main English-language publications include *Abortion and Protection of the Human Fetus: Legal Problems in a Cross-Cultural Perspective* (1987; coedited with George Cole) and "Mens Rea and Punishment in England: In Search of Interdependence of the Two Basic Components of Criminal Liability (A Historical Perspective)," *Detroit University Law Review* (1986). In the period 1972-1973, he was a senior Fellow at the Criminal Law Education and Research Center (New York University School of Law) and in 1982 he studied in Freiburg at Max-Planck Institute.

John C. Freeman, J. P., now lectures on criminal law, criminology, and penology at University of London King's College. He is Vice President of the Scientific Committee of the International Sociological, Penal and Penitentiary Research and Studies Centre, Messina, Treasurer of the British Society of Criminology, and a member of the Parole Board of England and Wales.

Marc G. Gertz holds a Ph.D. in political science from the University of Connecticut and is currently Associate Professor of Criminology at Florida State University. His published articles have appeared in *Justice Systems Journal* and *Journal of Criminal Justice*.

Joachim Herrmann has been Professor of Law at the University of Augsburg since 1972. He holds degrees from Freiburg and Tulane Universities and has been a Visiting Professor at the University of Virginia, University of Chicago, and University of Tokyo. His main publications in English include "The Rule of Compulsory Prosecution and the Scope of Prosecutorial Discretion in Germany," *University of Chicago Law Review* (1974) and "Reform of the German Penal Code-Sanctions: The German Law and Theory," *American Journal of Comparative Law* (1976).

Victor M. Kogan is a Senior Scientific Worker at the Criminal Law Section of the Institute of State and Law, the USSR Academy of Sciences. He is the author of many works in criminology and sociology of criminal law. His books include *Logical-Juridical Structure of the Soviet Criminal Law* (1966), *Social Characteristics of Crime* (1977), and *Social Mechanism of Criminal Law Influence (1983)*. Victor Kogan translated into Russian several foreign books such as *Punishment and Deterrence* by I. Andenaes (1979) and *Limits to Pain* by N. Christie (1983).

Kenichi Nakayama is Professor of Law at Kyoto University where he is a specialist in criminology and socialist law. His published books include *Soviet Criminal Law* (1958), *Causality in Criminal Law* (1970), and *Law and Society in Poland* (1978).

Alvar Nelson, born 1919, LLD 1950 in Uppsala, Sweden has been professor of Criminal Law in the Universities of Aarhus, Denmark (1952-1961), Lund, Sweden (1962-1964), and Uppsala (1965-1985). He has practiced law and served in the judiciary and on various public commissions in both countries. He is the author of many books and articles, for example, in the last few years in English *Potestas et Clementia* (on the prerogative of mercy, 1986), *From King's Men to Public Employees* (1986), *Social Defense and Human Rights* (1986), *Abortion* (1987), and *Responses to Crime* (1987).

Valery M. Savitsky is Professor at the Institute of State and Law of the Soviet Academy of Sciences in Moscow. As recognized expert in the field of criminal procedure, he is a member of several advisory bodies in the Soviet Union. Since 1974 he has served as Deputy Secretary General of the International Association of Penal Law (AIDP). His main publications include: *Procuratorial Supervision over the Investigation of Criminal Cases* (1959), *Theory of the Procuratorial Supervision* (1975), and *The Criminal Justice of the USSR* (1979, coedited with Ch. Bassiouni).